ascending
THE MOUNTAIN
Homilies for the year of Matthew

GEOFFREY PLANT

Published by
Garratt Publishing
32 Glenvale Crescent
Mulgrave Vic 3170
www.garrattpublishing.com.au

Copyright © 2010 Geoffrey Plant

Reprinted 2022

All rights reserved. Except as provided by the Australian copyright law, no part of this book may be reproduced in any way without permission in writing from the publisher.

Design and typesetting: JGD Graphic+Web www.jgd.com.au
Text editing: Helene Clarke

National Library of Australia Cataloguing-in-Publication entry
Author: Plant, Geoffrey Michael, 1947-
Title: Ascending the mountain : homilies for the year of Matthew / Geoffrey Plant.
ISBN: 9781920682255 (pbk.)
Subjects: Catholic Church--Sermons.
 Bible. N.T. Matthews--Sermons.
    Sermons, Australian.
Dewey Number: 226.406

With grateful thanks to Fr William Bausch

and in memory of Fr John McCrystal OFM,

mastercraftsmen of the Word.

Acknowledgements

The author and the publisher are grateful for permission
from the following people and sources to reproduce copyright material :
Michael Leunig ; 10 lines from Chapter One, from *Care of the Soul*
by Thomas Moore, © 1992 Thomas Moore. Reprinted by permission of
HarperCollins Publishers ; *Forgotten Among the Lilies* by Ronald Rolheiser
(Doubleday, 2005) ; *Necessary Losses* by Judith Viorst
(N.Y. :Simon &Schuster, 1986).

Excerpts from THE JERUSALEM BIBLE, copyright © 1966 by
Darton, Longman & Todd, Ltd. and Doubleday, a division
of Random House, Inc. Reprinted by Permission.

Excerpts from THE NEW JERUSALEM BIBLE, copyright © 1985 by
Darton, Longman & Todd, Ltd. and Doubleday, a division of
Random House, Inc. Reprinted by Permission.

Every attempt has been made to contact holders of copyright.
The author and publisher welcome inquiry from those where
this was not possible.

CONTENTS

Introduction	7
First Sunday of Advent	9
Second Sunday of Advent	12
Third Sunday of Advent	15
Fourth Sunday of Advent	18
Christmas Day	21
Holy Family	23
Epiphany	26
Ash Wednesday	29
First Sunday of Lent	32
Second Sunday of Lent	35
Third Sunday of Lent	38
Fourth Sunday of Lent	41
Fifth Sunday of Lent	45
Passion Sunday	48
Holy Thursday	51
Good Friday	54
Easter Sunday	57
Second Sunday of Easter	61
Third Sunday of Easter	64
Fourth Sunday of Easter	68
Fifth Sunday of Easter	71
Sixth Sunday of Easter	74
Seventh Sunday of Easter	78
Ascension of the Lord	81
Pentecost	84
Most Holy Trinity	88
Body and Blood of Christ	91
Assumption of the Blessed Virgin Mary	94
All Saints	97
Commemoration of all the Faithful Departed	100
Baptism of the Lord	103

Second Sunday in Ordinary Time 106
Third Sunday in Ordinary Time 109
Fourth Sunday in Ordinary Time 112
Fifth Sunday in Ordinary Time 115
Sixth Sunday in Ordinary Time 119
Seventh Sunday in Ordinary Time 123
Eighth Sunday in Ordinary Time 127
Ninth Sunday in Ordinary Time 131
Tenth Sunday in Ordinary Time 134
Eleventh Sunday in Ordinary Time 138
Twelfth Sunday in Ordinary Time 141
Thirteenth Sunday in Ordinary Time 145
Fourteenth Sunday in Ordinary Time 149
Fifteenth Sunday in Ordinary Time 152
Sixteenth Sunday in Ordinary Time 157
Seventeenth Sunday in Ordinary Time 161
Eighteenth Sunday in Ordinary Time 165
Nineteenth Sunday in Ordinary Time 168
Twentieth Sunday in Ordinary Time 171
Twenty-First Sunday in Ordinary Time 175
Twenty-Second Sunday in Ordinary Time 180
Twenty-third Sunday in Ordinary Time 184
Twenty-fourth Sunday in Ordinary Time 188
Twenty-fifth Sunday in Ordinary Time 191
Twenty-sixth Sunday in Ordinary Time 195
Twenty-seventh Sunday in Ordinary Time 198
Twenty-eighth Sunday in Ordinary Time 202
Twenty-ninth Sunday in Ordinary Time 206
Thirtieth Sunday in Ordinary Time 210
Thirty-first Sunday in Ordinary Time 213
Thirty-second Sunday in Ordinary Time 216
Thirty-third Sunday in Ordinary Time 219
Christ the King 223
Bibliography 227

INTRODUCTION

Ascending the Mountain is a collection of homilies for Year A of the liturgical cycle, the year of Matthew. It is a companion to a similar volume for Year C, the year of Luke, *Welcoming the Outsider*. Each of the evangelists offers us a different perspective on the life and ministry of Jesus, portraying him in a way that would meet the spiritual and pastoral needs of the community for which he was writing. We gain an insight into the distinctive perspective of each of the evangelists by looking at the story he places at the beginning of the public ministry of Jesus. In Mark's gospel it is an exorcism in the synagogue at Capernaum; for Luke it is Jesus' return to Nazareth and preaching in the synagogue; for John it is the wedding feast of Cana. Matthew's gospel places the Sermon on the Mount at the beginning of Jesus' public ministry, thereby presenting Jesus as the new Moses, a note first sounded in the infancy narrative (see the homily for the feast of the Holy Family).

Most scholars would agree that the evangelist was not Matthew, one of the Twelve apostles and an eyewitness to Jesus' ministry, but probably a Jewish convert of the second or third generation.[1] His community consisted of Jews who had accepted Jesus as their Messiah, but also of gentiles. These Jewish Christians were no longer welcome in the local Jewish synagogues and they were struggling to hold in tension their Jewish identity with the revelation of God in Christ, the old with the new. They're going through an identity crisis. In response to this pastoral situation the evangelist is like the "householder who brings out of his treasure new things and old" (Mt 13:52). In Matthew's gospel even the tiniest part of the ancient Jewish Law (jot and tittle) must remain, but only as radically interpreted by Jesus. Jesus, like Moses before him, ascends the mountain. Matthew then organises his teaching into five sermons, beginning with the Sermon on the Mount, thereby suggesting a new Torah, a fulfillment not an abrogation of the old.

In 1949 the American writer Joseph Campbell published a seminal work called *The Hero With a Thousand Faces*. Campbell observed that a central motif in storytelling is that of the journey, and the significance of his book's title lay in the realisation that the heroic figure in many of the great stories of humanity

---

[1] Raymond E. Brown, *Christ in the Gospels of the Ordinary Sundays*, The Liturgical Press, Collegeville, MI, 1998, p.18.

embarks upon what is essentially the same journey of discovery. Only the "face" of the hero and the setting of the story change. And ultimately, the story of the hero is our own story writ large! (Homily for the Eleventh Sunday in Ordinary Time). I have found Campbell's analysis of the heroic journey a useful lens for viewing the gospel, the greatest story ever told! It is "a recognition of a beautiful design, a set of principles that govern the conduct of life and the world of storytelling the way physics and chemistry govern the physical world."[2] For that reason I draw upon insights from novels and cinema as a way of entering into the gospel stories from a different perspective.

An earlier version of these homilies appeared in the *Australasian Catholic Record*, and I am grateful to Fr Gerard Kelly for permission to reproduce them here. I would like to express my gratitude to the parishioners of St Luke's Parish, Revesby, on whom these homilies have been road tested. I dedicate this book to Fr William Bausch and Fr John McCrystal OFM. I have never met Fr Bausch, but his many books have inspired my own preaching. The late Fr John McCrystal was my lecturer for homiletics in the seminary, and he introduced me to the power of story and patiently encouraged me to put flesh on my ideas when I preached.

---

[2] Christopher Vogler, *The Writer's Journey*, Michael Wiese Productions, Studio City, CA, 1998, p. xiii.

FIRST SUNDAY OF ADVENT

(YEAR A)

*So stay awake, because you do not know the day
when your master is coming.
(Mt 24:42)*

Today's gospel directs our attention ahead – to the Son of Man who is coming at an hour we do not expect. The language describing this coming is dramatic. We're told that of two men in the fields, one will be taken, one left; of two women at the millstone grinding, one will be taken, the other left. What's happening here? Some evangelical Christians interpret today's gospel literally and refer to this scenario as the Rapture. The phenomenal commercial success of the *Left Behind* series by American writers Tim LaHaye and Jerry B. Jenkins offers a disturbing insight into the fundamentalist fascination with the end time. This fictional series has sold more than 40 million copies since it first appeared in 1995 (plus an additional 10 million with the youth series spin-off). The twelfth and final novel in the series (*Glorious Appearing: The End of Days*) is set seven years after the Rapture and almost exactly seven years since the Antichrist's covenant with Israel. The Antichrist has assembled the armies of the world in the Valley of Megiddo, and this sets the scene for what he believes will be his ultimate triumph of the ages.

The opening scene of the first *Left Behind* novel introduces Captain Rayford Steele, a commercial pilot unhappily married to a woman who has become a religious zealot from listening to Christian radio. As he flies a Boeing 747 over the Atlantic his mind wanders to one of the female flight attendants he plans to seduce. Steele hands over the controls to his co-pilot and walks back to the cabin, only to find the flight attendant hysterical. Dozens of passengers have disappeared, their clothes left neatly behind on their seats. The reader soon discovers that millions of people worldwide have also disappeared. What has happened? Well, the rapture has just occurred and the seven year reign of the Antichrist is about to begin — a time of global tribulation. The *Left Behind* series chronicles those seven years. Of course not everyone is taken up in the rapture, only small children and true believers. Those who remain have a second chance at salvation.

The Illinois Catholic bishops have condemned the series not only because of its blatant anti-Catholicism, but also on the grounds that it reinforces an unhealthy and immature belief in a harshly judgmental God. The *Left Behind* series is a perfect example of interpreting apocalyptic writing as if it were intended to be an eyewitness account. In the fundamentalist worldview of *Left Behind* there is but one truth, derived from a literal reading of Scripture, and anyone who disagrees with that truth is deceived or evil.[3]

In 1993 the Pontifical Biblical Commission of the Catholic Church published a document entitled *The Interpretation of the Bible in the Church*, the preface to which was written by Cardinal Ratzinger, then head of the Vatican's Congregation for the Doctrine of the Faith. Cardinal Ratzinger, now Pope Benedict XVI, had this to say about fundamentalism: "The fundamentalist approach is dangerous, for it is attractive to people who look to the Bible for ready answers to the problem of life." The Cardinal warns that "the Bible does not necessarily contain an immediate answer to each and every problem", and he adds that "fundamentalism actually invites people to a kind of intellectual suicide. It injects into life a false certitude, for it unwittingly confuses the divine substance of the biblical message with what are in fact its human limitations."[4]

Today's gospel is alerting us to a fundamental truth. Each of us will have to give an account of our life, and we do not know when that moment will be. It may be sudden and unexpected. Today's gospel calls to mind a tragic event that occurred in 1997 at the Thredbo ski resort. Twenty-one-year-old ski instructor Stuart Diver was asleep beside his wife when a landslide destroyed the resort in which they were staying. Stuart survived; his wife died. One taken, one left – quite literally.

What, then, is Advent saying to us? Advent focuses upon the coming of the Lord. But if our gaze is constantly directed backwards to Bethlehem, or obsessed with the Second Coming, we may overlook a fundamental truth: Everyday is Advent. Christ comes into the lives of his disciples every day. Every day must therefore be a day of watching and waiting. But we are not watching and waiting for Christ's coming in spectacular and cataclysmic events, but rather in and through the tedium and mundane rhythm of everyday life. Ideally, of course, we should be ready for the Lord whenever and however he comes.

---

[3] Cf. Gershom Gorenberg, "Intolerance: The Best Seller", *The American Prospect*, 13, 17, September 23, 2002.

[4] Pontifical Biblical Commission, *The Interpretation of the Bible in the Church*, St Paul Book & Media, Strathfield,1993, p.75.

A pilgrim once journeyed far and wide to find a certain saintly monk to ask of him just one question: "If you had just one more day to live, how would you spend the day?" The monk stroked his long white beard and answered, "Well, after rising early in the morning I would wash and say my morning prayers. Then I would make a pot of tea, and perhaps potter around in the garden. I would set aside some time for *lectio divina* and study, and then I might go down the road to visit my neighbour. I would return home and prepare a light lunch, and perhaps lie down for an afternoon siesta, and then …" At this point the pilgrim became impatient and interrupted: "But isn't that the way you spend every day?" To which the monk replied, "Of course it is. Why should the last day be any different from the rest?"

And therein lays the truth of Advent. Those who wait on the Lord, those awake and on their guard are ready for the Lord whenever he comes, and in whatever guise he is to be found. The weight of eternity is borne by every moment of time.

SECOND SUNDAY OF ADVENT

(YEAR A)

A voice cries in the wilderness: Prepare a way for the Lord.
(Mt 3:3)

Christians didn't formally celebrate the birth of Christ until some time in the fourth century. The earliest record of Christmas being celebrated on December 25 is to be found in a document dated 354, the *Chronograph* or Calendar of Furius Dionysius Philocalus.[5] The reason Christians chose December 25 was almost certainly to coincide with the pagan festival of the birth of the unconquered or invincible sun (*Natalis Solis Invicti*). The cult of *Sol Invictus* was instituted by the emperor Aurelian in 275 and he placed this deity at the head of the pantheon. The emperor Constantine instituted the Day of the Sun, "Sun-day," as a weekly legal holiday in 321.[6] When Christianity came into the ascendancy the Church could have attempted to ban pagan festivals, just as Puritans attempted to abolish Christmas in England during the Cromwellian period (1649-1660). This proved to be an extremely unpopular measure and did little more than alienate the majority of English people from the Puritan experiment.[7] Wisely, then, the Church opted to "baptise" rather than ban the festival of the sun god. It's as though the Church said to the pagan world, "If you want a celebration at this time of the year, fine! Let's continue to celebrate." But instead of celebrating the birth of the sun god, the Church celebrated the birth of the Son of God. Christians identified Christ metaphorically as the sun. A key passage was Malachi 3:20 which speaks of "the Sun of justice (who) will rise with healing in his rays," and Psalm 19 was seen as an allusion to the resurrection when it likens the sun "who comes forth from his pavilion like a bridegroom, (and) delights like a champion in the course to be run." Gospel texts that referred to Christ as "the light of the world" (John 8:12), or Christ as the light shining in the darkness upon a people in the shadow of death (Lk 1:79) strengthened the identification of the birth of Christ with the turn of the

---

[5] Susan K. Roll, "Christmas Then and Now: Reflections on Its Origins and Contemporary Pastoral Problems," *Worship* 73,6, November 1999, p. 509.
[6] Ibid, p. 510.
[7] Reginald H. Fuller, "Sunday Scripture Readings: December 25 to January 16," *Worship* 45,10, December 1971, p. 599.

sun's course at the winter solstice.[8]

The Bible doesn't tell us when Jesus was born, but the symbolism of December 25 makes it an appropriate date to celebrate his birth. The pagan festival celebrated the winter solstice – that point in the calendar when nights are the longest.[9] The progressive lengthening of the day from then onwards mirrored the gradual growth of the sun god. Christians (living in the northern hemisphere) were able to say, "When nights are longest, when the world is darkest, there is born unto us Jesus Christ, who is the light of the world."

The Advent wreath is another example of the Church's adaptation of a pagan custom. Originally, the wreath was associated with the practice of placing candles around a wheel during the time of the winter solstice. When nights were the longest, it was a prayer that the sun might return in all its vigour. The wreath was usually surrounded or covered with evergreens, a symbol of the new life of spring.

Once the feast of Christmas took its place in the Christian calendar sometime in the fourth century, it was considered appropriate – and symmetrical – to have a period of preparation beforehand, just as Easter was preceded by the forty days of Lent. The first mention of a season called Advent can be traced back to Spain and Gaul in the fourth and fifth centuries. The Council of Saragossa in Spain (380 AD) referred to a three-week period of preparation for the celebration of Christmas. In the sixth century St Gregory of Tours (in France) mention a penitential period that lasted from the feast of St Martin (November 11) until Christmas. During this period the faithful fasted for three days during the week, and it was eventually called "St Martin's Lent." There is no mention of Advent in Rome until the middle of the sixth century, and the season lasted for six weeks.[10]

Advent, coming from the Latin word *adventus* meaning "coming", is a time of waiting – waiting for the coming of the Lord. Last week's gospel warned us: "Stay awake" because we do not know the day when our master is coming. Lent and Advent, the two great seasons of preparation in the Church's liturgical calendar, begin in the wilderness. Lent begins with Jesus being led by the Spirit into the desert, and in today's liturgy we encounter John the Baptist emerging from the Judean desert with the message, "Prepare a way for the Lord." The desert is a

---

[8] Roll, op. cit. p. 515.
[9] December 25 was the date of the winter solstice according to the Julian calendar. Today the northern hemisphere marks the solstice on December 21.
[10] Adrian Nocent, *The Liturgical Year: Advent, Christmas, Epiphany*, The Liturgical Press, Collegeville, MN, 1977, p. 66.

great teacher, but it is not primarily a place; it is an experience. The desert is not a setting; it is a state of soul. It is the *arena* (which is the Latin word for "sandy place") where God chooses to meet us. Alan Jones, the dean of Grace (Episcopal) Cathedral in San Francisco, describes the desert as "a place of silence, waiting, and temptation. It is also a place of revelation, conversion, and transformation." That can be confronting. "A true revelation is a very disturbing event because it demands a response; and to respond to it means some kind of inner revolution. It involves being 'made over,' being made new, being 'born again.' The desert, then, is a place of revelation and revolution."[11]

Joseph Conrad's novel *Heart of Darkness* is, on one level, about a journey into the heart of Africa, the so-called Dark Continent. On another level, it is a journey into the heart of an ivory hunter, Mr Kurtz. As Mr Kurtz ventured into the heart of the Dark Continent, he was also confronted by his own inner darkness. The narrator of the story makes this observation about Kurtz: "... the wilderness had found him out early, and had taken on him a terrible vengeance for the fantastic invasion. I think it had whispered to him things about himself which he did not know, things of which he had no conception till he took counsel with this great solitude."[12]

Ronan Kilgannon, an Australian priest living as a hermit, was interviewed for an ABC television program about Australian hermits called *Freedom or Madness?* During the course of the interview Fr Ronan had this to say: "Part of any serious prayer is to confront the false self, the false image that we have of ourselves. So there is a painful process of confronting the shadowy areas in our life — the sinfulness, the ingratitude, the ineptitude, the failures of the past, the long held resentments about things — being honest about those things. And for this to happen, one has to travel down into one's interior. But unless we do it, then we will always be alienated from our true selves. We will never be completely at peace." Pope John Paul II once said "No movement in religious life has any value unless it is also a movement inwards to the 'still centre' of your existence, where Christ is."[13] Today's liturgy summons us into the desert to prepare a way for the Lord.

---

[11] Alan Jones, *Soul Making*, HarperSan Francisco, 1989, p. 6.
[12] Joseph Conrad, *Heart of Darkness*, Penguin Books, Harmondsworth, 1973, p. 83.
[13] Adrian B. Smith, "The Spiritual Value of Transcendental Meditation", in *Spirituality*, Vol 3, Sept-Oct, 1977, p. 306.

THIRD SUNDAY OF ADVENT

(YEAR A)

Go back and tell John what you hear and see.
(Mt 11:4)

The first reading of today's Mass was written when the Jewish people were in exile in Babylon over 500 years before the time of Christ. Jerusalem had been devastated; the Temple destroyed, and for over 80 years the Jewish people languished "by the rivers of Babylon", longing to return home. The prophet Isaiah held out a vision of hope to these exiles, the vision of a land renewed: "Let the wasteland rejoice and bloom, let it bring forth flowers like the jonquil." A barren land transformed, a symbolic way of saying that the people themselves would be renewed – the eyes of the blind shall be opened, the ears of the deaf unsealed, the lame shall leap like a deer, and the tongues of the dumb sing for joy. And what happened? The Persian ruler Cyrus conquered the Babylonians and allowed the Jews to return home.

In time, this prophecy of Isaiah transcended its original context. Originally a vision of hope for exiles, it soon pointed to the time of the anointed one, the Messiah. When John the Baptist, imprisoned and awaiting execution, hears about Jesus he sends some of his disciples to ask the question: "Are you the one who is to come?" Jesus responds by making the text of Isaiah his own: "The blind see, the lame walk, lepers are cleansed, the deaf hear, dead are raised to life, and the Good News is proclaimed to the poor." Jesus invites John's messengers to look about them, to see what is happening and draw their own conclusions. In other words, the kingdom that you seek is already present in your midst, for those who have eyes to see.

The kingdom of God has been likened to treasure buried in a field, and it remains a perennial temptation to seek that treasure beyond distant horizons and in faraway places. There was a poor rabbi who lived in the city of Krakow. He lived in a hovel, the last dwelling on a street named the Lost Angel. There he lived with his wife and four children. He was extremely poor and every night dreamed of riches. But on one particular night his dream was exceptionally vivid. He dreamed that treasure was buried beneath a bridge in the city of Warsaw. When he awoke in the morning he excitedly told his family about the dream. He then set off on the long journey to find the bridge that seemed so clear in his dream. After a long and exhausting journey he finally arrived at Warsaw, startled to discover the bridge exactly as he had seen it in his dream. He approached the bridge cautiously, wary of the guard on duty. He must have been acting suspiciously because the guard challenged him, asking what he was doing lurking beneath the bridge. The rabbi was a simple man and couldn't lie. He told of his dream and the guard immediately began to laugh. "What a stupid fool you are to come so far in pursuit of a dream. Why only the other night I also dreamed of buried treasure in far away Krakow, but do you think I'm crazy enough to do anything about it? I've got to admit, though, my dream was incredibly vivid. I dreamed that in Krakow there was a street named the Lost Angel, and that treasure was buried beneath the fireplace in the last hovel in that street. But it was just a dream, it can't be true. Now get away from this bridge before I arrest you." The rabbi immediately set off for home, and as he entered his house, the last hovel on the street named the Lost Angel, he began removing the stones beneath the fireplace. And sure enough, he found the treasure.[14]

A similar point lies behind an ancient story about a famous monastery that had fallen on hard times. In bygone days its cloisters had been filled with young monks, and the monastery church resounded joyfully with chanting. But now, only a few elderly monks shuffled along the cloisters and praised God with heavy hearts. In the woods not far from the monastery an old hermit had built a little hut where he devoted himself to a life of prayer and penance. As long as he was there, the monks felt sustained by his prayerful presence. One day the abbot decided to visit the hermit and to open his heart to him and seek his advice. After Mass one morning he set out through the woods and came at last to the hermit's hut. As he approached the hut, the abbot saw the hermit standing in the doorway, his arms outstretched in welcome. It was as though he had been waiting there for a long time, and the two men embraced like long-lost brothers. The hermit then spoke to the abbot: "You and your brothers are serving God with heavy hearts, and I know that you have come to seek my counsel. As I prayed during the early hours of this morning the Lord revealed to me a special message for you and your brothers, but you can repeat it only once. After that, no one must ever say it aloud again." The hermit looked straight at the abbot and said, "There is one among you who is

---

[14] Adapted from William J. Bausch, *Storytelling: Imagination and Faith*, Twenty-Third publications, Mystic, CT, 1984, p. 76.

specially chosen by God." For a while, the two men stood there in silence. Then the hermit said, "Now you must go." The abbot left without a word and without even looking back. Later that day he called the monks together and told them of his meeting with the hermit. "The hermit has received a revelation from God. I will tell you what he said, but his words must never be repeated or spoken of again. One of us is specially chosen by God." The monks were startled by this saying, and each thought to himself, "What could it mean? Is Brother John the one specially chosen? Or Father Matthew? Or Brother Thomas? Or is it me; am I the one specially chosen?" They were all deeply puzzled by the hermit's teaching, but no one ever mentioned it again. As time went by, the monks began to treat one another with a very special reverence. Each thought to himself, "How privileged we are, that one of us should be specially chosen by God." And life in the monastery slowly changed. They now prayed with joyful hearts, and visitors were uplifted by their prayer. In no time at all young men were asking to join the community, and the cloisters once again resounded with the heartfelt praise of God, as they did in former days. The old hermit often chuckled to himself as he recalled the abbot's visit. What he had told the abbot was true indeed, that one of the monks had been specially chosen by God. But what he didn't tell the abbot was equally as true, that all of the monks had been specially chosen by God. The hermit's words had awakened the power of the gospel that lay dormant in that monastery.[15]

These two stories emphasise an obvious but often overlooked truth. Our treasure – the God whom we seek and his kingdom – is already present in our midst, but so often unrecognised. We search far and wide for that which is already before our eyes. Advent is a time of waiting for what is to come; but it is also a summons to recognise what already is. As Jesus said to the disciples of John the Baptist, "Look around you!"

---

[15] A slightly different version of this story may be found in William J. Bausch, *Storytelling: Imagination and Faith*, pp. 138-40.

FOURTH SUNDAY OF ADVENT

(YEAR A)

The virgin will conceive and give birth to a son.
(Mt 1:23, quoting Is 7:14)

"The virgin will conceive and give birth to a son and they will call him Emmanuel." In these words from today's gospel Matthew is quoting a passage from the prophet Isaiah, a passage that we heard as part of today's first reading. You'll notice one significant difference, though, in Matthew's version. Isaiah speaks of a *maiden* who is with child; Matthew calls her a *virgin*. We have here a case of mistranslation, but it's not Matthew's fault. In the original Hebrew text of Isaiah we find the word *almah*, which means a young woman – not necessarily a virgin. When, however, the Hebrew Bible was translated into Greek sometime around 200 BC, *almah* was translated by the Greek word *parthenos*, which means "virgin". Matthew quoted from the Greek translation, and not from the original Hebrew.

Today's first reading from the prophet Isaiah was written at some time during the eighth century BC. It was addressed to King Ahaz, and referred to events that were taking place there and then. In other words, Isaiah was not looking seven centuries into the future and foretelling the birth of Jesus. The prophet was telling King Ahaz that a maiden would soon give birth. There would be nothing miraculous about that birth – the maiden is not a virgin – but it would be a sign for the king.

Let us spend a few moments trying to understand what's happening here. Just over 700 years before the birth of Christ, the army of Assyria was on the move. The capital city of Assyria, the superpower of the region, was located in what is modern day Iraq. In the eighth century BC the area we now know as the state of Israel was divided. The northern part of modern Israel was then known as Israel and its capital was Samaria. The southern part was known as Judah and its capital was Jerusalem where King Ahaz ruled on the throne of David.

The kings of Syria and Israel had formed an alliance to protect themselves from Assyria, their common enemy. But they recognised that the odds were overwhelmingly against them, so they decided to enlist additional help. These two kings therefore sent envoys to King Ahaz in Judah, inviting him to join their mutual defence pact. Ahaz was no fool. He had assessed Assyria's military might far more realistically that the kings of Syria and Israel and concluded that if the kingdom of Judah had any chance of survival at all he would have to surrender to Assyria. This meant that Judah would lose its independence and have to pay tribute to Assyria. But at least Judah wouldn't be obliterated. Ahaz therefore refused to join the alliance.

The kings of Syria and Israel were not happy with Ahaz's refusal to join them, and they decided to use bullying tactics and attack Jerusalem. They mobilised their armies to march on Jerusalem with the intention of deposing Ahaz and placing a more cooperative king on the throne of Judah. So the armies of Syria and Israel are encamped outside the walled city of Jerusalem, and what does Ahaz decide to do? He decides to enlist the help of Assyria to defeat the armies of Syria and Israel. At this stage, enter the prophet Isaiah. Ahaz's kingdom is in a perilous position with hostile armies encamped on his doorstep. And what advice does Isaiah give? He says quite simply, "Don't seek Assyria's help. Trust in God, and everything will turn out alright." Ahaz dismisses this as pious humbug. So Isaiah then says, in so many words, "What I'm telling you is coming directly from God, and if you don't believe me, ask God for a sign." A sign would be a guarantee that Isaiah was speaking with divine authority. But Ahaz refuses to ask for a sign because if Isaiah's message is confirmed by a sign, he would then be acting directly against the will of God were he to go ahead with his plan. Ahaz has already made his decision – an alliance with Assyria – and nothing is going to change his mind. Certainly not the ramblings of some prophet. Isaiah isn't very happy at Ahaz's total disregard for what he's saying, so he tells the king, "Because you won't listen to me, because you won't ask God for a sign that what I'm saying does indeed come from God, God will give you a sign anyway, and here it is: 'The maiden is with child and will soon give birth to a son whom she will call Immanuel, a name that means God-is-with-us.'"

That sign obviously means something to Ahaz. Biblical commentators suggest that the young woman referred to is Ahaz's wife. The child soon to be born will therefore assure Ahaz of an heir, and therefore his dynasty will continue. End of story, as far as we're concerned today. What happened to Ahaz? Was Jerusalem destroyed by the armies of Israel and Syria? Did Assyria intervene on Judah's behalf? If you want to find out how things turned out, it's all recorded in the Second Book of Kings and the Second Book of Chronicles.

But what is all of this saying to us today? There is something of Ahaz in each of us. Ahaz is a perfect example of the person who is so determined to follow his own plans that he shuts out all dissenting voices, even the voice of God. Irving Stone's novel *The Agony and the Ecstasy* is the story of Michelangelo's life. At the age of thirteen Michelangelo tells his father, Lodovico, that he wishes to commence an apprenticeship as a painter. That is not part of Lodovico's plan for his son. Michelangelo is to be apprenticed to the Wool Guild. "I sent you to an expensive school, paid out money I could ill afford so that you would be educated and rise in the Guild until you had your own mills and ships … Do you think that I will now allow you to waste your life as a painter? To bring disgrace to the family name! …"[16] Like Ahaz, Lodovico is tunnel-visioned. He refuses to see beyond his own ambition; he is blind to his son's great gift. Each day is an Advent for those who have eyes to see, for those who have ears to hear.

---

[16] Irving Stone, *The Agony and the Ecstasy*, Fontana Books, London, 1961, p. 20.

CHRISTMAS DAY

(DECEMBER 25)

The Word became flesh and lived among us.
(Jn 1:14)

A certain parish was preparing a dramatic reenactment of the Christmas story for the children's Christmas Mass. The young children in the cast were exceptionally well behaved, with the exception of the young lad who had been chosen to play the part of Joseph. He'd been so naughty that the parish priest relegated him to the rather minor role of the innkeeper at Bethlehem. He was furious that Joseph's role had been given to someone else, and he began plotting his revenge.

The children's Mass had commenced, and the nativity play was progressing according to script. Mary and Joseph had finally reached Bethlehem, but, as you remember, they couldn't find anywhere to stay. Mary was soon to give birth, but the town was overcrowded. Finally, they came to an inn. If there was no accommodation at the inn, they'd have to bunk down for the night in a stable. Joseph knocked loudly at the door of the inn. The door opened, and there stood the innkeeper with a gleeful look in his eye. "Come on in," he said. "You're lucky. We've just had a cancellation!"

* * *

The gospel for the "Mass During the Day" is taken from the prologue of St John's gospel, a hymn that extols the Word through whom God created all things that came to be, the Word who became flesh and dwelt among us. "Word" is a translation of the ancient Greek word "logos," and it has a wide variety of meanings in Greek literature. In the Septuagint (the Greek translation of the Hebrew Scriptures commenced in the second century BC) *logos* is a translation of the Hebrew word *dābār*. Isaiah likens the all-powerful word (*dābār*) of God to the rain and the snow that come down from the sky "and do not return before having watered the earth, fertilising it and making it germinate to provide seed for the sower and food to eat, so it is with the word that goes from my mouth: it will not return to me unfulfilled or before having carried out my good pleasure and having achieved what it was sent to do (55:10,11). The book of Genesis begins with the words "In the beginning", and tells how God creates through his word. "God said ... and so it was." John's gospel also begins with the words "In the beginning", and it too tells the story of creation.

We're told in the book of Genesis that God rested after all his work of creating. God was proud of all that he had created, but he was especially proud of the man and woman he had created, because he had breathed into them a part of himself, his own spirit. But, according to an ancient legend, the devil was jealous and angry at the love God lavished on the man and the woman. So one day when God was walking with the man and the woman in the cool of the evening, the devil casually happened to walk by.

He walked up to God and asked him what he liked so much about these creatures. And when God opened his mouth to speak, the devil put a clamp upon God's tongue so that he could not speak! God could not speak! And since God's creative power was in his word, the devil had bound God's creative power. The devil laughed at God, and had his way with the man and the woman, leading them into all kinds of trouble. Aeons passed, and the devil returned to mock God — he couldn't resist. He scoffed at the silent deity and taunted this helpless God. God's only response was to hold up one finger. "One?" asked the devil. "Are you trying to tell me that you want to say just one word? Is that it?" Yes, God nodded, pleading with his soft eyes and urgent hands. The devil felt confident. "I don't suppose that even God could do very much harm with one word. OK." So the devil removed the clamp from God's tongue. And God spoke his one word, in a whisper. He spoke it for the man and the woman and it brought them great joy. It was a word that gathered up all the love, forgiveness and creativity God had been storing in his heart during the time of his silence.

The word he spoke was Jesus![17]

---

[17] Slightly adapted from William J. Bausch, *Storytelling: Imagination and Faith*, pp. 115-6.

THE HOLY FAMILY OF JESUS, MARY AND JOSEPH

(YEAR A)

I called my Son out of Egypt.
(Mt 15:15, quoting Ho 11:1)

The story of the flight into Egypt is recorded only in Matthew's gospel, which is strange because it would seem to be a major event in the life of the holy family. Herod is insanely jealous of any potential rivals to his throne, and commissions a heinous crime — the murder of all children the same age as the promised Messiah. Joseph is warned in a dream to escape into Egypt with Mary and the baby, and they remain there until the death of Herod. Joseph, Mary and the child Jesus then return to Israel and settle in Nazareth. Matthew tells us that this was to fulfil the words spoken through the prophet, "I called my son out of Egypt".

Those words give us a vital clue to interpreting the meaning of this strange episode. They were spoken by the prophet Hosea (11:1) some time in the eighth century before Christ. His words were not referring to an event some 800 years in the future — that is, God calling Jesus, Mary and Joseph back from Egypt. Hosea's words referred to God calling his people from slavery in Egypt to freedom in the Promised Land. In other words, Hosea was referring to that epic event we call the Exodus. And there is the clue we need.

Matthew wrote his gospel some fifty years after the death of Jesus.[18] He was writing for a community that included converts of both Jewish and Gentile descent.[19] And many of those Jewish converts were still trying to reconcile their ancient Jewish heritage with their newly found faith in Jesus as the Messiah. Matthew therefore attempts to show that Jesus is the fulfilment of all that God had promised to the Jewish people.

The great figure in the Jewish tradition was Moses, and the event that gave the Jews their identity as a nation was the Exodus. Matthew therefore presents Jesus as a new Moses, and his ministry as a new Exodus. But Matthew does

---

[18] Raymond Brown argues for a date in the 80s. Raymond Brown, *The Birth of the Messiah*, Doubleday, New York, 1979, p. 46.
[19] Ibid, p. 45.

it subtly. He uses a technique, familiar to the rabbis, called midrash. Midrash doesn't refer to a stomach rash. It's a technique that often involves telling a story against the backdrop of another story — a well known story — and inviting the audience to recognise the parallels.[20] One of the favourite techniques used by the New Testament writers "is to take significant events from the Old Testament and repeat or echo them in a different context to show that Jesus had assumed the role that was previously filled by the great figures of the Hebrew Scriptures, such as Moses."[21]

So, what are some of the key episodes in the Exodus story? Remember how Joseph the son of Jacob ended up in Egypt? Joseph's brothers were jealous of him, and sold him into slavery. He ended up in Egypt, and rose to become a high official in Pharaoh's household. His ability to interpret dreams was responsible, in large part, for his rise to prominence. During a time of famine, Joseph's family is forced to seek food in Egypt, and there the family is reunited. They remain in Egypt and grow in numbers.

The Jews prospered in Egypt, and a later Pharaoh regarded them as a potential threat. He therefore ordered the midwives to kill all Jewish boys as soon as they were born. One Jewish mother had just given birth to a son, before the arrival of the midwife. She kept the child hidden for some months, but when that was no longer possible she places the child in a papyrus basket and hides him among the reeds by the shore of the Nile river. Pharaoh's daughter comes across the baby, thinks he is very cute, and decides to keep him. She names him Moses. It is the adult Moses who eventually leads his people out of slavery in Egypt, and into the Promised Land.

And by now, you should have picked up a few of the parallels. The father of Jesus is called Joseph, and the Lord speaks to Joseph through dreams. Ring any bells? Pharaoh attempts to kill all Jewish babies because the Jews pose a potential threat to his sovereignty. Herod attempts to kill all Jewish children because one of them may grow up to usurp his throne. The Jewish people are led by Moses out of Israel. "I have called my son out of Egypt." The Holy Family is called out of Egypt. "I have called my son out of Egypt."

Does that mean that Matthew made up the story of what we call the "slaughter of the innocents", the flight into Egypt, and the return to Israel? Well, before

---

[20] According to Raymond Brown the term "midrash" does not do justice to the infancy narratives. The infancy narratives "were written to make Jesus' origins intelligible against the background of the fulfillment of OT expectations." (Brown, *The Birth of the Messiah*, p. 37).

[21] Richard Holloway, *Doubts and Loves*, Canongate, Edinburgh, 2001, p.150.

responding to that question, it's worth noting that there are certain elements in the story that ring true. Herod's slaughter of the innocents is mentioned only in Matthew's gospel. None of the other three gospel writers mentions it at all, nor is there any historical record of such a slaughter. There is, however, historical evidence that Herod was pathologically insecure, and had three of his own sons put to death. The Roman emperor Augustus once commented on Herod's brutality when he said that "It is safer to be Herod's pig than his son."[22] The Jewish historian Josephus tells us of an incident that occurred as Herod approached death. He instructed his soldiers to kill all notable political prisoners upon the news of his death. His idea was that the people's grief at the death of these prisoners would dampen their glee at the news of his own death.

Almost certainly, though, the events of today's gospel are not historical. The American Scripture scholar Fr Raymond Brown is a leading authority on the infancy narratives and he concludes: "There are serious reasons for thinking that the flight to Egypt and the massacre at Bethlehem may not be historical."[23] And that is not a radical point of view. Brown would be expressing the consensus view. In other words, when we hear this episode in the gospels, we have to be aware of Matthew's purpose. He is not conveying facts about the infancy of Jesus, but communicating a truth about Jesus' identity. Jesus is the new Moses. But Matthew is also attempting to describe the effect that Jesus had upon his contemporaries. In meeting Jesus, people felt liberated. The chains of oppression were cast off. He is truly the leader of a new Exodus.

---

[22] William Barclay points out that the saying is "even more epigrammatic in Greek, for in Greek *hus* is the word for a *pig*, and *huios* is the word for a *son*. William Barclay, *Gospel of Matthew*, Volume 1, The Saint Andrew Press, Edinburg, 1956, p. 20. The saying is found in Macrobius' *Saturnalia*, II iv 11 (cf. Brown, *The Birth of the Messiah, p.* 226).

[23] Raymond Brown, *The Birth of the Messiah*, p. 227.

FEAST OF THE EPIPHANY

(YEAR A)

Some wise men came to Jerusalem from the east. (Mt 2:1)

"Epiphany" comes from two Greek words meaning a "shining forth", "manifestation" or "appearance". In secular Greek the word indicated the appearance of the saving deity and the experience of the saving act.[24] There are many manifestations or epiphanies in the gospels — occasions on which something is manifested or revealed about Jesus. The visit of the magi is the first such manifestation: the wise men from the East recognise in Jesus "the infant King of the Jews" and come to do him homage. Epiphanies are therefore revelations, for those who have eyes to see. Max Bolliger tells the delightful story of a shepherd boy who was awaiting the appearance of the Great King. "Will the Great King wear a golden crown?", the young boy asked his grandfather. "And a rich cloak? And will he carry a shining sword?" How awesome and splendid the Great King would be. Every morning and evening the young shepherd boy played his flute, practising until he played better than anyone else. He wanted to be ready with a special tune when the Great King arrived. He would not play a tune for a king without a crown or a rich cloak or a sword. No, he thought, the Great King will make him rich with gold and silver. A king without a crown, a rich cloak or a sword would have nothing to give. Suddenly, angels appeared in the night sky. "Do not be afraid," they called, "for tonight your promised king is born." The shepherds set out at once with great haste, the young boy running fastest of all. He arrived first at the place over which the star had stopped and looked down at a babe in a manger. "These are poor people. This baby cannot be the Great King. I will not waste a king's tune on a baby." Although the other shepherds bowed low before the baby, the young boy turned away angry and disappointed. He no longer saw the deep, mysterious sky, nor the angels hovering above the stable. As he walked away through the snow he could hear the baby crying, but he did not want to hear the sound. He knew, though, that the baby was crying for something only he could give. The child's parents and the shepherds tried to soothe the crying

---

[24] Horst Balz and Gerhard Schneider, *Exegetical Dictionary of the New Testament, Volume 2*, William B. Eerdmans Publishing Company, Grand Rapids, MI, 1981, p. 44.

child, but without success. So, pulling out his flute, the shepherd boy began to play the tune he had prepared for the Great King. The baby began to cry less, and soon lay quietly in the manger. The child looked up at the boy and smiled, and that moment was a true epiphany. "Now I realise," the young shepherd thought to himself. "The Great King will not come wearing a golden crown and wearing a rich cloak and brandishing a shining sword. He has come as a helpless baby, not with gold and silver, but with love."[25]

In Matthew's story of the Epiphany there are two sets of wise men. When King Herod heard talk of a rival king of the Jews he immediately summoned his own wise men, the chief priests and scribes. He asked them where the child was to be born. The question didn't throw them into a spin. They didn't say, "Oh, Your Highness, give us some time to consult the scriptures and the writings of the rabbis." They didn't need to Google it! Without batting an eyelid, Herod's own wise men respond immediately — "at Bethlehem in Judea". And they even quoted chapter and verse: The prophet Micah, chapter five, verse one. But we never hear of Herod's wise men again. They knew exactly where the child was to be born — in Bethlehem, only ten kilometers from Jerusalem – but they didn't budge. They didn't do a thing. They refused to see what was virtually right in front of their eyes.

Dead Poets Society, a 1989 movie directed by Peter Weir, is set in 1959 at Welton Academy, a traditional and autocratic boys' college where the ethos is embodied in the four pillars: Tradition, Honour, Discipline and Excellence. This is the story of an English teacher, John Keating, who inspires his students to break out of their lives of conformity. At one point during a lesson Mr Keating leaps up into his desk and asks the class, "Why do I stand up here? Anybody?" One of the students replies, "To feel taller." "No!" replies Keating, and he explains. "I stand upon my desk to remind myself that we must constantly look at things in a different way. You see, the world looks very different from up here. You don't believe me? Come see for yourself. Come on. Come on!" Two of the students go to the front of the classroom and join him on the desk. Keating jumps down from the desk and tells the class, "Just when you think you know something, you have to look at it in another way. Even though it may seem silly or wrong, you must try!"[26]

---

[25] Adapted from Max Bolliger, *The Shepherd's Tune*, Macdonald Futura Publishers, London, 1981.

[26] The script of the screenplay can be downloaded from http://www.scifiscripts.com/msol/dead_poets_final.txt

Epiphanies demand that kind of openness, as the young shepherd boy was to discover. It was a lesson that Herod's wise men never learnt. They were so bound by Tradition that they couldn't look at what they knew in another way. The other wise men in Matthew's story — the magi — were prepared to take that risk. They set out to follow a star, not knowing where it might lead; not knowing who or what they might encounter; and not knowing how their journey might change their lives.

The magi have a lesson to teach us. If we truly seek God's will, we must take the same risk and step out into the unknown, not knowing where it might lead us, or how it might challenge us. There is, however, within all of us an ingrained reluctance to step out into the unknown. In Tolkien's modern classic, *The Hobbit*, there is an amusing scene in which the wizard Gandalf tells Bilbo that he is looking for someone to share in an adventure that he's arranging, but he's finding it very difficult to find anyone. "I should think so – in these parts!" replies Bilbo. "We are plain quiet folk and have no use for adventures. Nasty disturbing uncomfortable things! Make you late for dinner! I can't think what anybody sees in them ...".[27] John Keating encourages his students to take the risk — to follow their star, to search for the truth, and to struggle to remain faithful to the vision of that truth: "Boys, you must strive to find your own voice. Because the longer you wait to begin, the less likely you are to find it at all. Thoreau said, 'Most men lead lives of quiet desperation.' Don't be resigned to that. Break out!"

The magi, these seekers after truth, did "break out" and the truth they encountered unsettled them, but it also changed the way they saw life. In T.S. Eliot's poem *Journey of the Magi* one of the wise men looks back upon the journey from the vantage point of years afterwards: "this Birth was / Hard and bitter agony for us, like Death, our death. / We returned to our places, these Kingdoms, / But no longer at ease here, in the old dispensation, / With an alien people clutching their gods."[28]

---

[27] J.R.R. Tolkien, *The Hobbit*, HarperCollins Publishers, London, 1996, p. 6.
[28] T.S. Eliot, *Selected Poems*, Faber Paperbacks, London, Reprinted 1980, pp. 97-8.

ASH WEDNESDAY

(FEBRUARY 9)

Remember that you are dust and unto dust you shall return.

More than 20 tonnes of fireworks were ignited during Sydney's New Year's Eve celebrations to herald in the year 2000. At the very end of this spectacular display six billion television viewers worldwide beheld a single word fashioned in a style known as copperplate emblazoned across the Harbour Bridge. That single word was *Eternity*.

That word *Eternity*, written in chalk in the same elegant copperplate, appeared on Sydney's footpaths over half a million times between 1930 and 1967. It was written by a man named Arthur Stace. Arthur Stace was born in a Balmain slum in 1884. His mother and father were alcoholics as were his four siblings, two brothers and two sisters. His sisters operated a brothel and were constantly in trouble with the law. As a young boy Arthur slept on bags under the house and had to fend for himself because his parents were constantly drunk. He regularly stole milk from neighbours' doorsteps, picked food scraps from garbage cans, and stole cakes and sweets from local shops. At 12 years of age he was made a ward of the State, but his schooling was practically non-existent. At the age of 14 he was employed in a coal mine, squandered his first pay cheque in a local hotel. By the time he had turned 15 he was in jail for the first of many visits. By now he was well on the way to being an alcoholic himself.

In his 20s Arthur lived in Surry Hills running liquor between pubs and brothels, and he was also involved with illegal gambling and housebreaking. During the First World War he enlisted in the 19th Battalion and served in France. He returned from active service partially blind in one eye and suffering the effects of poisonous gas. Back in Surry Hills again, he soon lapsed into familiar ways. Drink gained an even stronger hold over him and he ended up living on handouts. Before long, the only drink he could afford was methylated spirits at sixpence a bottle.

On August 6, 1930, Stace attended a meeting for men at St Barnabas' Church on Broadway. Most of the 300 men present were down and outs, but it wasn't a sudden call to conversion that had brought them to church. St Barnabas served tea and rock cakes, but the men had first to sit through an hour-and-a-half sermon before refreshments were served. Six well-dressed men sat near the front of the church, quite apart from the rest of the congregation. Stace asked the man next to him, a well-known criminal: "Who are they?" And the reply: "I'd reckon they'd be Christians." Stace then said: "Well look at them and look at us. I'm having a go at what they've got." And he slipped down on his knees and prayed. From that moment onwards Arthur regained his self-respect and soon had a job working at the sand mills in Maroubra every alternate week for the grand sum of three pounds a week. Several months later he attended a service at the Burton Street Baptist Church at Darlinghurst. The preacher was the Reverend John Ridley, a Military Cross winner from World War One, and a noted fire and brimstone preacher. Ridley shouted from the pulpit, "I wish I could shout eternity through all the streets of Sydney!"

Recalling that day many years later in 1965, Stace remembered Mr Ridley repeating "Eternity, Eternity." "His words were ringing through my brain as I left the Church. Suddenly I began crying, and I felt a powerful call from the Lord to write 'Eternity'. I had a piece of chalk in my pocket and I bent down right there and wrote it. The funny thing is that before I wrote I could hardly have spelt my own name. I had no schooling and I couldn't have spelt Eternity for a hundred quid. But it came out smoothly in beautiful copperplate script. I couldn't understand it and I still can't."

From that day onwards, Stace began his unique ministry. He started early, usually before dawn, and wandered through all the streets of Sydney, bending down and writing on the pavement in large, elegant copperplate. He died of a stroke in a nursing home on July 30, 1967 at the age of 83 having written this one word at least 50 times each day for 37 years.

Two years after Stace died, the poet Douglas Stewart published the following reflection:

That shy mysterious poet Arthur Stace
Whose work was just one single mighty word ...

All night he walked and most nights of the week,
Treading with silent steps the silent town
Where none but drunks and whores were still awake,
His great word burning where he wrote it down;
ETERNITY he wrote, clear pure and pale,
And underlined it with the *y*'s long tail, ...

It was the greatest of all words he wrote
And if it hardly changed this wicked city
God rest his soul, his copperplate was pretty.[29]

During this Ash Wednesday liturgy we also will receive a reminder of eternity. Ash will be placed on our forehead and we shall hear the words, "Remember that thou art dust, and unto dust thou shalt return." This world, beautiful as it is, is not all there is. Our life is controlled and dominated by time, but our destiny is eternity. In the brief time entrusted to us let us repent with Arthur Stace, for — in the words of the prophet Joel — our God is all tenderness and compassion, slow to anger, rich in graciousness, and ready to relent.

---

[29] The complete poem may be found at http://oldpoetry.com/poetry/28269

FIRST SUNDAY OF LENT

(YEAR A)

Jesus was led by the Spirit out into the wilderness
to be tempted by the devil.
(Mt 4:1)

Some years ago a cartoon in the English Catholic magazine *The Tablet* showed a woman admiring a garment draped over a dummy in the window of a fashionable boutique. The boutique was advertising a "Lent Sale", and the garment displayed in the window was made of sackcloth. However, a sign attached to the garment read "Discontinued Line." Not only is penitential garb now a discontinued line, but penitential practices in general seem decidedly unfashionable. Asceticism has quietly slipped from the lexicon of contemporary Catholicism, but nothing is more essential to the Christian life. Catholics are now bound to fast and to abstain from meat on only two days of the year – Ash Wednesday and Good Friday. Ironically, though, diets of one kind or another proliferate in lifestyle magazines and television programmes, and many people have given up meat for health reasons. Margaret Hebblethwaite asks us to consider how much money people will spend on going to a health farm to be ritually starved of most things except bran and carrot juice for a week. "Yet they come away feeling so pure, so improved, so whole, so healed."[30] Alan Jones, dean of Grace (Episcopal) Cathedral in San Francisco, writes that we "know what a perfect body is supposed to look like. But what about the perfection or the wholeness of the inner life?"[31] In the words of Allan Bloom, "students have powerful images of what a perfect body is and pursue it incessantly. But ... they no longer have any image of the perfect soul, and hence do not long to have one. They do not even imagine there is such a thing."[32]

Perhaps fasting has fallen on hard times because it was trivialised by casuistry. Fr Edmund Campion reminisces on the time when Catholics fasted from midnight

---

[30] Margaret Hebblethwaite, "Repent and Believe" in *The Tablet*, 7 March 1998, p. 311. The cartoon mentioned in this homily is also to be found on this page.
[31] Alan Jones, *Passion for Pilgrimage*, Morehouse Publishing, Harrisburg, PA, 1999, p.18.
[32] Allan Bloom, *The Closing of the American Mind*, Simon and Schuster, New York, 1987, p. 381, quoted in Jones, p.18.

before receiving Holy Communion. "Yet what constituted food or drink? If you went to sleep with chewing gum in your mouth and then swallowed it, was the fast broken? Did toothpaste break the fast? And, for that matter, how did one compute midnight: summer time, metropolitan time, or Eastern Standard Time?"[33]

So, why should we fast? One obvious answer is that Jesus himself fasted. Matthew's gospel tells us that Jesus prepared for his public ministry by fasting for forty days and forty nights in the desert. At the end of the forty days Jesus encounters the tempter, and the temptations "revolve around the true understanding of what it means to be the Son of God and the royal Messiah."[34] That entails confronting the shadow side of his vocation. In psychological terms one could say that Jesus had to grapple with the tyranny of the ego. Daniel O'Leary points out that most of the "wise and holy people agree, that if we are to reach an appropriate maturity and responsible individuality, we must discern our egotism from our true self, and we begin to do this by keeping a vigilant watch over the arrogance and self-righteousness of the ego."[35] Asceticism arms us for the battle.

Arthur Miller's play *Death of a Salesman* is about Willy Loman, a tragic figure whose life of self-delusion ends in suicide. Willy's son Biff says of his father, "He never knew who he was." Shakespeare's *King Lear* is also about truth-telling. Stripped of all that he possessed, Lear laments, "Who is it that can tell me who I am?" Asceticism – from the Greek word *askesis* meaning "practice," "bodily exercise" or "athletic training" – is essentially about struggle. Asceticism – fasting is probably the most common ascetical practice – is a struggle in which "we deny ourselves to help us grow in self-knowledge: to show up our own attachments and compulsions and to assist us in letting go of them, and to see ourselves for who we truly are."[36]

Jesus is tempted to turn stones into bread. This is tantamount to doubting that God will provide, just as Israel rebelled in the wilderness. Fr Timothy Radcliffe, former Master General of the Dominicans, tells of a confrere, Brian Pierce, who fasted for twenty-eight days in New York on water alone. Pierce writes, "Fasting creates within us an openness, an emptiness, a space where God can surprise us with something new. ... (F)asting helps us to step back and allow a quiet, empty,

---

[33] Edmund Campion, *Rockchoppers*, Penguin Books, Ringwood, Vic, 1982, p. 69.
[34] John P. Meier, *A Marginal Jew, Volume Two: Mentor, Message, and Miracles*, Doubleday, New York, 1994, p. 271.
[35] Daniel J. O'Leary, *Travelling Light*, The Columba Press, Dublin, Reprinted 2002, p. 20.
[36] Megan Walker, "Why is fasting out of fashion?", *The Tablet*, 16 February 2002, p. 11.

sacred space of receptivity to be opened up."[37] Here in the quiet, empty space of the desert and later during the anguish of Gethsemane, Jesus is open to the will of his Father. As Messiah he will not use his anointing selfishly nor for his own advantage: "My Father ... let it be as you, not I, would have it" (Mt 26:39).

The tempter then challenges Jesus to throw himself down from the parapet of the Temple, thereby testing the truth of God's promise to protect him. Jesus refuses to test God's hand. Voltaire once observed "If God created us in His own image, we have certainly returned the compliment."[38] True trust, however, "includes an obedience which allows God to be God."[39]

Jesus is tempted to seek power: "I will give you all the kingdoms of the world." Alain de Botton's book *Status Anxiety* is based on the premise that status in the broad sense is determined by "one's value and importance in the eyes of the world." We become anxious when we are in "danger of failing to conform to the ideals of success laid down by our society." We may also worry that "we are currently occupying too modest a rung or are about to fall to a lower one."[40] In the words of Fr Timothy Radcliffe, fasting "loosens our greedy grasp on things. We cease to be consumers who must devour impulsively whatever is before us."[41] Tragically, though, many people measure success in terms of what they have rather than who they are. According to de Botton, once we have secured food and shelter our most basic need is love. Our desire to succeed in the social hierarchy "may lie not so much with the goods we can accrue or the power we can wield, as with the amount of love we stand to receive as a consequence of high status. Money, fame and influence may be valued more as tokens of — and as a means to – love rather than as ends in themselves."[42] The asceticism of Lent seeks to teach us quite a different lesson. "Lent is a time to practise dying by degrees, letting go of some things we love for a while so our souls learn the trick of it, ready for the real thing. The great mystery here is that the more we let go, the more we become what we really are."[43]

---

[37] Timothy Radcliffe, , "Why should we fast for Rwanda?", www.shineonline.net/mr2/pdf/timothy_radcliffe.pdf

[38] Quoted in M. Scott Peck, *Further Along the Road Less Travelled*, Simon & Schuster, New York, 1993, p. 230.

[39] Francis J. Moloney, *This is the Gospel of the Lord*, Year A, St Paul Publications, Homebush, NSW, 1992, p. 87.

[40] Alain de Botton, *Status Anxiety*, Hamish Hamilton, Camberwell, Vic, 2004, pp. 3-4,

[41] Quoted in Radcliffe.

[42] De Botton, p.11.

[43] Clifford Longley, "Giving up adjectives for Lent,", in *The Tablet*, 3 March 2001, p. 294.

SECOND SUNDAY OF LENT

(YEAR A)

There in their presence he was transfigured.
(Mt 17: 2)

On the first Sunday of Lent we accompanied Jesus as he entered the desert. On this second Sunday of Lent we accompany him up a high mountain. In the presence of Peter, James and John, Jesus is transfigured, an experience so powerful that the disciples do not want it to end. What does this experience say to us on our Lenten journey? The author of the book of *Ecclesiastes*, writing well over 2000 years ago, observed "there is a time for tears, a time for laughter; a time for mourning, a time for dancing" (Qo 3:4). Tears and laughter, mourning and dancing are mingled in every life, together with success and failure, pleasure and pain, joy and sorrow, triumph and suffering. For some people, though, the tears, mourning, failure, pain and suffering lead them to conclude that life itself is without any overall purpose or meaning. Journalist and broadcaster Philip Adams, for example, is able to say: "To me the universe is meaningless. There is no destiny, there's no author to creation. To me life is just a little brief flash in infinite darkness."[44]

Surely there are moments when all of us feel inclined to agree with Philip Adams. Life at times seems absurd, without any ultimate rhyme or reason. In 1989, a young Australian girl by the name of Melanie Woss took her own life at the age of 17. Her parents later found their daughter's reflections on a word processor, and they are now published under the title *Melanie*. At one point in her reflections Melanie wrote this: "Teenage suicides remind me of those old war movies where the biplanes get shot and spin out of control, faster and faster until, with a crash and a splash, they hit the dirt badly and leave only a few smouldering remains."[45]

Melanie is right. At times, life does seem like a biplane, shot and spinning out of control, hitting the ground with a crash and a splash. At times, life does seem absurd and irrational. But is that all there is? What about those moments in life, precious and few as they might be, that are charged with the promise of hope?

---

[44] Caroline Jones, *The Search for Meaning*, Collins Dove, Sydney, 1989, p. 78.
[45] Anabel Dean, "Melanie: Lost in the Dark", *The Sydney Morning Herald*, May 22, 1992.

Moments that often defy coherent description, but that leave an indelible impression of the sacred, of the holy? Moments like the birth of a child, a glorious sunset, falling in love, times of fun and laughter, experiences of conversion, fleeting encounters with beauty or goodness, feelings of divine assistance or guidance.

The Lutheran sociologist Peter Berger speaks of "signals of transcendence", a term which he uses to describe phenomena that are part of our ordinary everyday existence, but that somehow point beyond themselves.[46] The German scholar Rudolf Otto, in his important and influential book *The Idea of the Holy*,[47] coined the term "numinous" to describe these experiences. "Numinous" is an attempt to name the mystery and wonder (*mysterium*) that pervades human existence, that sense of mystery and wonder that is both awe-inspiring (*tremendum*) and fascinating or enticing (*fascinans*).[48] The Scottish-born American anthropologist Victor Turner and the Belgian anthropologist Arnold van Gennep speak of liminal or threshold experiences,[49] and Mircea Eliade, the doyen of historians of religion in North America, used the word "hierophany" to describe such moments.[50]

So, what are these numinous or liminal experiences, these signals of transcendence, these hierophanies? They may in fact be very ordinary human experiences, but in some indefinable way they appear to point beyond themselves. They transport us, however briefly, across the threshold between the sacred and the profane. They leave us with a feeling of awe. Whenever I've spoken about such experiences in discussion groups, it's never very long before people begin speaking about their own numinous experiences. I recall one nun talking about the moment she knew that she was called to religious life. As a young girl, she lived in a small country town, and was looking forward to the annual parish picnic. Unfortunately, the totally unexpected death of the local bishop meant that the picnic had to be postponed for several weeks. The young girl was very disappointed, but she looked forward to the postponed picnic with just as much eagerness. On the morning of the picnic, she remembers making her bed. It was at that moment that she was overcome by a powerful thought. "By the time I get into this bed tonight, the picnic will all be over." As an adult looking back on that

---

[46] Peter L. Berger, *A Rumour of Angels*, Penguin Press, Middlesex, 1970, p. 70.
[47] Rudolf Otto, *The Idea of the Holy*, Oxford University Press, 1958.
[48] See "Numen" in Mircea Eliade (ed) *The Encyclopedia of Religion*, Volume 11, Macmillan Publishing Company, New York, p. 21.
[49] Victor Turner, *The Ritual Process:Structure and Anti-Structure*, Routledge, London, 1969. See "Victor Turner" in Mircea Eliade (ed), Vol. 15, 94-6.
[50] Mircea Eliade, *Myths, Dreams and Mysteries*, Fontana, New York, 1968, p. 124.

experience, the nun was able to see the amusing side of the incident. But it was a powerful awareness of the transience of life. And it was from that moment that she felt called to the religious life.

Peter, James and John have yet to learn an important lesson. When Jesus is transfigured before their eyes they are overwhelmed by a sacred longing. Peter says, "Lord, it is wonderful for us to be here; if you wish, I will make three tents here, one for you, one for Moses and one for Elijah." They are covered by a bright cloud, and a voice says, "This is my Son, the Beloved; he enjoys my favour. Listen to him." That moment of majesty is fleeting, and when Jesus touches them they look up and see "no one but only Jesus." Writing about moments of enlightenment and awakening, Jack Kornfield makes the observation that "Most spiritual accounts end with illumination or enlightenment. But what if we ask what happens after that? What happens when the Zen master returns home to spouse and children? What happens when the Christian mystic goes shopping? What is life like after the ecstasy? How do we live our understanding with a full heart?"[51] Such experiences cannot endure. The title of Kornfield's book says it all: *After the Ecstasy, the Laundry*. These fleeting moments of sacred longing are signposts on our Lenten journey, Heavenly Messengers that remind us of the Divine Presence.

---

[51] Jack Kornfield, *After the Ecstasy, the Laundry*, Bantam Books, New York, 2000, pp. xiii-xiv.

THIRD SUNDAY OF LENT

(YEAR A)

When a Samaritan woman came to draw water, Jesus said to her,
'Give me a drink'. (Jn 4: 7)

On this Third Sunday of Lent, we commence the scrutinies, another step in the Rite of Christian Initiation of Adults. "Scrutinies" is a term that applied to the formal testing of catechumens before their baptism in the early church. When the Catechumenate was reintroduced in 1972 the rite included three scrutinies that take place after the homily on the third, fourth and fifth Sundays in Lent.[52] The first two scrutinies are followed by a presentation. After the first scrutiny, the candidates are presented with a copy of the Creed. Following the second scrutiny the candidates will receive a copy of the Lord's Prayer. The Church "lovingly entrusts to (the catechumens) ... the ancient texts that have always been regarded as expressing the heart of the Church's faith and prayer."[53]

Today's liturgy has something important to say to our catechumens and candidates in these final weeks leading up to their baptism or reception into full communion with the Catholic Church. The copy of the Creed that the catechumens receive is a succinct summary of all that we hold dear as Catholics; it offers in a nutshell the essence of our faith. The word Creed comes from two Latin words 'Cor' meaning 'heart; and 'dare' meaning 'to give'. The Creed, therefore, is a statement of truths to which we give our heart rather than a list of theological propositions to which we give intellectual assent. By accepting the Creed the catechumen is now located in a tradition and a story.

Today's gospel story offers a map for the journey of faith. The Samaritan woman whom Jesus meets at the well has no idea at first what he is trying to say to her. "How on earth can you get water from such deep well without a bucket?" Jesus is, of course, speaking about water of quite a different kind. She then moves to a partial faith because she is startled and amazed at what Jesus tells her about herself. She concludes that he is a prophet, and then wonders if he is the Christ? We'll never know if she ever got past wondering. Were the doubts that held her

---

[52] "Scrutiny", in F. L. Cross and E. A. Livingstone (eds) *The Oxford Dictionary of the Christian Church*, Oxford University Press, 1997, p. 1475.
[53] Rite of Christian Initiation of Adults, n. 134.

back ever resolved? Whatever about the woman, the Samaritan villagers are aroused by her curious story and go to the well to see Jesus for themselves. They invite him to their town and he remained with them for two days. They were at first drawn to Jesus because of the woman's testimony, but after hearing him for themselves they came to believe. They saw in Jesus something more than a prophet. "He really is the saviour of the world."

The journey of faith is not without doubts, misgivings and struggle. A young boy who came across a cocoon decided to keep it, just to see what kind of butterfly or moth would emerge. But he soon became impatient with the long wait. He decided to place the cocoon under a lamp, hoping that the warmth would speed up the process. And sure enough, after about a week a small opening began to appear on the underside of the cocoon. Suddenly little antennae emerged, followed by the head and tiny front feet. After a few hours, the creature had struggled to free its listless wings, and the colours revealed that it was a monarch butterfly. It wiggled, shook, and struggled, but then it seemed to be stuck. The butterfly couldn't seem to force its body through the small opening in the cocoon. So the young boy decided to give nature a hand. With his scissors, he began snipping the cocoon to free the butterfly. But once separated from the cocoon the creature crawled around dragging its wings and swollen body. Within a short time it died. The boy told his biology teacher what had happened, and the teacher then explained why the creature had died. The butterfly's struggle to get through the tiny opening was necessary in order to force fluids from its swollen body into its wings. Unless that happened it would not be strong enough to fly. Unless the butterfly struggles, its wings will never develop, it will never fly.

This story is an apt metaphor for our journey of faith. Today's first reading recalls the Israelite's struggle in the wilderness. They are tormented by thirst and regret having left Egypt. They complain against Moses: "Why did you bring us out of Egypt?" They complained when they were slaves in Egypt; now they complain about hardships in the wilderness and long to return. The Book of Numbers records their complaints in these words: "Think of the fish we used to eat free in Egypt, the cucumbers, melons, leeks, onions and garlic! But now we are withering away ..." (11:5,6).

How often on the journey of faith are we tempted to look backwards, craving for the cucumbers, melons, leeks, onions and garlic of our former life? A Leunig cartoon has a man proposing a toast: "Gentlemen, charge your glasses for a toast! Gentlemen, here's to the future." To which all gathered enthusiastically assent,

"To the future." And the drinking begins, and continues, and continues. And so, within a short time after the triumphant toast to the future, the conversation revolves around: "Whatever happened to ... Remember the time we .... We used to ... Who was the bloke who ... I'll never forget when we ... I used to have..." [54] In the ensuing alcoholic haze, they forsake the future and take refuge in the past.

Like the butterfly emerging from the cocoon, the Israelites' struggle in the wilderness of Sinai was essential. The desert purified them, and later generations were to look back upon the Exodus as a time of great intimacy with the Lord. Perhaps we can locate ourselves somewhere in today's stories: grumbling in the desert — craving for cucumbers, melons, leeks, onions and garlic and wanting to turn back; or with the woman sitting by the well, at first confused, then fascinated, but ultimately left wondering; or perhaps among the Samaritans who invited Jesus into their town and tasted for themselves the spring welling up to eternal life. The desert, the well or the town — where are you standing?

---

[54] Michael Leunig, *The Travelling Leunig*, Penguin Books, Ringwood, Vic, 1990, pages unnumbered.

FOURTH SUNDAY OF LENT

(YEAR A)

As Jesus went along, he saw a man who had been blind from birth.
(Jn 9:1)

I couldn't help smiling at a television advertisement for the new Mercedes-Benz E-Klasse. The scene is a public library. An attractive young woman approaches the librarian and places an order: "French fries, a burger and a milkshake." With a look of utter disdain the librarian replies, "This is a library." Somewhat taken aback the young woman looks about her and the reality of the situation gradually seems to sink in. So, somewhat chastened, she repeats her order – "French fries, a burger and a milkshake" – but in a whisper! "Beauty is nothing without brains," the advertisement tells us – so unlike a Mercedes! Beauty without brains, perhaps, but also a good example of sight without perception. And that could be the theme of today's readings.[55]

Let us review our Lenten journey so far. On the first Sunday of Lent we joined the Lord as the Spirit led him into the wilderness. There he prayed and fasted for forty days and forty nights. On the second Sunday of Lent we accompanied the Lord as he ascended a high mountain. There in the company of Peter, James and John he was transfigured. Last Sunday we travelled with Jesus on a journey through Samaria. His meeting with the villagers in a Samaritan town was the story of a journey from no faith to partial faith to full faith.

Today's gospel about the cure of a man born blind is about blindness and sight, about seeing and not seeing. That theme is announced in the first reading from the first book of Samuel. When the prophet Samuel came to Jesse with instructions from God to anoint one of his sons as the future king, all of Jesse's sons were paraded before the prophet. As Samuel looked over these fine young men he could not sense a future king of Israel standing before him. "Have you any other sons?" the prophet asked. And the answer, "Well, there's David, the youngest. He's out in the fields tending the flock." So David was summoned, and Samuel immediately recognised the future king of Israel in the least likely of all Jesse's sons. So often we cannot see what is right in front of us.

---

[55] See for yourself on Youtube: http://www.youtube.com/watch?v=fXT3Sma4-rg

In the later half of the nineteenth century the president of a small college on the west coast of America invited a bishop of the Evangelical United Brethren Church to dine with faculty members. During the course of the meal the president expressed his firmly held belief that humanity was on the threshold of brilliant new discoveries. "What did you have in mind?" the bishop asked. The president said he expected that flying machines would be invented sometime within the next fifty years. To which the bishop replied, "Rubbish, my dear man. If God had intended us to fly, He would have provided us with wings. Flight is reserved for the birds and the angels." The bishop's name was Milton Wright, and he had two sons named Orville and Wilbur — the inventors of the first airplane.

The cure of the man born blind is the sixth of seven signs in John's gospel. A man who is born blind can see again, and in the process of receiving physical sight he also becomes a believer. His belief in Jesus is contrasted with the Pharisees' lack of faith; his sight with their unwillingness or inability to see. They had eyes but could not see. Some time ago I was doing some research on anexoria nervosa, an eating disorder in which an individual fails to maintain a body weight that is normal for his or her age and height and suffers from a fear of becoming fat.[56] When I Googled "anexoria nervosa" I came across a video clip of a woman in late adolescence unenthusiastically pushing food around a plate but not eating. She constantly looks at herself in the mirror with a frown of disapproval, works out on an exercise bike, and then goes to the bathroom. The image that the viewer sees reflected in the bathroom mirror is that of a young woman, perhaps a little overweight, but certainly attractive. When the young woman herself comes into view, she is disturbingly thin. The body that she sees reflected back to her in the mirror bears no resemblance to her actual shape and weight. She refuses to see what is before her very eyes.

The Pharisees we read of in today's gospel were probably not wicked or evil people. But they were the Establishment, and they felt threatened by Jesus. He was offering them a different vision of life, a new way of seeing. Their present way of life was comfortable and familiar, and change would be challenging and painful. All establishments, be they secular or sacred, are reluctant to change. There is usually too much self-interest invested in maintaining the status quo. The former US Vice-President Al Gore has become an environmental activist, the harbinger of what he calls "an inconvenient truth." He argues that many oil and coal

---

[56] Elizabeth Rieger (Ed), *Abnormal Psychology*, McGraw Hill Educational, North Ryde NSW, 2008, p. 499.

companies are currently employing tactics adopted decades ago by the tobacco companies. Despite the US Surgeon General's report that made it abundantly clear that smoking can cause lung cancer, "the tobacco companies were working overtime to encourage Americans not to believe the science — to create doubts about whether there was any real cause for concern." As a result, people were tempted to take the report less seriously than they should have, with the result that "almost 40 years after the landmark Surgeon General's report linking smoking to lung cancer, emphysema, and other diseases in United States, more Americans continued to die from smoking-related causes than were killed during World War II." Gore concludes that "the clever and deceitful approach the tobacco companies used to confuse people about what the science really demonstrated added up to a model for the campaign that many oil and coal companies are using today to confuse people about what the science of global warming is really telling us."[57]

Consider another example. In 1630 the Holy Office condemned Galileo in these words: "The said Galileo (is) ... in the judgment of the Holy Office vehemently suspected of heresy, namely, of having believed and held the doctrine which is false and contrary to the Sacred and Divine Scriptures, that the sun is the centre of the world and does not move from the east to the west and that the earth moves and is not the centre of the world ..."[58] Galileo, then in his seventies, was called upon to "abjure, curse, and detest the said error and heresies." But it should be noted that it was not only the Church that should be blamed for the way in which Galileo was treated. Galileo also had many critics in the scientific world, many of whom sought to use the Church's influence to silence and discredit him because their own vested interests were threatened. The scientific world is not exactly innocent in this affair![59] Ecclesiastics and scientists, each for their own reasons, failed to see things as they are. They feared any challenge to the prevailing paradigm because it would upset their own tidy and comfortable universe.

Umberto Eco's novel *The Name of the Rose*[60] is a story of mystery and intrigue set in a monastery in fourteenth century Europe. The protagonist, Fr Jorge, will do all in his power, even kill, to prevent a certain manuscript from falling into the wrong hands.[61] The manuscript is a treatise on laughter by the ancient Greek philosopher Aristotle. Fr Jorge is a rigid and orthodox man and, ironically, he is

---

[57] Al Gore, *An Inconvenient Truth*, Bloomsbury, London, 2006, p. 256.
[58] Peter de Rosa, *Vicars of Christ*, Corgi Books, London, 1989, p. 319.
[59] Michael Morwood, *Tomorrow's Catholics*, Spectrum Publications, Melbourne, 1997, p. 19.
[60] Umberto Eco, *The Name of the Rose*, Picador, London, 1983.
[61] cf. Michael Whelan, *Without God All Things Are Lawful*, St Pauls, Homebush, 1994, p. 144.

blind. The irony of his blindness consists, I believe, in this: Laughter is subversive, because it occurs in that sudden, explosive moment when we see the gap between reality and appearance. We laugh at a well told joke because the punch line takes us by surprise. We see things in a totally unexpected way. Fr Jorge does not have a sense of humour. He is totally unwilling to view the world except through the spectacles of his own inflexibility. And that is the blindness that Jesus seeks to heal — the blindness of self-deception — a refusal to see things as they are.

FIFTH SUNDAY OF LENT

(YEAR A)

Lazarus, here! Come out!
(Jn 11: 43)

***The Diving-Bell & the Butterfly* by Jean-Dominique Bauby** is a remarkable book, not only for the story it tells, but also because of the extraordinary way in which it was written.[62] On Friday, 8 December, 1995, the author, aged in his early 40s, suffered a massive stroke that left him completely paralysed, speechless, and able to move only a single eyelid. With that one eyelid he "dictated" the book. And how did he dictate the book? Someone would read aloud the letters of the alphabet, not from A to Z, but according to the frequency of each letter as it is used in the French language. With a blink of the eye, Bauby would stop the reader at the appropriate letter. The book was therefore dictated letter by letter.

There was a time when people would have died after suffering a massive stroke. But, as Bauby observes, improved resuscitation techniques have now prolonged and refined the agony. "You survive," he writes, "but you survive with what is so aptly known as "locked-in syndrome." Paralysed from head to toe, the patient, his mind intact, is imprisoned inside his own body, but unable to speak or move. In my case, blinking my left eyelid is my only means of communication."[63]

Bauby had been editor-in-chief of the French magazine *Elle*, and the father of two young children. He now lay helplessly alive in the prison, in the tomb of his own body, like a diver encased in a diving-bell. He described his predicament in these words: "exiled, paralysed, mute, half deaf, deprived of all pleasures and reduced to a jellyfish existence...".[64] His former life is "reduced to the ashes of memory."[65]

Janine Shepherd was a gifted and dedicated athlete in a number of sports. She held national records in athletics, played State-level softball and netball, and had been NSW triathlon champion. She would almost certainly have represented Australia in cross-country skiing in the 1988 winter Olympics in Calgary. In her

---

[62] Jean-Dominique Bauby, *The Diving-Bell & the Butterfly*, Fourth Estate, London, 1997.
[63] Ibid, p.12.
[64] Ibid, p.33.
[65] Ibid, p.85.

own words, "My entire life had been devoted to sport. That was what I did best and what I lived for. I was fortunate that whatever sport I tried my hand at, it all came very easily. I couldn't imagine a life without sport. It was my passion."[66]

In a tragic split second Janine's life took an entirely new and unforeseen direction. One afternoon over ten years ago Janine set out on a bike ride with friends in Sydney's Blue Mountains. Her life was irrevocably altered when she was hit by a truck and flung from her bicycle. Her neck and back were broken. She had very serious internal bleeding that doctors were at first unable to stop. She was not expected to live. Even if, by some small chance, she recovered, it seemed unlikely that she would ever walk again.

Janine writes of her recovery in a book entitled *Never Tell Me Never*. It is the story of how she came to terms with her shattered Olympic dreams, and how she focused every sinew of her being on healing a broken body and crushed morale. *Never Tell Me Never* is the story of great courage and determination; it is also a story about death and new life; not a physical death, but the death of dreams, hopes, ambitions and plans for the future.

Janine was confined to bed for 13 weeks before she was ready to take her first step. On her first attempt at walking she shuffled and slided, centimetre by centimetre until she collapsed into a wheelchair, exhausted. She had taken four steps! Learning to walk again was a tremendous challenge, and living for months on end in a plaster cast was a great ordeal. It was, she said, as if she were wearing a straitjacket.

Improvement over the next few months was slow. She writes: "I began to feel frustrated at plodding along without any real progress. Each day became a boring repetition of the same old thing and it started to affect me."[67] While still in a plaster cast Janine decided that she was going to learn to fly. She booked in for a trial instructional flight and had a friend drive her out to Bankstown airport. After the flight she was more determined than ever that she was going to get a pilot's certificate, even though it would be a long time before she could pass the prerequisite medical examination.

Janine's situation mirrors that of the Jewish people in today's first reading from the prophet Ezekiel. Jerusalem had been destroyed, the Temple lay in ruins; they sat by the rivers of Babylon, exiles languishing in a foreign land. The prophet Ezekiel offers them hope: "The Lord says this: I am now going to open your

---

[66] Janine Shepherd, *Never Tell Me Never*, Sun, Sydney, Reprinted 1995, p. 8.
[67] Ibid, pp.147-8.

graves; I mean to raise you from your graves, my people, and lead you back to the soil of Israel."

And what became of Janine? Yes, she did eventually gain a pilot's licence, and exactly two years and nine days after the accident, she herself became a flying instructor. But not satisfied with conventional flying, Janine was fascinated by aerobatics. And not content with merely performing aerobatics, she signed up for a course to become an aerobatics instructor. And in the process Janine met her future husband. She is now the mother of two daughters and the final words of *Never Tell Me Never* express her joy: "I love my family, I love my life. It really is a wonderful time to be alive."[68]

"Jesus said to them, 'Unbind him, let him go free.'" Like Lazarus, freed from the shroud, Janine emerged from her plaster straitjacket to a new life. After despair and dashed hopes, she discovered a life immeasurably richer than anything she could have imagined before her accident.

Jean-Dominique's life did not have the same happy ending. But before his death on March 9, 1997, he had set up the Association of Locked-In Syndrome, thereby offering hope to others like himself of escaping in some way from the diving-bell, from the tomb, from the prison of their own bodies.

St Paul writing to the Christians of Rome in today's second reading reminds them "that he who raised Jesus from the dead will give life to your own mortal bodies through his Spirit living in you." In one way or another, we are all encased in a diving-bell body or a plaster straitjacket, waiting to be set free, like a butterfly emerging from its cocoon, waiting to be set free to soar through the skies. "Unbind him, let him go free."

---

[68] Ibid, p.313.

PASSION SUNDAY

(YEAR A)

But Jesus, again crying out in a loud voice, yielded up his spirit.
(Mt 7:50)

Jesus is betrayed with a kiss, and immediately armed soldiers seize him. Matthew's gospel tells us that one of the followers of Jesus (Peter, according to John's gospel) leapt to his defence and cut off the ear of the high priest's servant. Jesus tells him to put his sword back, for all who draw the sword will die by the sword. Matthew then informs us that Jesus tells his disciples that if he wished he could appeal to his Father, who would promptly send more than twelve legions of angels to his defence.

What would have happened if Jesus had called upon those twelve legions to defend him? Graham Greene's Monsignor Quixote had just such a dream. As the result of a humorous fiasco, Fr Quixote, the parish priest of a small Spanish town, is honoured by the Pope and made a monsignor, much to the chagrin of his local bishop. In need of a short holiday, Monsignor Quixote sets out for Madrid in the company of his close friend Zancas, the town's ex-mayor and an avowed Communist.

The terrible dream that profoundly disturbed Monsignor Quixote was that Christ had been saved from the Cross by a legion of angels. "So there was no final agony, no heavy stone which had to be rolled away, no discovery of an empty tomb. Father Quixote stood there watching on Golgotha as Christ stepped down from the Cross triumphant and acclaimed. The Roman soldiers, even the Centurion, knelt in His honour, and the people of Jerusalem poured up the hill to worship Him. The disciples clustered happily around. His mother smiled through her tears of joy."[69]

Christ's coming down from the cross in triumph would have done away with the need for genuine faith. Doubt, uncertainty and ambiguity would be banished from the Christian lexicon, and that leaves Monsignor Quixote uneasy. He awoke from his dream with "the chill of despair felt by a man who realises suddenly that he has taken up a profession which is of use to no one, who must continue to

---
[69] Graham Greene, *Monsignor Quixote*, Vintage Classics, London, 2000, p. 76.

live in a kind of Saharan desert without doubt or faith, where everyone is certain that the same belief is true." He found himself whispering, "God save me from such a belief."[70] Even the Marxist Zancas (whom Quixote affectionately calls Sancho) is not immune from doubt. The ghost of his professor haunts him: "I dream I am sitting in his lecture room and he is reading to us from one of his own books. I hear him saying, 'There is a muffled voice, a voice of uncertainty which whispers in the ears of the believer. Who knows? Without this uncertainty how could we live?'"[71] While both men try not to doubt, the Monsignor reflects that "sharing a sense of doubt can bring men together perhaps even more than sharing a faith."[72] And Quixote is riddled with doubt. "I am sure of nothing, not even of the existence of God, ... Doubt is human."[73]

There is undoubtedly a great deal of Greene himself in Monsignor Quixote's struggle with belief and doubt. Matthew, following Mark, has Jesus cry out from the cross in a loud voice, "My God, my God, why have you deserted me?" Fr Raymond Brown makes the observation that "Those who exalt the divinity of Jesus to the point where they cannot allow him to be truly human interpret away this verse to fit their christology. They insist that Psalm 22 ends with God delivering the suffering figure. That may well be, but the verse that Jesus is portrayed as quoting is not the verse of deliverance but the verse of abandonment — a verse by a suffering psalmist who is puzzled because up to now God has always supported and heard him ... Matthew, following Mark, does not hesitate to show Jesus in the utter agony of feeling forsaken as he faces a terrible death."[74] Alan Jones, Dean of San Francisco's (Episcopal) Grace cathedral, writes that "Graham Greene (and he is not alone) would have us believe that our doubts and ambiguities are sanctified, since God took us on in Jesus Christ so that our despair and failure are part of God's life as shown forth on the Cross."[75]

If Jesus were rescued from the cross by a legion of angels there would be no room for doubt and uncertainty. But neither, would there be room for that perfect love by which a person lays down his life for his friends. Today's reading of the Passion is the reading of a love story, and the wounds of the Passion reveal the depth of that love. An ancient legend recounts how the Devil tried to get

---

[70] Ibid, p. 77.
[71] Ibid, p. 112.
[72] Ibid, p. 59.
[73] Ibid, p. 205.
[74] Raymond E. Brown, "The Passion According to Matthew", *Worship*, 58,2, March 1984, pp. 105-6.
[75] Alan Jones, *Soul Making*, pp. 116-7.

into heaven by pretending to be the risen Christ. The Devil, being a master of disguises, took with him a contingent of demons made up as angels of light and stood before the gates of heaven and intoned the words of Psalm 24: "O gates, lift high your heads; grow higher, ancient doors. Let him enter, the king of glory!" The angels looked down on the one whom they thought was their king returning triumphant from the dead. So they shouted back with joy the next line of the psalm, "Who is the King of glory?" Then the Devil made a fatal mistake. In every particular save one he was just like Christ. When the angels in heaven thundered, "Who is the King of glory?" the devil opened his arms and said, "I am the King of Glory!" In that very act of arrogance he showed the angels he was an impostor, and they refused to let him enter. The angels knew he was an impostor because they saw no wounds in his hands.[76]

---

[76] Adapted from Alan Jones, *Passion for Pilgrimage*, p.155.

HOLY THURSDAY

He had always loved those who were his in the world, but now he showed how perfect his love was. (Jn 13: 1)

Babette's Feast is a charming short story by the Danish writer Isak Dinesen (a pseudonym for Karen Blixen) that first appeared in the *Ladies Home Journal* of May 1950. It was eventually made into a movie directed by Gabriel Axel, receiving the Academy Award in 1986 for Best Foreign Film.[77] Dinesen's story is set in Norway, but Axel located the movie in Norre Vosburg, an impoverished fishing village on the coast of Denmark. The story is set in the late 19th century and is essentially the tale of two pious sisters whose lives are defined solely by their religious beliefs, and the enigmatic Babette who lives with them as a domestic servant.

Martina and Philippa are the daughters of the charismatic founder of an austere Lutheran sect. After their father's death the sisters preside over the small community of disciples who are bound together by his memory, although much of the sect's early vitality has dwindled with the passing of time. The remaining members are elderly and their lives are blighted by the bitterness of past sins and disagreements. The community lives a frugal existence, their diet consisting of boiled cod and gruel made from bread boiled in water with a splash of ale. Their spiritual compass is set on the New Jerusalem, and they seem wary of the secular world and its values. It is difficult not to sympathise with the sisters' untiring dedication to good works and living a moral life, but something is clearly lacking. As young women they were both extremely attractive, but neither married. Martina successfully resisted the advances of a young cavalry officer, and Philippa rebuffed a famous operatic singer who was smitten by her beauty and her exquisite voice.

Thirty-five years pass, and during a stormy night a young woman arrives unannounced on their doorstep. Her name is Babette and she had lost her husband and son during the terrors of the French civil war. Speaking only French, Babette presents a letter of introduction from Achille Papin, the famous singer whom

---

[77] I have drawn liberally on the film *Babette's Feast*, and also from Wendy M. Wright, "*Babette's Feast:* A Religious Film", *Journal of Religion and Film*, (1, 2, October 1997), and from Philip Yancey, *What's so Amazing About Grace?* Zondervan, Grand Rapids, MI, 1997, pp. 19-26.

Philippa had spurned so many years before. The letter implored the sisters to give her refuge and assured them that "Babette can cook." Martina and Philippa have neither the money nor the inclination to employ a maid, but Babette softens their hearts. She offers to work for them in exchange for room and board.

Twelve years pass, and the sisters become extremely fond of her. One senses that Babette is dismayed by their simple diet, yet she never questions the tasks they assign her. On the occasion of what would have been their father's one-hundredth birthday, Martina and Philippa plan to hold a simple celebration. As the date approaches Babette receives word that she has won ten thousand francs in the French lottery thanks to a ticket renewed annually by an old friend. The sisters congratulate her, but with heavy hearts because they are sure that Babette will now return to France.

However, Babette makes a request that leaves the sisters feeling uneasy. She offers to prepare and pay for the anniversary meal for their father. Once the money arrives Babette begins to make preparations for what shapes up to be a sumptuous banquet – turtle and quail, pastries of lightness, sauces of unutterable delicacy, a gateau cradled in a nest of ripe fruits and drizzled with sweet liquor, grapes and figs, and an abundance of vintage wine – all served on a table draped with fine linen and adorned with gleaming silver candlesticks and elegant china.

The sisters are fearful that something akin to a witches' Sabbath is about to take place in their own home. They alert their guests who unanimously decide to attend the dinner, but not to comment on the food and to keep their minds resolutely fixed on higher things. All of them, that is, except Lorenz Lowenhielm, the dissolute young soldier who had been infatuated by Martina years earlier. Now a general, he attends the dinner as a guest of his aunt, and is overwhelmed by the exquisite fare that unfolds in magnificence before them. The food reminds him, he tells the guests, of a famous Parisian chef at the Café Anglais, a woman renowned for her culinary artistry in the years prior to the civil war.

The fine food and choice wines slowly prevail, and the guests — twelve of them — begin to respond, not only to the feast but also to each other. Old quarrels are healed and past grievances genuinely forgiven. When the feast comes to an end, the disciples join hands in a circle and dance together in the village square. Inside, Martina and Philippa thank Babette for the feast. They learn that she was the fabled chef of the Café Anglais. Moreover, she will not be returning to France for she has spent her entire lottery winnings on the meal.

On this Holy Thursday night we gather around the table of the Lord to celebrate a sacred banquet that is the "summit and source of the Christian life."[78] Like Babette's feast, this banquet is grace, it is "the gift par excellence", for it is the gift of the Lord himself, "of his person in his sacred humanity, as well as the gift of his saving work."[79] *Babette's Feast* is a parable of grace. Twelve people gather to celebrate a meal in honour of a revered pastor, and during the course of that banquet they are transformed. The exquisite food and fine wine is freely and graciously given to people who scarcely knew how to appreciate the feast that is laid before them. These people had "heard sermons on grace nearly every Sunday and the rest of the week tried to earn God's favour with their pieties and renunciations. Grace came to them in the form of a feast, Babette's feast, a meal of a lifetime lavished on those who had in no way earned it, who barely possessed the faculties to receive it. Grace came to Noore Vosburg as it always comes: free of charge, no strings attached, on the house."[80] So, too, does the ineffable mystery we celebrate on this holy night

---

[78] Second Vatican Ecumenical Council, *Dogmatic Constitution on the Church (Lumen Gentium)*, n.11.
[79] Pope John Paul II, *Ecclesia De Eucharistica*, n.11.
[80] Yancey, *What's so Amazing About Grace?*, p. 26.

GOOD FRIDAY

It is accomplished. (Jn 19:30)

We have four rather different accounts of the trial and crucifixion of Jesus in the gospels of Matthew, Mark, Luke and John. Each of these four accounts, written 30 to 60 years after the life of Jesus, reflects considerable theological development.[81] The key principle of any intelligent approach to the gospels must acknowledge that they are not literal or eyewitness accounts of what happened. The earliest of the four accounts is that of Mark, written about thirty years after the actual event. The last of the four gospel accounts to be written is the one we have just heard. John's gospel was written about sixty years after the death of Jesus. There is a dramatic contrast between the two accounts — that of Mark and that of John.

The starkest version of the Passion of Jesus is to be found in the gospel of Mark. In Mark's gospel all the disciples fail Jesus at the crucial moment. While Jesus prays in the Garden of Gethsemane, the disciples fall asleep, not once, but three times. Judas betrays Jesus, and Peter denies ever having known him. When Jesus is arrested and brought to trial all the disciples run away. One even leaves his clothes behind in a desperate bid to flee.

When Jesus is brought to trial in Mark's gospel, both Jewish and Roman judges are cynical. Jesus hangs on the cross for six hours. During the first three hours, he is mocked, taunted and scorned. During the second three hours, the land is covered with darkness. The only words Jesus speaks from the cross are, "My God, my God, why have you forsaken me?"

When Maria Richards died from cancer at the age of 42, she left behind a husband and four children aged between five and 11. The family was left reeling from the savage, destructive waste of Maria's death. Somehow the usual explanations that Jesus loved her so much that he'd taken her to heaven didn't seem adequate. If that were so, why did he allow her to suffer so much and for so long?" Maria had struggled with cancer for three years, but the last few months had been pain without end. Her last few weeks were agony. The last nights of her life were something like we might imagine hell to be. The cancer first appeared in

---

[81] My chief source for the contrast between the various biblical accounts of the passion is Raymond E. Brown, *The Death of the Messiah*, Volumes 1 & 2 Doubleday, New York, 1993.

a breast and spread rapidly into her bones, hips, pelvic girdle, spine and skull. She couldn't feed herself, nor in the final week could she even swallow. Death when it came was harrowing, a long night of agony in which Maria was screaming to her mother and sister to do something to take the pain away. The neighbours were awakened by her cries, which were not stilled by the saying of decades and decades of the rosary.

Maria had just 10 minutes of peace before she died, unable to breathe, and leaving her family shattered. The church in which Maria's funeral was celebrated was packed to the doors, a final testament to the love in which she was held. Maria had been crucified on the cross with Mark's Jesus, her life shrouded in darkness. Her last words could well have been, "My God, my God, why have you forsaken me."[82]

The account of the trial and death of Jesus in the gospel of John is quite different. John's portrait of Jesus is that of a self-assured sovereign, reigning victoriously from the cross. Jesus is in control of all that happens. "You have no power over me at all", he tells Pilate during the trial. He doesn't pray, as he does in Mark's gospel: "Father, if it be possible, let this cup pass from me." No, in John's gospel this is his "hour", his destiny, the whole purpose of his life. There is no Simon of Cyrene to help Jesus carry his cross in John's gospel. It is a burden he bears alone. Jesus' final words from the cross are a solemn proclamation. "It is finished." These are not words of abandonment. Even in death, water, a symbol of life, flowed from his pierced side.

Lorraine Cibilic died just after celebrating her 50th birthday in April 1995. Early in 1982 Lorraine Cibilic was taking her family on a Sunday picnic when she was critically injured in a car crash. The crash crushed Lorraine's body, leaving her with minimal chances of survival. It also claimed the life of her 10-year-old daughter.

Lorraine survived, but four years later her life was plunged into deeper tragedy. Tests proved that the blood transfusions she'd received in hospital had been contaminated with the AIDS virus. It was then that she contemplated taking her own life. But what followed instead were ten years of sheer, unrivalled dedication as a relentless campaigner for justice on behalf of Australia's 430 sufferers of medically acquired HIV.

Somehow, this extraordinary woman, together with her husband and son, found a wonderful reservoir of strength. An obituary, written by television

---

[82] Robin Richards, "Where is God in this?", *The Tablet*, 29 January, 1994.

journalist Chris Smith, said of Lorraine: "Day in, day out, she'd come to sit by the deathbeds of other sufferers to listen and encourage. Thousands of hours were spent letter writing and phone-calling as she discovered a secret, nationwide network of sufferers. Through dogged investigation, she uncovered evidence that in the early 1980s, despite official warnings, authorities had acted far too slowly to prevent further contamination of the blood supply. She was incensed to find others needlessly infected, and so given a death sentence."[83]

Lorraine lobbied government ministers and bureaucrats, and even led a concerned group of people in storming the NSW Parliament. In 1991, almost single-handedly, Lorraine forced a NSW Parliamentary inquiry into medically acquired HIV, which in turn led to little more than token financial settlements. In April of 1994, Lorraine achieved her ultimate victory. The High Court granted a just payment to the people she'd been fighting for. Lorraine herself was never in the legal category for financial assistance. This 10-year battle was all for others.

Two months before her death, Lorraine went blind and became paralysed. She decided to cease taking any more drugs and told a friend, "I'm ready to go now." Lorraine's final years were marked by courage, compassion and commitment. Her long journey to death had given life to so many others. At the hour of death her final words could well have been those of Jesus in John's gospel: "It is finished."

Maria lay in death with Mark's Jesus, abandoned and in darkness. Lorraine gave up her spirit, gloriously triumphant with John's Jesus. But herein lies the mystery we celebrate during these three sacred days. The body abandoned in darkness, the body gloriously triumphant, is laid to rest in the tomb. And on the third day, God raised Jesus from the dead.

---

[83] Chris K. Smith, "Campaigner inspired AIDS justice triumph", *The Australian*, April 17, 1995, p.10.

EASTER SUNDAY (YEAR A)

It was very early on the first day of the week and still dark,
when Mary of Magdala came to the tomb.
(Jn 20:1)

On the first day of the week, while it was still dark, Mary of Magdala came to the tomb – alone in John's gospel, and in the company of "the other Mary" in Matthew's account. According to John's gospel, once Mary of Magdala saw that the stone had been moved away she then ran to Simon Peter and the other disciple, the one Jesus loved, and told them "They have taken the Lord out of the tomb and we don't know where they have put him." Peter and the other disciple then set out together and saw for themselves that the tomb was indeed empty. The verse immediately following tells us that the two disciples then went home. Mary, however, remained standing outside the tomb, weeping. As she stooped to look inside the tomb she saw two angels in white sitting where the body of Jesus had been, and they ask her why she is weeping. She is weeping, she tells the angels, because "They have taken my Lord away and I don't know where they have put him." Mary then turns around and sees Jesus, although she does not recognise him. When he asks her why she is weeping and who she is looking for, she supposes he is the gardener: "Sir, if you have taken him away, tell me where you have put him, and I will go and remove him." Jesus then calls her by name — "Mary!" — and she turns around and address him in Hebrew — "Rabbuni!" — which means Master.

Following the publication of Dan Brown's 2003 best seller *The Da Vinci Code* there was a great deal of interest in Mary of Magdala. The central thesis of Brown's novel is a conspiracy theory! The Christian Church has been hiding a secret for almost two millennia: Mary Magdalene was the wife of Jesus and she carried his child with her when she fled to the south of France after the crucifixion. Their progeny intermarried with the locals, eventually founding the Merovingian dynasty.

What can be said of Mary of Magdala, the woman whom Christian tradition has often portrayed as a penitent, a reformed prostitute? Her name suggests that she came from Magdala, a city situated on the shore of the Lake of Galilee. The New Testament does not call Mary a prostitute. Mark 16:9 and Luke 8:2 tell us that Jesus had cast out seven devils from her, indicating the severity of the possession and nothing more. Mary is a prominent member among a group of women who followed Jesus on his preaching tours of Galilee and accompanied him to Jerusalem. According to Luke's gospel (8:3), Mary and other women of substance supported Jesus' travelling band with their money and their personal service. John P. Meier argues that Luke has preserved a valuable historical memory, suggested by the fact that "unchaperoned women sharing the preaching tours of a celibate male teacher is discontinuous with both the Judaism of the time and with what Luke presents — and with what we know — of the first-generation Christian mission."[84] This would almost certainly have offended and disturbed the stringently pious among Jesus' contemporaries.[85] The synoptic gospels and the gospel of John also place certain women followers at the scene of the crucifixion and at the finding of the empty tomb. Despite discrepancies in the names of the women in the four Gospels, Mary Magdalene is common to all the lists.[86] It is interesting to note, however, that none of the evangelists ever calls these women, including Mary Magdalene, a disciple, even though they literally and physically followed Jesus. It is true, though, that even if they are not given the title "disciple", the women "proved themselves disciples in deed if not in word not only by the economic support they gave Jesus during his journeys but also by their following him even to the cross, after the male disciples had betrayed, denied, or abandoned him."[87]

For many feminists Mary Magdalene "is an example of the woman's voice lost or suppressed in the male-dominated structures of the early church."[88] This is not feminist paranoia! It's interesting to note that while the evangelists restrict the title "apostle" to males, Paul mentions "Junia (*Iounian*, in the Greek text), prominent among the apostles" (Romans 16:7). The Patristic tradition had

---

[84] John P. Meier, *A Marginal Jew, Volume 3: Companions and Competitors*, Doubleday, New York, 2001, p. 76.

[85] Ibid, p. 247.

[86] Ibid, p. 75.

[87] Ibid, p. 247. Meier looks at a number of explanations that might explain why the women were not called disciples: (a) the evangelists' androcentric point of view; (b) the evangelists may have lacked any narratives of specific women being called by Jesus to follow him; (c) the evangelists may simply be echoing in wooden fashion their Aramaic sources, which had no feminine form of the word "disciple" (pp. 77, 247).

[88] Howard Clarke, *The Gospel of Matthew and Its Readers*, Indiana University Press, Bloomington, IN, 2003, p. 207.

no difficulty in accepting this name as feminine, but in the course of time the name was turned into the masculine form, perhaps because of a reluctance to acknowledge that a woman could be named as "prominent among the apostles." *The New Jerusalem Bible* gives the masculine form of the name, Junias, but a number of other contemporary translations, including *The New Revised Standard Version*, have reverted to the feminine, *Junia*.[89]

Mary is a relatively common name in the New Testament. Apart from Mary the mother of Jesus and Mary Magdalene, there are five women named Mary, leaving ample room for confusion. It would appear that Mary Magdalene should be suing Pope Gregory the Great (540-604) for defamation. While the Eastern Orthodox Church always separated Mary of Magdala, Mary of Bethany and the unnamed sinner in Luke, Pope Gregory identified the unnamed woman who anointed the feet of Jesus with Mary of Bethany and Mary Magdalene: "She whom Luke calls the sinful woman, whom John calls Mary (of Bethany), we believe to be the Mary from whom seven devils were ejected according to Mark."[90] This identity stuck, and so began and enduring tradition that Mary Magdalene was a penitent, an image that has been hard to shake off. As recently as 1970 Andrew Lloyd Weber's popular musical *Jesus Christ Superstar* portrayed Mary as a harlot, and in Mel Gibson's movie *The Passion of the Christ* the reputation of Mary Magdalene is slighted yet again by identifying her with the woman caught in adultery (Jn 8), both roles being played by Monica Bellucci. Until the reform of the liturgy following the Second Vatican Council, the *Missale Romanum* referred to Mary as *poenitentis* (penitent), and the gospel for her feast day was Luke 7:36-50, the story of the "woman who had a bad name in town" anointing the feet of Jesus. She has, however, finally been rehabilitated in the revised Roman Missal.

Mary of Magdala's most important role in the gospels is her being the first witness to the resurrection. Her encounter with the risen Lord is the scene that follows immediately after the story told in today's gospel; it is difficult to understand why this pericope has not been included as part of today's gospel reading. It has an important lesson to teach us about the meaning of the resurrection. In her joy at seeing the risen Lord, Mary must have reached out to touch him. Jesus replies, "Do not cling to me ('hold on to me', in some translations), because I have not yet ascended to the Father."

---

[89] Joseph A. Fitzmyer, *Romans*, The Anchor Bible: Doubleday, New York, 1993, pp. 737-8; cf. also Brendan Byrne, *Romans*, The Liturgical Press, Collegeville, MN, 1996, p. 453.

[90] Quoted in David Van Biema, "Mary Magdalene: Saint or Sinner?", in Dan Burstein (Ed), *Secrets of the Code*, Weidenfeld & Nicolson, London, 2004, p. 11.

Firstly, Mary fails to recognise Jesus immediately – a motif present in several post-resurrection appearances. She recognises him when he calls her name, calling to mind the Good Shepherd who knows his sheep and whose sheep know him: "The sheep hear his voice as he calls by name those that belong to him" (Jn 10:3). If Luke's story of the disciples on the road to Emmaus is telling his readers that they will recognise the risen Lord in the breaking of the bread, John may be telling his readers "that in the spoken word of Jesus they have the means of recognising his presence."[91]

Secondly, Mary's reaction to Jesus may be a response to his promise at the Last Supper: "I am coming back to you. In just a little while the world will not see me any more, but you will see me" (Jn 14:18-19). She is overcome with joy at seeing his promise fulfilled, but she has yet to learn that she cannot resume their former relationship. He will indeed be with her, but not as before. His enduring presence "is not by way of appearance, but by way of the gift of the Spirit that can come only after he has ascended to the Father."[92]

---

[91] Raymond E. Brown, *The Gospel According to John XIII-XXI*, Doubleday & Company, New York, 1970, p. 1009.
[92] Ibid, p.1012.

SECOND SUNDAY OF EASTER

(YEAR A)

Happy are those who have not seen and yet believe.
(Jn 20:29)

A Christian exists only as a member of a community. Jesus likens our relationship to him as a vine and its branches. Cut off from the vine the branch withers and dies. St Paul uses the image of a body. The church is the mystical Body of Christ. Jesus is the head of the body, and we are the various limbs and organs of the body. None of our limbs or organs can survive if severed from the body. Likewise, if one part of the body is infected, the whole body suffers.

Today's first reading presents an idyllic picture of the first Christian community in Jerusalem. We're told that they all lived together, sharing everything in common. They all sold their goods and possessions, and shared out the proceeds among themselves according to what each one needed. They shared their food gladly and generously, and they went as a body to the Temple every day. As far as we know, no other Christian community that we read about in the New Testament imitated the example of the church in Jerusalem. But Christians elsewhere were still part of a community, even if they didn't sell all their possessions and live a communal life. So, as we reflect upon that unique experience of the Jerusalem community, let us reflect upon the role of community in human and spiritual development.

The French playwright Jean-Paul Satre (1905–80) wrote a play in 1945 called *No Exit*.[93] Taking a few liberties with the plot, the play goes something like this. The curtains open on what we are led to believe is the waiting room of hell. Three people, two women and one man, are seated in the waiting room. The windows are bricked up; there are no mirrors; the lights can never be turned off. We presume that these three people have lived evil and wicked lives, and, having died, they are now awaiting their fate. They're expecting someone to come through the door at any moment, and to usher them into ... well, what is there in hell? Furnaces? Torture chambers?

For the time being, no one comes, and the three people begin to interact, as people often do in waiting rooms. But it's not long before all the bitterness, all the

---
[93] Jean-Paul Sartre, *No Exit*, Samuel French, New York, 1958.

evil, all the spite, all the vindictiveness, all the hate, which had been part of their lives on earth, begins to seethe to the surface. So heated does their interaction become that one of them takes out a knife and attempts to stab one of the others, who has to remind him, "Look, the reason we're here is because we're dead already!" Within a short span of time, each of these three characters has come to loathe, hate and despise the others.

Pounding on the door, one of the characters, Cradeau, pleads: "Open up! Open us there! I'll take them all, the tweezers, the boots, the tongs, the molten lead, whatever you've got! I want some real suffering! Let's have a thousand gashes. Let's have the acid and the whips, anything but this pain!"[94] But here is the moment of enlightenment in the play. For all eternity, for ever, and ever, and ever, each of these three people is condemned to remain in that waiting room with two other people whom, in such a short span of time, they have come to loathe, hate and despise. And so it is that one of the characters finally realises that hell has nothing to do with furnaces and torture chambers. Hell is other people![95]

We can do that to each other. We can make living together in families sheer hell. But there is a far more hope-filled vision of living together in families in the writings of the Jewish mystic, Martin Buber. One of Buber's many books is called quite simply *I and Thou*, and his insight is simple yet profound. Just as we know what our physical self is like by looking into a mirror and having that image reflected back to us, so at a more profound level we come to understand and appreciate the beauty that is ours as a human being, not in isolation, not in the solitude of a mountain top, but in communion with a Thou. "I require a You to become."[96]

That is the insight of that well-known, but hair-raising fairytale, *Rapunzel*. Once upon a time, a little baby named Rapunzel, is kidnapped by an ugly old hag of a witch and taken to a tower in a secluded part of the forest. There Rapunzel grows up to be an exceedingly beautiful person is every way. But the witch, envious of her beauty, continually tells her: "You're ugly, you're hideous, you're repulsive. In fact, I've done you a favour by locking you away from the sight of other people, because if they saw you they would tell you how ugly you are, and, my dear, your heart would be broken." Rapunzel is a prisoner, not so much of the stone tower, but rather of the image of herself created by the witch.

---

[94] Ibid. pp. 47,48.
[95] Ibid. p. 52.
[96] Martin Buber, *I and Thou*, Trans Walter Kaufmann, T & T. Clark, Edinburgh, 1970, p. 62.

Well, no fairy tale is allowed to end quite like that, and so it happens that a handsome young prince, strolling through the forest, happens perchance to come across this strange tower. And it was a strange tower because it had no doors. As the young prince look towards an upper window, he happened to see the face of Rapunzel, and immediately falls in love. But how to gain access? The prince remains hidden and observes how the witch leaves and returns: "Rapunzel, Rapunzel, let down your hair, and I shall climb your golden stair." Thus the witch comes and goes. Rapunzel, you realise, had not been to the hairdressers for a long time!

And so, when the witch departs to do the shopping, the prince tries his luck. "Rapunzel, Rapunzel, let down your hair and I shall climb your golden stair." Rapunzel lets down her hair, and up he climbs. I did warn you that this was a hair-raising story! And what happens when Rapunzel and her prince meet? In meeting her prince Rapunzel perceives an image of herself that she had not thought possible. In the encounter with her beloved, she is recreated. This is true not only in the case of Rapunzel, but with all of us. We desperately need to see in the mirror of another's eyes our own goodness and beauty, if we are to be truly free. Until that moment, we, too, will remain locked inside the towers of ourselves.[97]

The Easter season is a celebration of new life. That first community of Christians in Jerusalem was united heart and soul, and they ministered the new life of Easter to each other. Nothing has changed. In our relationships — in our families, in our parish community — we can imprison each other in a tower of ugliness, or we can awaken each other to the beauty of new life so that our inner selves may grow strong (cf. Eph 3:16).

---

[97] John Powell, *Why Am I Afraid to Love?*, Argus Communications, Chicago, 1967, p. 29.

THIRD SUNDAY OF EASTER

(YEAR A)

Then they told their story of what had happened on the road and how they had recognised him at the breaking of bread.
(Lk 24:35)

One of the unfortunate legacies of the 16th century Reformation was the way in which the Catholic tradition focused almost exclusively upon the presence of Christ in Sacrament, while the Protestant tradition emphasised the presence of Christ in the Word. Even the architectural style of churches built in the post-Reformation period affirmed these emphases. The high altar and, specifically, the tabernacle was the focus of attention in Catholic churches, while the grand pulpit dominated Protestant churches. Catholics were not encouraged to read the Bible; Protestants rarely celebrated the Eucharist. The liturgical renewal in both Catholic and Protestant churches has attempted to redress this imbalance.

Any tradition that fails to recognise the importance of both Word and Sacrament has embarked upon a handicapped pilgrimage into the sacred. While Protestant traditions are rediscovering the ancient Christian rhythm of Word and Sacrament, the Catholic church has affirmed that "sacred Scripture is of the greatest importance in the celebration of the liturgy".[98] Catholic Christianity now faces the challenge of breathing life into rituals that had been hidebound by a Tridentine insistence upon liturgical precision. But when ritual is unbound and allowed to come forth, it reveals the power of the Lord to transform his people.

Today's gospel records an incident that took place on the road to Emmaus very soon after the death and burial of Jesus. Two disciples were travelling together discussing all that had just taken place in Jerusalem. A stranger joins them on the journey and asks: "What are all these things that you are discussing as you walk along?" The disciples are amazed that the stranger seems to be totally unaware of the dramatic events which had just transpired: "You must be the only person staying in Jerusalem who does not know the things that have been happening there these last few days." The stranger feigns ignorance: "What things?" And so the disciples proceed to give an account of the events that have made them

---

[98] *The Constitution on the Sacred Liturgy* (Sacrosanctum Concilium), n. 24.

so downcast.

The stranger then attempts to show the disciples how these recent events have been an unfolding of the great story that begins with Moses and continues through the prophets. Perhaps the disciples were consoled at hearing the Word of God explained with such authority, but a veil still remained before their eyes. It was only through the ritual gesture of breaking bread that the disciples recognised their Lord in the mysterious stranger who has accompanied them. They experienced the life-giving power of story when it was celebrated in ritual. Why is that so? Why did the disciples not recognise their Lord until the breaking of the bread? It is difficult to give a rational explanation precisely because ritual carries us across the threshold of the spoken word, beyond the boundaries of empirical verification or scientific testing.

In cultures both ancient and contemporary, the stories that give a society its identity are celebrated in ritual. Such rituals express feelings and emotions that the written or spoken word cannot adequately describe. Rituals, like dance, which is so often an integral component of ritual celebrations, cannot be reduced to linguistic equivalents. When the great dancer Anna Pavlova was asked what she was trying to say in a particular dance, she replied "If I could tell you, I would not dance."[99] As J.G. Davies notes, dance "is not just one more language expressing that which could equally well be said in another."[100] This is equally true of ritual. Not all human experiences can be expressed or communicated adequately in words, and the tyranny or dictatorship of the word restricts human experience.[101] Ritual takes us across a threshold where words fall silent.

The power of ritual to express strong emotions is evident in the annual Anzac Day march in most Australian cities and towns. The ritual of Anzac Day usually begins with a dawn service at the cenotaph. Later in the morning, war veterans, wearing service medals, join their former regiments to parade through city streets along a designated route. While Anzac Day finds its origin in a series of futile World War I military engagements in remote Turkey, it has come to enshrine certain fundamental and perennial values that are important to many Australians. This day is a ritual affirmation of mateship, a day on which the ordinary person becomes a hero. It is also a celebration of patriotism and sacrifice.

---

[99] Quoted in J.G. Davies, *Liturgical Dance*, SCM Press, London, 1984, p. 100.
[100] Ibid.
[101] Ibid.

Alan Seymour's play about Anzac Day[102], *The One Day of the Year*, focuses on a conflict between a father and his son. Alf, the father, lives an uneventful life that is momentarily transformed through the rituals of this one day of the year. Hughie, his son, sees Anzac Day as nothing more than "a great big meaningless booze-up."[103] It was little more than a "Waste of lives, waste of men. That whole thing — Anzac — Gallipoli — was a waste. Certainly nothing to glorify. God, there's been another war since then! Dozens of wars everywhere, thousands of lousy little victories and defeats to forget. But they go on an on about this one year after year, as though it really was something."[104]

Seymour's character Alf expresses a number of values which Anzac Day celebrates. On a personal level, Alf, who is "just an ordinary little man"[105], whose life literally has its continual ups and downs (he's a lift operator), can for once feel superior to the "jumped-up little clerks" and others who despise him as "a lumpa dirt"[106]. On this one day of the year he can say, "I don't need no excuse today. It's my day, see."[107] Anzac Day is "the ordinary bloke's right to feel a bit proud of 'imself for once."[108] For people who are "nothin' much" for most of the year, Anzac Day transforms them into "someth'n'". Alf cannot express adequately in words the effect this one day of the year has upon him: "They make a fuss of y' for once. The speeches and the march ... and y're all mates. Y're mates an' everyth'n' seems all right. The whole year round I look forward to it. Me mates, some grogs, and — and the feelin' y're not just ... not just ... Y'know. It's the one day .. the one day ... I ever feel ..."[109]

Here we see the transformative power of ritual, a power beyond the grasp of rational manipulation. It is a power that evokes feelings of transcendence and awe, reverence and holiness. The 1987 Vietnam Veterans' march through the streets of Sydney was an actual example of the power of ritual to bring

---

[102] Anzac is an acronym for Australia and New Zealand Army Corps. Anzac Day, April 25, is probably Australia's most important national occasion. It marks the anniversary of the first major military action fought by Australian and New Zealand forces during the First World War.
[103] Alan Seymour, "The One Day of the Year", in Alrene Sykes (ed), *Five Plays*, (University of Queensland Press, Brisbane, 1977, p. 67.
[104] Ibid, p. 37.
[105] Ibid, p. 77.
[106] Ibid, p. 30.
[107] Ibid, p. 55.
[108] Ibid, p. 75.
[109] Ibid, p. 78.

healing and reconciliation. Newspaper accounts described the march as "one of the greatest emotional outpourings Sydney has witnessed in decades."[110] A crowd of 150,000 people lined the city streets and cheered the 25,000 veterans who "revelled in the applause for which they had waited so long."

One newspaper account described the event as "an emotional purging of anger, frustration, bitterness, confusion and rejection which has possessed these men since they returned from that terrible Asian war." The march had a deep emotional impact upon many of the veterans. One veteran, Phil Holmes, now confined to a wheelchair after being severely injured by a mine, felt rejected when he returned from Vietnam: "They didn't want to know us when we came back. You got abused if anyone found out you had been there. I told people I had been injured in a car accident. Oh God, how I have waited for this day. It is everything to me. I can't walk but I tell you right now I feel I could fly."

This rejection came from the most unexpected quarters. Peter Kilby, a Vietnam veteran from Grafton, went to a Returned Soldiers' League club "and one of the bastards there said he didn't want us in the club. "Why don't you go fight a real war?" he said ... I got pig's blood thrown at me the last time I marched in the Sydney streets. I didn't know if we were supposed to be there or not but, right or wrong, we did the best we bloody well could ... For years I walked the streets being ashamed of who I was. Not any more. Not after today."

The Vietnam War left deep and enduring emotional scars, and hundreds of Australian soldiers have committed suicide since returning home. On this day, marchers and spectators were united in a ritual of reconciliation and healing. It gave veterans a chance to tell their story at last. It was a day on which, according to Walker, "thousands of personal ghosts were laid to rest." The throngs of spectators, the ranks of veterans, bands, flags and banners, medals and military insignia all combined to create an impact which any number of speeches by national leaders could never have achieved. A marvellous example of the power of ritual!

At each liturgical celebration we celebrate our story, in word and ritual, and worship before the throne of the transcendent God who is present in our midst. At the breaking of the bread may we, too, recognise our Lord and Saviour.

---

[110] Frank Walker, "Vietnam vets weep as nation says thanks", *Sun-Herald*, October 4, 1987.

FOURTH SUNDAY OF EASTER

(YEAR A)

I am the gate of the sheepfold. (Jn 10:7)

The central image in chapter 10 of John's gospel is that of the shepherd. Jesus is the good shepherd who is prepared to lay down his life for his sheep. And the sheep listen to the voice of their shepherd. For that reason the fourth Sunday of Easter is known as vocation Sunday. The word "vocation" comes from the Latin *vocare*, meaning "to call." Vocation Sunday has traditionally been an opportunity to talk about the call to priesthood and religious life. But each of us has a vocation. We are all called by God. Fr John Powell writes, "God sends each person into this world with a special message to deliver, with a special song to sing ... with a special act of love to bestow." And Cardinal Newman expressed the same insight in these words: "God has committed some work to me which he has not committed to another."[111]

Behind the gospel image of the Good Shepherd lies the figure of the first century Palestinian shepherd. The shepherd knew his flock well, giving names to each of the sheep as we would to a pet dog or cat. By night shepherds sought refuge in sheepfolds. They were simple enclosures consisting of a stone wall, but with only one entrance. Having ushered their flocks into the sheepfold, the shepherds slept across the entrance, thus deterring bandits or marauding beasts at the risk of their own lives. At sunrise, each shepherd stood at the entrance and with his own distinctive call summoned his sheep. The sheep recognised the call of their shepherd and followed him alone.

I would like to focus on that image of the shepherd calling his sheep from the enclosure, because in one sense or another all of us live in an enclosure. The Australian psychologist and social commentator Hugh Mackay has written a book entitled *Why Don't People Listen?* in which he speaks, not of the enclosure but of the cage which surrounds each of us. The cage is our world view, forged from all our experiences and memories of life. We are both a product and a prisoner of our experiences.[112]

---

[111] Quoted in Mark Link, *Vision 2000*, Tabor Publishing, Allen, TX, 1992, p. 367.
[112] Hugh Mackay, *Why Don't People Listen?* Pan Macmillan, Sydney, 1994, p. 61.

Our cage gives us a much needed framework for making sense of the world around us. We store, organise and learn from all of our previous experiences, and that helps us to understand and cope with life. To take but a simple example, could you imagine trying to cross a busy road without having learnt from all of your previous experiences of crossing busy roads?

We are engaged in a lifelong process of constructing personal "cages" around ourselves. The bars of our cages are all the things that life has taught us: our knowledge, our attitudes, our values, our beliefs, our convictions. As the cage becomes stronger and more complex, we feel increasingly comfortable inside it and increasingly confident in our ability to cope with the world beyond the cage.[113] The cage is our storehouse of meaning, and we can only look out at the world through the bars of the cage.

But of course, we are seldom conscious of the bars. In *The Extended Phenotype*, Richard Dawkins tells the story of an African pygmy who was taken out of the forest for the first time in his life by the British author Colin Turnbull. Turnbull and the pygmy, named Kenge, climbed a mountain and looked down at the plains below. Kenge had never climbed a mountain in his life, and when he spotted some buffalo grazing on the plains below several miles away, he asked Turnbull, "What insects are those?" It took Turnbull a moment to realise what Kenge meant, but then he realised that forest vision is so limited that Kenge had never learnt to make an allowance for distance when judging size. When Turnbull told him that they were buffalo, Kenge expressed his disbelief with a roar of laughter.[114] In other words, Kenge was caged by his own experience.

We are all imprisoned in a cage or, using the image of today's gospel, we are like sheep in an enclosure. It is secure in the enclosure; we are safe from danger. But the voice of the shepherd summons us. Sadly, many people refuse to listen. A family member had suffered from acute deafness, and was offered hope through a transplant — a new ear drum. But the specialist explained that it was a rather expensive exercise. If you choose a male ear drum, it will cost $50,000. On the other hand, we can implant a female ear drum for only $500. "Why the staggering difference in prices?" a family member inquired. "Well, the male ear drum is so expensive because, unlike the female ear drum, the male ear drum has seldom been used."

Psychologists make a distinction between hearing and listening. When we hear

---

[113] Ibid.
[114] Ibid, p. 63.

our ear drum is responding to certain frequencies that we may or may not think about. Listening means that we are not just hearing what someone else says; we are also attending, understanding and interpreting what is said.

Mackay points out that our reluctance to listen is legendary, and there are many physical and psychological reasons why that is so. The first and most important reason why we so often fail to listen is that we don't have the courage to do it. Courage? Why does listening require courage? In fact, listening is one of the most psychologically courageous things we ever do in our normal relationships simply because listening, real listening, involves seriously entertaining the ideas of the other person. That entails the risk of having to change our minds in response to what we hear. If we listen properly, if we listen attentively, if we listen as if we were truly entertaining — trying out — the ideas of the other person, we may find that we will have to take what is said into account, and that may well involve some cage-work on our part.[115] Cage-work is the task set before us on this vocation Sunday!

---

[115] Ibid, pp. 143-4.

FIFTH SUNDAY OF EASTER

(YEAR A)

To have seen me is to have seen the Father (Jn 14:9)

Six blind men once visited a zoo to "see" an elephant. Being blind, of course, they had to rely upon the sense of touch. The first of the blind men grabbed the elephant's leg, and declared, "Ah! The elephant is very like a tree trunk." The second man grabbed the elephant's tail, and decided that the elephant was like a piece of rope. The third man reached up and touched the elephant's ear. "You're all wrong, the elephant is like a large fan." The fourth man grabbed hold of the elephant's trunk and concluded that the elephant was very similar to a snake. The fifth man touched one of the elephant's tusks and argued that the elephant was like a sword. Finally, the sixth man touched the elephant's body, and feeling the huge expanse of rough skin said, "You're all horribly mistaken. The elephant is like a brick wall." And so the six blind men disputed loudly and at great length, each one adamant that he was right and all the rest were wrong. And though each was partly in the right, they all were in the wrong.

The story of the six blind men and the elephant has often been used to describe the human search for God. If God will pardon the analogy, God is the elephant. Each of the blind men represents one of the world's religions — Hinduism, Buddhism, Judaism, Christianity, Islam, to name but a few. Just as each of the blind men experienced only a small part of the elephant, so, the argument goes, each of the world's religions experiences only one facet of the Divine. Just as each of the blind men claimed to know exactly what an elephant was like, so, the analogy goes, some of the world's religions claim to have a privileged insight into the nature of God. The blind men were all wrong, and so by implication, is any religion that claims to know the essential nature of God.

Well, there is a great deal of truth in this analogy. Words are utterly inadequate even to begin describing the ineffable mystery of God. God is transcendent, forever beyond the grasp of the human mind or imagination. St Augustine once observed, "If you have understood, then what you have understood is not God!"[116]

Our Christian faith often asks us to hold two apparently contradictory truths

---

[116] Alan Jones, *Passion for Pilgrimage*, p. 131.

in creative tension with each other, what psychologists call cognitive dissonance. On the one hand, we acknowledge that God is transcendent. But on the other hand, we also believe that God is immanent. That is, God is present, here and now, among us. God is the very ground of our being.

That is the message of today's gospel. Jesus has been talking about the Father, and so Philip asks, 'Lord, let us see the Father.' And Jesus replies, 'Philip, to have seen me is to have seen the Father.' What an astounding claim! Jesus is saying that insofar as we can know anything at all about God, God becomes visible to us in his life and ministry, in his words and deeds.

That doesn't mean that other world religions are totally misguided. It does mean though, that the clearest image we will ever have of God in this life is to be found in the person of Jesus. Take the example of my reading glasses. They were prescribed for me, and even though I can sometimes read with other people's glasses, my vision is never as crisp and clear as when I use my own. And so, by analogy, we can see something of the mystery of God through other world religions, but never as clearly or truly as we can through the revelation of God in Christ.

Sadly, many Christians have a blurred vision of God; they need to have the prescription for their spiritual glasses adjusted. Some of us treat God as if the deity were a vending machine. I put the requisite number of coins into the slot, press the button indicating which item I want, and hey bingo, it falls into the tray below. I want a God like that! I want to be able to say an appropriate prayer, indicate clearly what I require, and find my prayer answered as soon as possible. Some of us see God as the all-seeing scorekeeper. "I know what you did. I know your darkest secrets, and they are all written in my book. On the Day of Judgment, I shall read every single one of them out aloud in the presence of everyone you've ever known. I know!"

Allied to the all-seeing God is God the vindictive and spiteful punisher. The "I'm-gonna-getcha" God. [117] I remember being told a story in primary school about a boy who used sin, sin, sin relentlessly and unashamedly from Sunday to Friday, but on Saturday he always went to Confession. He treated Confession as if it were a kind of spiritual dry-cleaning service. But on one particular Saturday afternoon, the story goes, just as he was about to cross the road to go to confession, he recklessly stepped out without first looking. He was instantly dispatched to

---

[117] Patty Fawkner, "A Big Enough God", *Inform*, No. 63, Catholic Adult Education Centre, 1999, p. 4.

the fires of hell by a double-decker bus hurtling down the road. In my young impressionable mind, I imagined the bus parked in a side street, just up the road from the church, with St Michael sitting at the wheel and God standing behind him. As the sin-burdened youth approached the curb, I imagined God tapping St Michael on the wing and saying, "Rev her up, Mick. Let's get him!"

Or some of us see God as an insurance policy. I don't know if God exists, but I'll do all the right things here on earth, just in case it's true after all. I'll grovel and pray here on earth, so that I'm well looked after in heaven, if there is one. And some of us see God as Mr One Hundred Per Cent. This God only loves me when I'm perfect. This God loves me conditionally.

And some people treat God as a frail old maiden aunt who can't cope with our dark side, our grief, despair and anger.[118] And others of us worship the Panadol God. Just as we only take a Panadol when we're not feeling well, some people worship God only when something is going wrong in their lives.

How do you see God? Perhaps some of us need to have our spiritual eyes tested. The great fourteenth century theologian and preacher, Meister Eckhart, once wrote: "The ultimate leave-taking is the leaving of god for God."[119] Perhaps we need to do that. We need to take leave of a god who is too small, too restrictive, too petty and vindictive, too blurred. Let us look to Jesus that we may gaze upon the mystery of the eternal God, made visible to us in his Son. "To have seen me is to have seen the Father."

---

[118] Bruce Wilson, *The Human Journey*, Ronald N. Haynes Publishers, Palm Springs, CA, 1980, p. 251.

[119] Quoted in Jospeh Campbell (with Bill Moyers), *The Power of Myth*, Doubleday, New York, 1988, p. 49.

SIXTH SUNDAY OF EASTER

(YEAR A)

I shall ask the Father, and he will give you another Advocate to be with you for ever. (Jn 14: 16)

First I read the book, and then I saw the movie - *Into the Wild*, a compelling but exasperating story about a romantic idealist allured by the Alaskan wilderness. The movie — winner of a 2007 Golden Globe and nominated for an Academy Award — is based upon a book written by Jon Krakauer about the adventures of Christopher McCandless, a 22-year old who loads all of his belongings into his cherished old Datsun and heads off on a voyage of self-discovery without an itinerary and without even saying goodbye to family or friends. Rejecting a privileged life, his family, and even his own identity, McCandless donates his entire savings of $24,000 to charity and adopts the name Alexander Supertramp. Before long he abandons the car and ceremoniously burns all the money in his wallet. After almost two years travelling throughout the American West and south into Mexico he arrives at last in Alaska.

In the grey Alaskan dawn of April 28, 1992, a local by the name of Jim Gallien stopped to pick up McCandless, a shivering hitchhiker trudging along a snow covered road. During the course of their three hour drive together, Gallien, an experienced bushman, tried repeatedly to dissuade "Alex" from his planned trek into the wilderness, but to no avail. He was concerned that his passenger seemed woefully ill-equipped for such an ordeal. McCandless's gear was exceedingly minimal for the rugged conditions of the bush, which in April still lay buried beneath the winter snowpack, and he admitted that the only food in his pack was a ten-pound bag of rice. He had a .22 caliber rifle, a camera, several boxes of ammunition, some camping gear, and a small selection of literature—including a field guide to the region's edible plants. He didn't have a compass, and his only navigational aid was a tattered road map that he'd scrounged at a petrol station and eventually left in Gallien's truck, along with his watch, his comb, and all his money, a grand total of 85 cents. "I don't want to know what time it is," Alex declared cheerfully. "I don't want to know what day it is, or where I am. None of that matters."

Feeling an affinity for the young man, Gallien offered to drive Alex all the way to Anchorage to buy him some decent gear. "No, thanks anyway," Alex replied. "I'll be fine with what I've got." When Gallien asked whether his parents or a friend knew what he was up to — anyone who could sound the alarm if he got into trouble and was overdue — Alex answered calmly that, no, nobody knew of his plans, that in fact he hadn't spoken to his family in nearly two years. "I'm absolutely positive," he assured Gallien, "I won't run into anything I can't deal with on my own."[120] McCandless died sometime during August, 1992, having survived the wintery wilderness for about one hundred and twelve days; his decomposed body was found by moose hunters in early September.

Perhaps we find Chris McCandless's story so fascinating because there is something of the romantic idealist in all of us. I've certainly fantasised about casting off cares and responsibilities, of putting aside all commitments, of being beholden to no-one and adventuring into the unknown without map, timetable or compass. "I won't run into anything I can't deal with on my own" is the mantra of the rugged individualist, and it has a beguiling appeal. Was it rugged individualism, stubbornness, the brashness of youth, inexperience, naivety, *hubris,* or just bad luck — perhaps a cocktail of the lot — that led to McCandless's death?

Without wanting to paint an overly pessimistic portrait of human nature, the Scriptures acknowledge that we are flawed, and that we need to be saved — from the folly of our aberrant ego that clouds our perception and weakens our resolve. And there are times when we are overwhelmed by forces beyond our control. We constantly run into obstacles that we can't deal with on our own, and we need help.

In today's Gospel Jesus promises his disciples that he will ask the Father to give them another Advocate. That word "Advocate" is a translation of the Greek *parakletos. Parakletos* is a difficult word to translate precisely into English. The *Jerusalem Bible*, the *New Revised Standard Version* and the *New American Bible* prefer "Advocate", but it is also rendered into English as "Comforter" (*King James*), "Helper" (*New Century* and the *New King James Version*), "Counselor" (*Revised Standard Version, New Living Translation*), and "Paraclete" (*New Jerusalem Bible*). It's interesting to note that the 1966 *Jerusalem Bible* translation used "Advocate", but the *New Jerusalem Bible*, published in 1985, opted for the more obscure word "Paraclete".

---

[120] John Krakauer, *Into the Wild*, Pan Books, London, 1996. I have also drawn freely on Jon Krakauer's original article, "Death of an Innocent: How Christopher McCandless lost his way in the wilds," reproduced in *Outside Online*, January 1993. http://outside.away.com/outside/features/1993/1993_into_the_wild_1.html

How would John's contemporaries have understood the word? In secular Greek the most characteristic usage of both *paraklein* (the verb) and *paraklētos* refers to help given during a legal trial. The *paraklētos* was a friend of the accused, called in to give a favourable character reference, and also a legal adviser or helper in the relevant court.[121] The Jewish philosopher Philo (c.20BC-c.AD 50), a contemporary of Jesus, tells how the Jews of Alexandria (in Egypt) wished to plead a case before the Roman Emperor Caligula. To obtain a favourable outcome they needed someone with influence and clout at the imperial court. They referred to such a person as a *paraklētos*.[122] A *paraklētos* is therefore an intercessor, a mediator, a spokesperson.[123] Like the fictional defence attorney Perry Mason created by Erle Stanley Gardner, the *paraklētos* stands alongside the helpless and intervenes on their behalf. Perry Mason's description of himself in Gardner's first novel (*The Case of the Velvet Claws*, 1933) is an apt portrayal of a *paraklētos*: "I'm a specialist on getting people out of trouble. They come to me when they're in all sorts of trouble, and I work them out." Such is the Spirit promised by Jesus.

In the 1997 Australian movie *The Castle*, Bud Tingwell plays the part of a *paraklētos* in his role as Lawrence Hammill. Darryl Kerrigan and his family are typical Aussie battlers who live right next to Melbourne airport. Not only is their house adjacent to one of the runways, but it's built on toxic landfill and located beneath power lines. For Darryl, though, "It's not a house; it's a home ... people love each other, care for each other ... it's got memories, great memories."

When a valuer with the local council arrives to inspect the property Darryl proudly points out all of the house's salient features, even though he has no intention of selling. Soon after, he receives a letter informing him that the site has been compulsorily acquired because the airport intends to build one of the largest freight handling facilities in the Southern Hemisphere. Darryl is not at all happy because "his house is his home, his castle", and he decides to fight the decision. When agents from the airport try to bribe and bully the family into giving up, Darryl bands together with fellow neighbours and hires a small time lawyer Dennis Denuto (Tiriel Mora). Darryl attempts to fight the eviction by putting his faith in the principle that the government cannot evict him unwilling from his home.

---

[121] William Barclay, *New Testament Words*, p. 218; W. E Vine, M. F. Unger, & W. White, *Vine's Complete Expository Dictionary of Old and New Testament Words* T. Nelson, 1996), on *Nelson's Ultimate Bible Reference CD-ROM*, Thomas Nelson, 2003.
[122] *In Flaccum* 4, 22-23, F.H. Colson (Tr), *Philo*, Vol IX, Harvard University Press, 1985, p. 315.
[123] Raymond E. Brown, *The Gospel According to John, XIII – XXI*, p.1136.

Denuto is hopelessly out of his league appearing before the Federal Court ("He does conveyancing mainly, you know, wills, petty theft, that kind of thing"), and his threadbare argument that the eviction goes against the "vibe" of the Constitution fails to make an impression. While awaiting the court's decision, Darryl starts chatting with Lawrence Hammill, a retired lawyer. Having turned down the family's appeal, the court gives them two weeks to vacate the premises. The money offered to the family is scarcely enough to cover the purchase of a small apartment, yet alone another house. Dejected in defeat, the family begins to pack.

Lawrence, a former Queen's Counsel, takes an interest in the Kerrigans' case and offers to argue the matter before the High Court of Australia on their behalf, *pro bono*. He makes a persuasive case that the Kerrigans have the right to just compensation for the acquisition of property under Section 51(xxxi) of the Australian Constitution. He closes by paraphrasing Darryl's own comments that his house is more than just a structure of bricks and mortar, but a home built with love and shared memories. The court rules in favour of the Kerrigans, and their case becomes a landmark precedent on the subject. An epilogue shows that the Kerrigans continue to prosper happily, and Lawrence becomes a lasting friend of the family.[124] But without Lawrence's advocacy the outcome would have been quite different. He interceded on the Kerrigans' behalf when they themselves were powerless.

---

[124] I am indebted to *Wikipedia* for the plot summary (See http://en.wikipedia.org/wiki/The_Castle_(film) and also http://wwwmcc.murdoch.edu.au/ReadingRoom/film/dbase/2000/Castle.html

SEVENTH SUNDAY OF EASTER

(YEAR A)

I am not in the world any longer, but they are in the world.
(Jn 17:11)

What does John's gospel mean by "the world"? On the one hand we read that "God loved the world" (Jn 3:16), and that "God sent his Son into the world not to judge the world, but so that through him the world might be saved" (3:17). And yet, the world hates Jesus because he gives evidence that its ways are evil (7:7). Moreover, Jesus tells his disciples that by choosing them he has drawn them out of the world, and that is why the world hates them (15:19). Let's be clear about one thing: the world was not created evil, a belief held by different Gnostic groups. Gnostics were extreme dualists, believing that the created world was inherently evil, as opposed to the world of the spirit, which is good.[125] The word "world" (*kósmos* in Greek) occurs 186 times in the New Testament as a whole and 78 times in John's gospel[126] where it "doesn't simply mean the physical universe as we know it. It means the world insofar as it has rebelled against God, has chosen darkness rather than light, and has organised itself to opposed the creator."[127] The world is thereby alienated from God and antagonistic towards God and the things of God.

Although Jesus is sitting at table with his disciples his presence and mission in and to "the world" has now come to an end, but that of the disciples is about to begin.[128] What can we say about their mission? They are to share with others the teaching that has come from Jesus, just as we are. And just as Jesus prays for the disciples, he also empowers us to be his witnesses in the world. Rick Warren writes that whenever God gives us an assignment, "he always equips us with what we need to accomplish it." To illustrate his point he uses the acronym SHAPE,

---

[125] cf. Bart D. Ehrman, *Lost Christianities*, Oxford University Press, 2003, p. 116.
[126] Horst Balz and Gerhard Schneider, *Exegetical Dictionary of the New Testament, Volume 2*, William B. Eerdmans Publishing Company, Grand Rapids, MI, 1991, p. 310.
[127] Tom Wright, *John for Everyone, Part 2*, SPCK, London, 2002, p. 95.
[128] Francis J. Moloney, *Glory Not Dishonor: Reading John 13-21*, Wips & Stock Publishers, Eugene, OR, 1998, p. 113.

which refers to the Spiritual gifts, Heart, Abilities, Personality and Experience that are unique to each individual.[129]

Every disciple of Jesus is called to ministry, a word that derives from the Latin verb *ministrare*, which means "to serve." When Jesus washed the feet of his disciples, a very menial task in first century Palestine, usually undertaken by a slave or a servant, he reminded them that the Son of Man came not to be served but to serve. God entrusts spiritual gifts to each of us that are "not given for your own benefit but for the benefit of *others*, just as other people were given gifts for your benefit."[130] We don't deserve or earn these spiritual gifts, which is why they're called *gifts*! Some people are called to minister to others within the liturgy, as lectors, acolytes, extraordinary ministers of the eucharist, musicians or altar servers. But most of us are called to serve God in very ordinary ways. As a student for the priesthood, I was rostered to assist at a refuge for men run by the Missionaries of Charity in the Melbourne suburb of Fitzroy. The Missionaries of Charity are the Congregation founded by Mother Teresa, and their refuge provided meals and a bed for the city's down and outs. After the evening meal, the sisters returned to their convent, only a block away, and we seminarians stayed overnight to maintain order. One morning, after the nuns had finished serving breakfast, they told us that Mother Teresa had just arrived from India and was staying at their convent. Would we like to call in and say hello? The two of us leapt at the opportunity and with some trepidation made our way to the convent. Mother Teresa, confidante of popes, presidents and royalty welcomed us as if we were visiting cardinals. She smiled as she told us about something that had happened the previous day. No sooner had she stepped off the plane than a young man approached her in all earnestness, assuring her that he wanted to love and serve God with all his heart. He was prepared to return with her to India to work among the poorest of the poor in the slums of Calcutta. "I could tell that he was a very sincere and devout young man," Mother Teresa said, "but I said to him, 'If you really want to love and serve God with all your heart, you don't need to travel any further than Melbourne.'" How true! A handful of people, like Mother Teresa herself, are called to love and serve God in faraway places, but for most of us the call to serve others is right where we are, here and now. And for most of the time its about doing very ordinary things. But what gifts do I have, you might ask? Warren argues that studies tell us "the average person possesses from 500 to

---

[129] Rick Warren, *The Purpose Driven Life*, Zondervan, Grand Rapids, MI, 2002, p. 236.
[130] Ibid.

700 different skills and abilities" — far more than we realise.[131] We are called to use these abilities (the natural talents we were born with) to serve God from the heart (the A and H in SHAPE), not out of sense of duty or obligation, but with joy and enthusiasm.

God also uses all types of personalities (the P in SHAPE) for ministry. I'm called to preach, but I'd be hopeless in the music ministry because I'm almost tone deaf. Nor do I have the patience and creativity to work effectively in youth ministry. But, thankfully, we have dedicated and gifted youth ministers in our parish who do a marvellous job supporting and encouraging the faith of young people. It's obvious, Warren points out, that "God loves variety — just look around! He created each of us with a unique combination of personality traits. God made *introverts* and *extroverts*. He made people who love *routine* and those who love *variety*. He made some people *'thinkers'* and others *'feelers'*. Some people work best when given an individual assignment while others work better with a team."[132] All of our life experiences (the E in SHAPE) have fashioned us into the unique individual each of us is. The body of Christ, to use St Paul's metaphor, functions well when each part of the body does what it's supposed to do. It would be chaotic if the nose went on strike because it was tired of smelling and yearned to hear a Beethoven sonata, or if the ear decided it would like to smell exotic aromas. God has shaped us for a purpose and he expects us to make the most of the gifts entrusted to us. There is no use-by date on our call to service, nor should we stop searching for the dozens of hidden gifts that we don't know that we have. Warren says that he encourages people to try doing some things they've never done before. "No matter how old you are, I urge you to never stop experimenting. I have met people who discovered hidden talents in their seventies and eighties. I know a woman in her nineties who runs and wins 10K races and didn't discover that she enjoyed running until she was seventy-eight!"[133] Jesus entrusted to his disciples, and to us, the teaching that he received from the Father. May we in turn share from the heart that same teaching, using all the spiritual gifts, abilities and experiences the Lord has entrusted uniquely to each of us.

---

[131] Ibid, p. 242.
[132] Ibid, p. 245.
[133] Ibid, p. 251.

THE ASCENSION OF THE LORD

(YEAR A)

And know that I am with you always; yes, to the end of time.
(Mt 28:20)

Flying from Melbourne to Sydney a businessman found himself seated next to a stunningly attractive woman. Before long they began chatting, and during the course of the conversation she revealed that she was a clinical psychologist researching aspects of sexual attraction. "The popular perception is that French and Italian men are the best lovers," she explained. "But according to my research, that's not the case. Greek and Irish men are by far and away the best lovers." "Oh, that's very interesting," he replied. "I'd love to hear more about your research. Perhaps you'd like to join me for dinner in Sydney tonight? By the way, my name is Demetrios O'Shaughnessy!"

Why did I tell you that story on the feast of the Ascension? I appeal to the authority of the Australian theologian Fr Gerald O'Collins, who writes that it was once customary in parts of central Europe for the preacher to tell jokes during his Easter Sunday sermon. He had to make the congregation laugh and show that they truly shared the joy of Christ's victorious resurrection.[134] I realise that we're not in central Europe, and the Easter season is almost at end — but surely we can still laugh and rejoice that Jesus is truly risen! And for the disciples that joy continued once he had ascended. You'd think that they might have been sorrowful and despondent once Jesus had parted from them and was carried up into heaven. But Luke's Gospel tells us that they returned to Jerusalem "with great joy." And we, too, should be filled with great joy. Why? Because he is with us always; yes, to the end of time.

***

A four-year-old child awoke during the night, frightened, convinced that in the darkness around her there were all kinds of spooks and monsters. Terrified and in tears, she ran into her parents' bedroom. He mother calmed her down and, taking

---
[134] Gerard O'Collins, *Experiencing Jesus*, E.J. Dwyer, Sydney, 1994, p. 98.

her by the hand, led her back to her own room where she put on a light, tucked her back into bed, and gently reassured the child with these words: "You needn't be afraid, you are not alone here. God is in the room with you." The child replied: "I know that God is here, but I need someone in this room who has some skin!"[135]

That lovely story offers us the reason for the Incarnation. God takes on flesh because, like the young girl in the story, we need someone with us who has some skin. And that is what the word "incarnation" means. It comes from the Latin word carnus, meaning "flesh", physical flesh. In Jesus, God became human, and that is another interesting image, because the English word "human" also comes from a Latin word, humus, meaning soil or earth. The Book of Genesis calls the first human being Adam, a name coming from the Hebrew for the ground, admah.[136]

The Incarnation reminds us of a central truth of our faith — that in Jesus, God is physically present among us. The feast of the Ascension takes us one step further; it reminds us the "incarnation began with Jesus and it has never stopped. The ascension of Jesus did not end, nor fundamentally change, the Incarnation." The incarnation "is not a thirty-three year experiment by God in history, a one-shot, physical incursion into our lives."[137] As Fr Ronald Rolheiser reminds us, "God's physical body is still among us. God is still present, as physical and as real today, as he/she was in the historical Jesus. God still has skin, human skin, and physically walks on this earth just as Jesus did. In a certain manner of speaking, it is true to say that, at the ascension, the physical body of Jesus left this earth, but the body of Christ did not. God's incarnational presence among us continues as before."[138]

This is obvious from Jesus' parable about the sheep and goats in Matthew's gospel: "Whatsoever you did to the least of my brothers and sisters, that you did unto me." And again, when St Paul (then known as Saul) had set out for Damascus to arrest any followers of the Way that he found there, he encountered the risen Lord who asked, "Saul, Saul, why are you persecuting me?" Saul then asked, "Who are you, Lord?" The answer he received was: "I am Jesus, whom you are persecuting." Now as far as we know Saul had never seen or even met Jesus, so how could he have persecuted him? Jesus makes it quite clear. He is persecuted when his disciples are persecuted. In other words, we are the body of Christ. The incarnation continues into the present in and through us. We are the

---

[135] Slightly adapted from Ronald Rolheiser, *Seeking Spirituality*, p. 72.
[136] Christopher Jamison, *Finding Sanctuary*, Phoenix Paperback, London, 2006, pp. 94-5.
[137] Rolheiser, p.74.
[138] Ibid, pp.74-5.

skin of God. When a cloud had taken Jesus from the apostles' sight, they remained there staring into the sky. Two men in white appear and ask, "Why are you men from Galilee standing here looking into the sky?" In other words, get moving! From now on you are the presence of Christ in this world.

Fr Ronald Rolheiser tells of an elderly nun who came to see a spiritual director. She shared with him the story of a young nun who had just left their community. The elderly nun had very much liked her younger confrere and appreciated the spark and vigour she brought to the community. For a year she noticed that the young nun was obviously in distress, agonising as to whether or not she should leave the community and as to whether indeed the community even wanted her. So the elderly nun prayed for the young nun, prayed that she might stay, prayed that she might realise that she was wanted and valued, prayed that God might give her the strength to see beyond her doubts. But she never went, at any time, and talked to the young nun. She never ever told her how much she appreciated the gift that she, the young nun, was to the community. Now she was upset that the young nun had left. In other words, she never put skin to her prayer. She never concretely involved herself in trying to bring about what she was asking God to do.[139] These sentiments are beautifully expressed in a prayer attributed to St Teresa of Avila: "Christ has no body now, but yours. No hands, no feet on earth, but yours. Yours are the eyes through which Christ looks compassion into the world. Yours are the feet with which Christ walks to do good. Yours are the hands with which Christ blesses the world."

In her memoir *Out of Africa*, the Danish author Karen Blixen (also known by her pseudonym Isak Dinesen) tells the story of a young man from the Kikuyu tribe (in Kenya) whom she had employed as a farm worker. After only three months he surprised Karen by announcing that he intended leaving her to go and work for a Muslim man nearby. She asked if he'd been unhappy working for her. He assured her that all was well, but that he had decided to work for a Christian for three months to study the Christian way of life, and then work for a Muslim for three months to study the ways of a Muslim. After experiencing both, he would decide whether to be a Christian or a Muslim.[140] I find that story a little daunting, because I've wondered what decision a person might come to if they were to spend some time working with me, as the young man had worked with Blixen. Perhaps there would be an increase in the Muslim population!

---

[139] Ibid, pp. 79-80.
[140] Adapted from William J. Bausch, *The Word In and Out of Season*, Twenty-Third Publications, Mystic CT, 2000, p. 122.

PENTECOST SUNDAY

(YEAR A)

*Receive the Holy Spirit.
For those whose sins you forgive, they are forgiven.
(Jn 20: 22)*

I can still recall my first Confession at Our Lady Star of the Sea, Watsons Bay. With a sense of excitement tinged with trepidation I entered the confessional box and knelt in darkness, waiting for the priest to open the slide. And then it began, "Bless me, Father, for I have sinned. This is my first confession, and these are my sins." To be honest, I can't recall what sins I confessed, but it would almost certainly have been something like: "Disobedience to my parents, telling lies, and not doing what the teacher tells me." Heavy stuff! I think my penance was to say one Our Father and one Hail Mary. At times we might be forgiven for wondering if this is really what our Lord had in mind when he breathed on his disciples and said, "Receive the Holy Spirit. For those whose sins you forgive, they are forgiven; for those whose sins you retain, they are retained." One thing is certain though: the gospels record that the call to repentance was central to the message of Jesus. In fact, the name "Jesus" means literally "God saves". We read in the gospels that Jesus didn't come to call the virtuous, but sinners, to repentance. Much of his teaching focused on God's forgiveness and the need to forgive others their failings. He was constantly accused of being a friend of sinners, and the gospels record that he ate with tax collectors and sinners.

Jesus not only forgave sins; he also bestowed upon his disciples the power to forgive sins, as we have heard in today's gospel. But nowhere do we hear of Jesus giving any explicit instructions about how his disciples are to implement this commission to forgive sins. And history records that the way in which the Christian church has celebrated the forgiveness of sins has varied enormously throughout the ages.

The earliest forms of the Sacrament of Penance were rigorous and severe, nothing like the sacrament as we know it today. By the end of the third century the Sacrament of Penance could be celebrated only once after baptism. Those guilty of serious sin who sought forgiveness through the Sacrament of Penance were enrolled into what was called the Order of Penitents. The process was long and usually quite severe. The penitent would confess his or her sins to the bishop, and a penance would be imposed. Penances included fasting, almsgiving, prayer, abstinence from marital intercourse, and sometimes the adoption of penitential dress. Often the penitent was forbidden to hold public office, or to attend public amusements. Nor could the penitent receive Holy Communion until the completion of this lengthy penitential period that might last for several years. Absolution was granted by the bishop only when the period of penance had been completed, and that usually occurred at Easter. St Jerome (c.347–419/420) tells us of an aristocratic Roman lady by the name of Fabiola who had completed a lengthy period of penance and was about to receive absolution from the bishop. In Jerome's own words: "On the day before Easter, when the whole city was looking on, Fabiola took her place in the ranks of the penitents, with dishevelled hair, a ghastly countenance and soiled hands. She prostrated herself before the bishop, the priests, and all the people, as they wept along with her ... The sides of her garment were unfastened, her head was bared, her lips tightly drawn. She did not enter the church of the Lord, but ... sat apart, in order that the priest who had cast her forth might personally call her back again."[141]

Well, how did Christians of the time react to such severity? One common response was to postpone baptism until later in life, until the storms of youth had passed by. Baptism, of course, is the sacrament of forgiveness, par excellence — we can be baptised only once. When, in the fourth century, St Ambrose was elected bishop of Milan, at the age of 35, he was not even baptised. Within the brief span of eight days he went from being an unbaptised layman to bishop. St Augustine, who lived in the fourth and fifth centuries, was not baptised until he was 33 years of age. His struggle to live the Christian life is reflected in his well-known prayer: "Lord, make me chaste, but not yet!"[142] The Emperor Constantine postponed his baptism until he lay dying in 337 AD. Why did he delay baptism until he was on his deathbed? John Julius Norwich suggests that the most obvious and likely answer is that offered by Gibbon: "The sacrament of baptism was supposed to contain a full and absolute expiation of sin; and the soul was instantly restored to its original purity, and entitled to the promise of eternal salvation. Among the proselytes of Christianity, there were many who judged

---

[141] Quoted in William J. Bausch, *A New Look at the Sacraments*, Twenty-Third Publications, Mystic, CT, Revised 1983, p. 171.

[142] *Confessions*, Book 8, Chapter 7.

it imprudent to precipitate a salutary rite, which could not be repeated; to throw away an inestimable privilege, which could never be recovered."[143]

This severe penitential practice continued for some six centuries, but the rigour of it varied from place to place. It was eventually challenged and slowly displaced by a different form of the sacrament of penance that originated in the Irish church. The early church in Ireland was focused around the abbot and his monastery, rather than around the bishop and his cathedral. Monastic spirituality was therefore highly influential in the Celtic church. It was the normal practice for each monk to have a spiritual director — an older and wiser monk who offered guidance and support on the spiritual journey. As part of this spiritual guidance, the monk would disclose to his spiritual director those areas of his life where he felt he had failed, those areas where he sought God's forgiveness and healing. It was this experience of the Sacrament of Penance that the Irish monks took with them on their missionary journeys throughout Europe. The hierarchy at first banned this new form of the sacrament of penance, but as usually happens in the church, people voted with their feet. They found this new approach infinitely more appealing than the severe penance that they were accustomed to. And so, within a comparatively short period of time, this Irish monastic form of the Sacrament of Penance became normative in the Church.

Jesus breathed on the disciples and said, "Receive the Holy Spirit. If you forgive anyone's sins, they are forgiven. If you retain anyone's sins, they are retained." Symbolically, John is proclaiming that "just as in the first creation God breathed a living spirit onto man, so now in the moment of the new creation Jesus breathes his own Holy Spirit into the disciples, giving them eternal life."[144] The new creation is about the forgiveness of sins and being reborn into a new life through the waters of baptism. But the power to forgive sin granted by the risen Lord cannot be confined to baptism or the sacrament of penance. "These are but partial manifestations of a much larger power, namely, the power to isolate, repel, and negate evil and sin, a power given to Jesus in his mission by the Father and given in turn by Jesus through the Spirit to those whom he commissions."[145]

The rituals through which the Church has celebrated Divine forgiveness have varied enormously down through the ages. And they will undoubtedly continue to evolve. But whatever rituals the church has used down through the ages, they

---

[143] John Julius Norwich, *Byzantium: The Early Centuries*, Penguin Books, Harmondsworth, Middlesex, 1988, p. 76.
[144] Raymond E. Brown, *The Gospel According to John XIII-XXI*, p. 1037.
[145] Ibid, p. 1044.

are all an attempt to make present in the here and now the Lord's power to forgive and to heal. And this is, indeed, a precious gift.

THE MOST HOLY TRINITY

(YEAR A)

God loved the world so much that he gave his only Son. (Jn 3:16)

Every child, and the child in every one of us, is always ready to plead, "Tell me a story." The role of stories is to explore the meaning of life with all its ambiguity and uncertainty. Among my favourite stories is that of the great Jewish rabbi who lay dying, surrounded by his disciples. The rabbi's disciples gathered around his bed, hoping for a word of wisdom before he died. The senior disciple leaned over and whispered into the rabbi's ear, "Rabbi, what is the meaning of life?" The rabbi thought for a moment, and then replied, "Life is like a cup of tea." The rabbi's words were reverently whispered from disciple to disciple, until the message finally reached a pleasant but rather slow-witted disciple standing towards the back of the room. More than a little puzzled, he asked: "What does the rabbi mean, 'life is like a cup of tea?'" And so, this question was whispered back from one disciple to another until it finally reached the senior disciple who was still standing by the rabbi's bedside. A second time he leaned over and whispered into the rabbi's ear. "Rabbi, with the greatest respect, what do you mean, 'life is like a cup of tea?'" The rabbi shrugged, "All right, then, maybe life is *not* like a cup of tea!"[146]

The paradox and uncertainty of life continually taunts our desire for security and certainty. Life is like a cup of tea; life is not like a cup of tea. Our faith so often asks us to hold two apparently contradictory truths in tension with each other. On this festival of the Holy Trinity we stand before the mystery of God, aware of the total inability of human words and concepts to describe the ineffable nature of God. On the one hand, God is wrapped in cloud, transcendent and beyond human knowing, and yet he is also a God of tenderness and compassion, slow to anger, rich in kindness and faithfulness. St Augustine of Hippo put it this way, "Let human voices keep silent, let human thoughts take their rest; they reach out to incomprehensible things not as if they could take them in their grasp, but only to share in them; and share in them we shall."[147] So let us not be daunted. Today's

---

[146] Adapted from William Bausch, *Storytelling: Imagination and Faith*, p. 77.
[147] Augustine, *Enarratio in Ps. 146*, 11 (PL 37:1906).

gospel assures us of God's immanence; he loved the world so much that he gave his only Son, so that everyone who believes in him may not be lost but may have eternal life.

We feel uncomfortable and uneasy in the realm of mystery, a terrain in which there are no clear and decisive answers. The great thirteenth century theologian, St Thomas Aquinas, was wandering along a seashore, deep in thought. He was pondering the mystery of the Holy Trinity, for he had almost completed his great work entitled *De Trinitate*. He was wholly lost in thought and almost tripped over a small child playing in the sand. The little child had dug a small hole in the sand, and was running back and forth between the sea and his hole, filling a small bucket with water and emptying the water into the hole. Unable to contain his curiosity St Thomas asked the child what he was doing. "I'm emptying the ocean into this hole." St Thomas chuckled to himself and offered the child a word of wisdom: "You'll never empty the ocean into that hole, even if you kept running back and forth for the next thousand years. The sea is so vast and your hole so small!" But with an uncanny confidence, the child replied: "Father Thomas, I have as much chance of doing this as you have of explaining the vast mystery of the Holy Trinity."[148]

It was a moment of enlightenment, for in his own way Thomas also had been attempting to fill a small hole with the infinite mystery of God. Later, the saint would write in his work *De Veritate*: "The essence of God Himself remains forever hidden from us. The most we can know of God during our present life is that he transcends everything that we can conceive of him."[149]

In the film *The Heart Is a Lonely Hunter*, there is a sequence in which a person who has been deaf from birth asks a young girl what music sounds like. She stands in front of the deaf man so that he can read her lips. She gestures with her hands, but nothing works. Finally, they both laugh and give up.[150] Is it possible to describe music in words? Can you, for example, tell me in words about one of Beethoven's late quartets? Nor can we capture the reality of the ineffable God in human words and concepts.

In 1995, the American journalist and former Jesuit Jack Miles wrote a bestseller entitled, *God: A Biography*.[151] Miles based this so-called biography on the Hebrew Bible rather than the Old Testament. The contents of the Hebrew Bible

---

[148] A delightful but undoubtedly apocryphal story, sometimes also told about St Augustine.
[149] *De Veritate*, Q2, Art I.
[150] Mark Link, *Vision 2000*, p. 227.
[151] Jack Miles, *God: A Biography*, Sondon, Simon & Schuster, London, 1996.

and what Christians call the Old Testament are essentially the same, but they are arranged in a different order. His aim is to examine God, not as the object of religious belief, but as the protagonist of a classic of world literature. To cut a long story short, Miles observes an interesting sequence. God in the Hebrew Bible begins as a God of action. Action then yields to speech — God becomes a God of speech. Speech yields in its turn to silence. In fact, in the ten closing books of the Hebrew Bible, God hardly says a word.

What conclusion can we draw from that observation? The Bible has often been called the word of God in human words. This does not mean that God dictated a message that was faithfully and accurately transcribed, word for word, by human scribes. The Bible is indeed divine revelation, but it also reveals a great deal about humanity, and about our growing understanding of God. The more we enter into the mystery of God, the quieter we become. If words cannot describe music, neither can they lay bare the mystery of God. Words, however noble and eloquent, are little more than skirmishes with silence, raids on the unspeakable. The mystery of God cannot be captured in words.

Towards the end of his life St Thomas Aquinas was still writing his monumental work, the *Summa Theologica*. While celebrating Mass in the chapel of Saint Nicholas on December 6, 1273, he underwent an astonishing transformation. After celebrating that Mass, Thomas neither wrote nor dictated another word. He had been working on the third part of the *Summa*, the treatise concerning Penance, when he put down his pen for the last time. His secretary, Br Reginald of Piperno, was obviously distressed and asked why he was abandoning the work. The master responded simply, "Br Reginald, I cannot do any more." Brother Reginald waited awhile before raising the matter yet again. He received the same reply: "I cannot do any more. Everything I have written seems to me as straw in comparison with what I have seen."[152] Shortly afterwards, at the age of 49, and having written more than 40 volumes, Thomas died. In the early hours of March 7, 1274, he at last beheld the Divine Mystery that he had so faithfully worshipped "shrouded here below."[153]

---

[152] "Processus Canonizationis S. Thomae", Neapoli, quoted in Jean-Pierre Torrell OP, *Saint Thomas Aquinas, Volume 1, The Person and his Work* (Tr Robert Royal), The Catholic University of America Press, Washington DC, 1996, p. 289.

[153] From his hymn, *Adoro Te Devote*, tr. Gerard Manley Hopkins.

THE BODY AND BLOOD OF CHRIST

(YEAR A)

Anyone who eats this bread will live for ever. (Jn 6:58)

The oldest known European grave in Australia is that of a Franciscan friar, Claude-François-Joseph Receveur. He lies buried on the shores of Botany Bay, and the epitaph lists the date of his death as February 17, 1788. At 28 years of age Fr Receveur was selected as a scientist and chaplain to accompany La Perouse's voyage of exploration which set sail from France on August 1, 1785. Commanding the *Boussole*, La Perouse was accompanied by the *Astrolabe*, the ship to which Receveur was assigned. On the morning of December 11, 1787 the crew of the *Astrolabe* encountered trouble at the Navigators' Islands (now Samoa) when they tried to procure drinking water from a local village. Without warning the Samoans attacked, and the commander and eleven of his men were killed. Receveur almost lost an eye, but he made light of his wound in a letter he wrote to his brother from Botany Bay: "You can rest quite reassured. My wounds, which were very unimportant, have healed". Ten days later, he was dead.[154] When the French arrived at Botany Bay on January 26 they found British ships already at anchor. Captain Arthur Phillip had arrived in the *Supply* a few days earlier, and while the British fleet moved to Port Jackson, the French remained at Botany Bay for a further six weeks.

We can be reasonably certain that Receveur celebrated Mass aboard the *Astrolabe* while it lay at anchor, or perhaps even on the shore of Botany Bay, but we have no records. We can also assume that Fr Jean-Andre Monges, a scientist and chaplain appointed to the *Boussole*, celebrated a Requiem Mass for his brother priest, but again we have no records. However, the first recorded celebration of Mass in the penal colony of New South Wales was in 1803, fifteen years after the colony's foundation. The congregation was made up of prisoners, and the celebrant was Fr Dixon, an Irish convict priest allegedly complicit in the 1798

---

[154] John Dunmore, *Pacific Explorer: The Life of Jean-Francois de La Perouse 1741-1788*, The Dunmore Press, Palmerston North, NZ, 1985, p. 209. Letters and reports from the French were taken back to Europe by the English.

Irish rebellion. This cautious toleration of Catholic worship was withdrawn the following year, and although Fr Dixon, and after him Fr Harold, were able to exercise their ministry in a private capacity, public Mass was not celebrated in the colony again until 1820.[155]

When Fr Jeremiah O'Flynn arrived in Sydney in November 1817 he did so without authorisation from the British Government, although the Sacred Congregation of the Propagation of the Faith (Propaganda) had appointed him Prefect Apostolic. Governor Macquarie allowed O'Flynn to remain in the colony on the understanding that his credentials from the Colonial Office were to arrive on the next ship. In the meantime, he could not minister publicly. The credentials never arrived, and O'Flynn was expelled from the colony in May 1818. By accident or design, O'Flynn left the Blessed Sacrament behind in Sydney, and the host was constantly venerated and became the centre of Catholic life in Sydney. The consecrated host remained in the Kent Street house of James Dempsey where a room had been converted into a little chapel.[156] Columbus Fitzpatrick, who was a boy at the time, recalled that "it was no unusual thing on a Sunday, when Catholics could assemble to join the prayers at Mass which were being read in that room, to see many of them kneeling under the verandah, and even in the street, much to the amusement of the scoffers, who said we ought to be sunstruck."[157]

In the vast and dreadful wilderness God sustained the people of Israel with manna; in the even vaster wilderness of a convict colony the faith of our forebears was sustained and nourished by the presence of the living bread which has come down from heaven, the bread that is the life of the world. Their reverence for the Blessed Sacrament intuitively grasped a fundamental truth that was expressed at the Second Vatican Council over two centuries later — "no Christian community can be built up unless it has its basis and centre in the celebration of the most Holy Eucharist".[158] The Eucharist "stands at the centre of the Church's life."[159]

At the beginning of the Year of the Eucharist Pope John Paul II recalled the many times and places in which he had celebrated the Eucharist. "I have been able to celebrate Holy Mass in chapels built along mountain paths, on lakeshores and seacoasts; I have celebrated it on altars built in stadiums and in city squares."

---

[155] Cf. Patrick O'Farrell, *The Catholic Church and Community in Australia: A History*, Nelson, West Melbourne, 1977, pp. 1-2.
[156] Ibid, pp. 15-16.
[157] Edmund Campion, *Australian Catholics*, Penguin Books, Ringwood, Vic, 1988, p. 5.
[158] Decree on the Ministry and Life of Priests *Presbyterorum Ordinis*, n.6.
[159] Pope John Paul II, *Ecclesia De Eucharistia*, n.1.

These varied scenarios left the pope with a powerful experience of the universal and cosmic character of the Eucharist.

During the celebration of Mass the priest "breaks the bread" while the *Lamb of God* is sung or said. He then places a small particle of the consecrated host into the chalice, a liturgical gesture that probably goes unnoticed. It is, however, rich in significance and its origin goes back to the old papal Masses when a particle of the Eucharist reserved from the previous Mass was placed in the chalice. This commingling signified the unity and continuity of the present celebration with that which had preceded it. Also, on Sundays and feastdays the bishop of Rome would send a small piece of his consecrated host to other churches in the city where Mass was being celebrated. This particle, called the *fermentum*, was a token of communion with the Apostolic See. Newly ordained priests also received a consecrated host from the Pope, and for eight days they broke off a particle from it and mingled it in the chalice.[160] This very ancient custom is an expression of our unity, in time and place, when we celebrate the Eucharist. This sacramental memorial of the once-for-all death of Jesus, intimately unites us with the Lord, but also with the communion of saints — those who have gone before us, and those yet unborn. Anton Baumstark observes that when we celebrate the Eucharist we are at one with those who "since the very earliest days of Christianity, have offered prayer and sacrifice", and we are at one "with those who in time to come will be offering the same prayer and the same sacrifice, long after the last fragments of (our) mortal remains have crumbled to dust."[161] Whether Mass is celebrated in a Cathedral or in a country church, in the first or the twenty-first century, it is "always in some way celebrated *on the altar of the world*. It unites heaven and earth. It embraces and permeates all creation."[162]

---

[160] Pius Parsch, *The Liturgy of the Mass*, B. Herder, London, 1957, p. 288.
[161] Quoted in Theodor Klauser, *A Short History of the Western Liturgy*, Oxford University Press, Second edition 1979, p. 18.
[162] *Ecclesia De Eucharistia*, n.8.

THE ASSUMPTION OF THE BLESSED VIRGIN MARY

My soul proclaims the greatness of the Lord.
(Lk 1:46)

An elderly lady near to death sat in the rocking chair of her nursing home. "You know I believe, always have, and lived a good life. But now the time is getting close and sometimes I get to wondering."[163] Human beings are creatures who wonder, and our Christian faith provides us with a way of seeing, a context for our wondering. People often claim, "I am not religious", and by that they usually mean that they are not affiliated with a particular religion, or if they are, they no longer practise their faith. Religion, though, is far more encompassing than an explicit affiliation to a particular religious tradition. Keith Yandell defines religion as "a conceptual system that provides an interpretation of the world and the place of human beings in it, that builds on that interpretation an account of how life should be lived in that world, and that expresses this interpretation and life-style in a set of rituals, institutions, and practices."[164] If religion is so defined, most people are religious, even if they have never formally articulated the conceptual system which for them expresses the meaning of the world and their own lives. As M. Scott Peck observes, we all have "an explicit or implicit set of ideas and beliefs as to the essential nature of the world.[165] Our view of reality "is like a map with which to negotiate the terrain of life. If the map is true and accurate, we will generally know where we are ... If the map is false and inaccurate, we generally will be lost."[166]

Stories help us negotiate the terrain of life, especially by offering hope. On the occasion of the sixtieth anniversary of the liberation of the concentration camp at Bergen-Belsen, Rabbi Jonathan Sacks, the Chief Rabbi of Great Britain, spoke on the BBC Radio 4's *Thought for the Day*. "How did Jews survive all those centuries of persecution," he asked his listeners, "knowing all the pain and

---

[163] John Shea, *Stories of Faith*, The Thomas More Press, Chicago, IL, 1980, p. 61.
[164] Keith E. Yandell, *The Epistemology of Religious Experience*, Cambridge University Press, 1993, p. 15.
[165] M. Scott Peck, *The Road Less Travelled*, p. 200.
[166] Ibid, p 45.

persecution, why didn't they just give up? The answer, it seems to me, lies in Passover itself. We never forgot the story; we taught it to our children; and we always told it in such a way as to end on a note of hope: 'this year we are slaves, next year we'll be free.' Passover kept hope alive, and hope kept the Jewish people alive."[167]

The book of Revelation is addressed to persecuted Christian communities during the reign of the megalomaniac and tyrannical Roman emperor Domitian. These communities were small and helpless, and "the tide of the Roman world flowed steadily against them."[168] The prophet John depicts history "as a stark struggle between the forces of evil and worshipers of God and of the Lamb."[169] In the midst of persecution he reminds them of the story that sustains their faith. He assures them of the ultimate triumph of the kingdom of God: "Victory and power and empire for ever have been won by our God, and all authority for his Christ." This does not mean that the Christian has been inoculated against persecution and suffering, but it assures us that in the end all will be well. The Jewish author Steve Zeitlin tells a story about his father-in-law, a pediatric anaesthesiologist who was working with a young boy named Brian who suffered from continually recurring cancer. "The treatments were very painful, but, in this boy's case, my father-in-law could usually alleviate that pain." On one day that Brian was due to receive treatment he had caught a cold, and it would have been extremely dangerous to give him anaesthesia. "So my father-in-law sits the boy down and he says, 'You know, Brian, I love you very much, and I have to give you this treatment. But I can't give you the anaesthetic this time. I can't take the pain away. But every time I apply the treatment, I'm going to hold you, I'm going to hold you through the whole thing. And each time the pain comes, I'm going to be there and hold you, and you'll feel better.' And sure enough, it worked." As Zeitlin rightly observes, story is important because it illustrates a fundamental truth. No one can ever take away all the pain in our life. "There are times when there's nothing to do but say to someone — I can hold you when the pain is there, but this time I can't take it away."[170]

Where is God in the midst of human suffering and where is God at the moment of death? He is with us, embracing us with his presence and sustaining us with

---

[167] Quoted in Catherine Pepinster, "Sacks' plaintive melody" in *The Tablet*, 21 May 2005, p. 14.
[168] Wilfrid J. Harrington, *Revelation*, The Liturgical Press, Collegeville, MN, 1993, p. 12.
[169] Ibid, p. 13.
[170] Steve Zeitlin, *Because God Loves Stories*, Simon & Schuster, New York, 1997, p. 292.

his promise. Today's feast of the Assumption affirms our belief that Christ has been raised from the dead, the first fruits of all who have fallen asleep. First fruits are "the first portion of an agricultural harvest, the thing that precedes the rest of the harvest. As such it is a harbinger of things to come. The idea of first fruits implies that other fruits will be harvested at a later time."[171] The ancient tradition of Mary's Assumption must be seen within "the realm of discipleship and redemption by Jesus." She has received a privilege "that will ultimately be given to all Christians. All believers in Christ will be raised from the dead and take bodily to heaven."[172]

John Shea tells the story of a young man whose eighty-three year old father has been dying for about three weeks. For the last two weeks he's been in hospital, although he is conscious about half the time. His son, Jim, comes each day after work and sits by the bedside, wishing his father would open his eyes so they could talk. On Friday night just before he left the hospital, Jim leaned over to his father. "Oh, Pa, for God's sake let go! Let go! It's got to be better."[173] The message of the Assumption resonates within the mystery of the Resurrection. It says to us, "Let go!"

---

[171] Raymond F. Collins, *First Corinthians*, The Liturgical Press, Collegeville, MN, 1999, pp. 547-8.
[172] Raymond E. Brown, *Responses to 101 Questions on the Bible*, Paulist Press, New York, 1990, pp. 87-8.
[173] John Shea, p. 14.

FEAST OF ALL SAINTS

(YEAR A)

How happy are the poor in spirit. (Mt 5:3)

Some time ago an article in the *Sydney Morning Herald*[174] looked at the celebration of Halloween in Australia — fun for some people and anathema to others. A spokeswoman from Arndell Anglican College is quoted as saying: "We're a Christian school and Halloween is everything against Christianity so we don't recognise it." It would seem that the school's spokeswoman wasn't aware that Halloween simply means the eve of All Hallows, in other words, the evening before the feast of All Saints, October 31. All Saints Day is celebrated in a number of Christian churches, including the Anglican Church.

Most of us would probably consider Halloween an American phenomenon, together with the custom of young children dressing up in costume, going from door to door asking "trick or treat?". While the ritual of Halloween may have developed some American characteristics, it is essentially a Gaelic celebration. In ancient Britain and Ireland, October 31 was observed as the end of summer. This date was also the eve of the new year in both Celtic and Anglo-Saxon times. In popular mythology there was a crack between the end of the old year and the commencement of the new year — a crack that allowed spirits, both good and bad, to enter our world. It was customary for people to leave small offerings of food in their homes, offerings for the spirits of their deceased ancestors.

On the eve of All Saints it was also customary for some people to travel from door to door, offering to pray for deceased ancestors, for a small offering. If, perchance, they were turned away without an offering some people turned a little nasty and became mischievous. Hence the custom of "trick or treat". Immigrants to America, particularly the Irish, introduced Halloween customs that became popular in the late 19th century. In time the custom was observed mainly by small children who go from house to house, often in costume, demanding "trick or treat" (the treat, often lollies, is generally given and the trick rarely played).

The belief that on life's journey we are accompanied and supported by those

---

[174] Jacqueline Maley, "Lollies and fun drive pagan import from God-loving land", *The Sydney Morning Herald*, Weekend Edition, November 1-2, 2003.

who have gone before us is enshrined in many cultures. In the Christian tradition we call such a belief the Communion of Saints — the belief that those countless millions of men and women who have gone before us on the journey of faith intercede for us before the throne of God. The feast of All Saints is also a reminder that the saints are set before us to inspire us on our own journey of faith.

John's apocalyptic vision of 144,000 servants of God is clearly symbolic, an example of the highly metaphoric and poetic language of the Book of Revelation. The number twelve immediately calls to mind the twelve tribes of Israel, but once it is squared and multiplied by a thousand it suggests a vast multitude impossible to count. This is a vision of hope addressed to persecuted Christian communities during the reign of Domitian. This megalomaniac and tyrannical Roman emperor demanded that the populace acclaim him as "Lord and God' and participate in his worship. Christians, therefore, "were bound to experience increasing conflicts with the Roman civil religion since they acclaimed Jesus Christ and not the emperor as their 'Lord and God'".[175] The seer's vision is not a promise that they will be spared persecution, but it does assure them that they will be "sealed for protection *through* the great tribulation."[176] Our faith gives us an assurance of victory, through the victory of Christ.

There was a man whose lifelong desire had been to see the famous stained-glass windows of Chartres cathedral. Late in life, he was finally able to undertake the great journey. After travelling for many days, he at last reached the town of Chartres. It was close to evening. Upon entering the cathedral, he found it dark and gloomy. The famous stained-glass windows were black, opaque, cold and lifeless. Night had fallen. He left that evening disappointed. When he returned to the cathedral the following morning, it was a festival of colour and light, of warmth and brightness. And yet, these were the same stained-glass windows that he beheld the previous evening, but with one difference. When he entered the cathedral that morning, the sun had risen.

The disciple of Jesus is not cocooned or inoculated from the absurdities of life; from suffering; death and destruction. Believer and unbeliever alike look upon the same windows. But our faith gives us a way of seeing. Our lives are transformed by our belief that the Son has risen. The fanfare of apocalyptic proclaims this truth boldly: "Victory to our God, who sits on the throne, and to the Lamb!" The

---

[175] Elisabeth Schussler Fiorenza, *Invitation to the Book of Revelation*, Doubleday, Garden City, NY, 1981, p. 62.
[176] Wilfrid J. Harrington, *Revelation*, p. 99.

cartoonist Michael Leunig uses more gentle imagery: "Dear God, We struggle, we grow weary, we grow tired. We are exhausted, we are distressed, we despair. We give up, we fall down, we let go. We cry. We are empty, we grow calm, we are ready. We wait quietly. A small, shy truth arrives. Arrives from without and within. Arrives and is born. Simple, steady, clear. Like a mirror, like a bell, like a flame. Like rain in the summer. A precious truth arrives and is born within us. Within our emptiness. We accept it, we observe it, we absorb it. We surrender to our bare truth. We are nourished, we are changed. We are blessed. We rise up. For this we give thanks. Amen."[177]

---

[177] Michael Leunig, *A Common Prayer*, Collins Dove, North Blackburn, Vic, Reprinted 1992.

COMMEMORATION OF ALL THE FAITHFUL DEPARTED

But our homeland is in heaven (Phil 3:19)

On the afternoon of January 26, 1788, a fleet of 11 ships sailed into Sydney Harbour after a journey lasting more than eight months. The fleet, under the command of Captain Arthur Phillip, carried 1030 people. Seven hundred and thirty-six of them were convicts. Few of these prisoners were dangerous criminals by today's standards. They had been condemned to the new penal colony of Australia for offences that in this day and age would scarcely warrant a custodial sentence. The oldest of the prisoners, Dorothy Handland, was 82 years of age, a dealer in rags and old clothes. She had been sentenced to seven years for perjury. The youngest convict was a nine-year-old chimney sweep, John Hudson, sentenced to seven years for stealing some clothes and a pistol.[178]

Once the convicts landed, the British flag was unfurled, thereby marking the beginning of European civilisation in Australia. The first religious ceremony in the newly founded colony was held on Sunday, February 3, 1788. It was led by an Anglican minister, the Reverend Richard Johnson, under a large tree situated at what is now the intersection of Hunter, Bligh and Castlereagh Streets. With what can only have been unconscious irony he chose as the text for his sermon a verse from Psalm 116: "What shall I render unto the Lord for all his benefits toward me?"[179]

It is difficult to imagine the sense of desolation and abandonment that these convicts experienced in this ancient, yet alien, land. Few people in England at that time had travelled more than 10 miles from their home. A 15,000-mile journey to the other side of the world was beyond their comprehension, an inconceivable distance.

The sentence of transportation severed the convicts from their homeland and from their family. Their anguish and despair is painfully evident in letters home. A letter from prisoner Peter Withers to his brother is a heart-wringing plea for information about his wife: "I have sent two letters to my wife and can't get any

---

[178] Robert Hughes, *The Fatal Shore*, Pan Books, London, 1988, p. 73.
[179] Edmund Campion, *Rockchoppers*, p. 44.

answer from her which causeth me a great deal of unhappiness, for I think she have quite forgotten me and I think she is got married to some other man ...". Eleven years were to pass before Withers heard from his wife.[180]

Exiled in a penal colony, all their thoughts were of home. When St Paul wrote to the Philippians, he reminded them, "For us, our homeland is in heaven." They understood what he meant, for Philippi was a Roman colony. When Rome wished to extend its influence it established colonies that lived under Roman law and custom, and steadfastly maintained their allegiance to Rome. Even while living at the ends of the earth, these colonists remained Roman through and through. Rome was their homeland. Paul was reminding the Philippians that we all live in a colony, a colony of time, but our ultimate allegiance is to our eternal homeland, the empire of eternity.

I recently celebrated the funeral of a parishioner who died at the age of ninety-four. He and his wife had migrated from Italy following the Second World War, and although they had returned to visit Italy several times, they considered Australia their true home. Their English was heavily accented, and people referred to them as "Italian", although they had lived in this country for the greater part of their lives. It takes great courage to leave one's own homeland and launch out into the unknown — to leave family and friends behind, to learn a new language, and to find your bearings in an alien culture. The price a migrant pays is that of never truly being at home anywhere on the face of the earth. People in Australia refer to you as a migrant or a new Australian (or worse!), and if you visit your homeland, things have moved on since you left, they're not as you remember them; you're an alien there as well. It's a familiar experience for many people now living in Australia because twenty-five percent of our population was born overseas.

In one sense, we are all migrants. This passing world is not our homeland. The crypt of the Capuchin church of Santa Maria della Concezione on the Via Veneto in Rome contains the bones of thousands of Capuchin friars interred there between 1528 and 1870. At one point the visitor is confronted by a skeleton wearing the Capuchin habit. Attached to the habit that the skeleton is wearing is a sign bearing a message for the onlooker: "As you are, I was; and as I am, you will be!" A stark reminder that this world, beautiful as it is, is not all that there is. We are travellers through this colony of time, and our homeland is in heaven. This is not to deny the beauty of this world, for all creation is a gift from God. In the thirteenth century, St Francis of Assisi sang the praises of God's creation in his *Canticle of Brother*

---

[180] Hughes, p. 131.

Sun.[181] Francis joined with all creation in singing the praises of God, and yet his final salutation was for our Sister, Bodily Death, from whom no living person can escape. The great mystic of Assisi saw the fundamental unity of all creation, and rejoiced in its beauty. And yet he greeted his own death with the lovely salutation, "Welcome, my Sister Death."

A little while ago I spent many hours with a forty year old parishioner who was close to death. He had reached a stage of acceptance, no longer fearful of death, no longer denying the reality of his illness, no longer angry, no longer bargaining with God, and no longer depressed. He described the past few months as being like a journey, initially of fear, but now of incredible happiness and joy. "It is as if God had stripped me of everything that was unessential in life: it has been a journey into my inner self." On my last visit he asked me to read a few lines from the Bengali poet Rabindranath Tagore. The words, he said, applied profoundly to his own life, and they are words eminently suitable for this commemoration of All the Faithful Departed:

I have got my leave. Bid me farewell, my brothers!
I bow to you all and take my departure.
  Here I give back the keys of my door — and I give up
all claims to my house. I only ask for last kind words from you.
  We were neighbours for long,
but I received more than I could give. Now the day has dawned
and the lamp that lit my dark corner is out. A summons has come
and I am ready for my journey.[182]

---

[181] Regis J. Armstrong and Ignatius C. Brady (Tr), *Francis and Clare: The Complete Works*, Paulist Press, New York, 1982, p. 38.

[182] "Gitanjali", XCIII, in *Collected Poems & Plays of Rabindranath Tagore*, Macmillan, London, 1962, p. 43.

BAPTISM OF THE LORD

(YEAR A)

This is my Son, the Beloved; my favour rests on him. (Mt 3:17)

It would appear that Matthew found Jesus' baptism by John something of an embarrassment. Because it seems to make Jesus inferior to John, Matthew adds a disclaimer before the baptism. The Baptist insists that it is he who ought to be baptised by Jesus, and the strange inversion of roles proceeds only at Jesus' bidding. Luke's Gospel "dodges rather than denies" the fact that John baptised Jesus. In an offhanded way Luke mentions that Jesus was baptised, but omits the name of the baptiser, and moves immediately into his account of the theophany. The Fourth Gospel suppresses the event of the baptism altogether, although it retains the theophany with the spirit descending as a dove on Jesus. After all, how could the eternal Word made flesh receive baptism from John?[183]

Why was Jesus baptised, and what does it tell us about Jesus? At some time around the beginning of 28 AD Jesus set out from Nazareth to the Jordan River and there received baptism from John. By submitting to John's baptism, was Jesus making a confession of sin? Well, it's impossible to know; we have no way of looking into the conscience of the historical Jesus. Nevertheless, by posing such a question we have to confront the cultural and religious gap between the first and twenty-first centuries. Meier observes that "Modern Christians, especially Catholics, think of repentance and confession of sins very much in terms of the personal sins of the individual penitent with an uneasy conscience." Some Catholics who frequent the confessional "still tend to see confession as a time for excessive introspection and the dredging up of every past peccadillo that can be recalled. The spotlight is focused on the private conscience of the individual, judging in isolation his or her actions." By contrast, the confession of sin in Israel "was a God-centred act of worship that included praise and thanksgiving. Confession of sin often meant recalling God's gracious deeds for an ungrateful Israel, a humble admission that one was a member of this sinful people, a recounting of the infidelities and apostasies of Israel from early on down to one's own day, and a final resolve to change and be different from one's ancestors.

---

[183] John P. Meier, *A Marginal Jew: Volume 2: Mentor, Message, and Miracles*, p. 102.

Even apart from the question of one's particular personal sins, one was part of this history of sin simply because one was part of this sinful people."[184] In other words, reality is social. A rabbi once asked his students, "How can you tell when day is breaking?" One of them replied, "It's when you look in the orchard and you just make out the difference between a pear tree and an apple tree." The rabbi replied, "No, that's not the answer." Another pupil said, "It's when you're looking down the road and you can tell whether the animal ahead is a dog or a fox." "No, that's not the answer either," the rabbi said. "Light comes when you look into the eye of another human being and know that he or she is your brother or your sister. Until you can do that, it is *always* night, no matter what time of day it is!"[185] By going down into the waters of the Jordan Jesus symbolically entered into the world of sinful humanity; rising from the waters he prophetically proclaimed his triumph over sin and death.

At the very least, according to John P. Meier, "Jesus' baptism meant a fundamental break in his life: baptism as a watershed." From our meagre sources about the life of Jesus prior to his baptism it would seem that "Jesus was a respectable, unexceptional, and unnoticed woodworker in Nazareth. Both family and neighbours were shocked and offended by Jesus once he undertook his ministry, and not without reason. Apparently there was nothing in his previous life that foreshadowed or ostensibly prepared for his decision to dedicate himself totally to a religious mission to all Israel, a mission lacking any official sanction."[186] Jesus' baptism was a symbolic and public celebration of a radical turnaround in his life's direction — a conversion in the literal sense of the word.

In the early church, when catechumens were baptised, they took off their old clothes and went down naked into the waters of baptism. The clothes they had just discarded were symbolic of the old way of life that they have left behind. Baptism is a radical turnaround. *Twenty-Eight Days*, starring Sandra Bullock, is the story of Gwen Cummings, a successful newspaper columnist with a serious drug and alcohol problem, although she would be the last person to admit that she had an addiction. Her boyfriend Jasper is part and parcel of a lifestyle of excess. Getting "wasted" is his way of dealing with the pain of life: "No one adult human being is happy! People are born, they have a limited amount of time going around thinking life is dandy but then, inevitably, tragedy strikes and they realise life equals loss!

---

[184] Meier, pp. 113-4.
[185] Alan Jones, *Living the Truth*, Cowley Publications, Cambridge, MA, 2000, pp. 57-58.
[186] Meier, 108-9.

The whole point of the game is to minimise the pain caused by that equation! Now some people do it by having kids, or making money, or taking up coin collecting, others do it by getting wasted."

At the reception following her sister's wedding, Gwen prances around the dance-floor in an alcoholic stupor and crashes into the wedding cake, totally demolishing it. In no fit state to drive, she hijacks one of the wedding limousines in a futile attempt to buy a replacement cake. She crashes the car, and is subsequently given a choice of prison or a rehabilitation centre. She chooses rehabilitation, but is extremely resistant to taking part in any of the programmes on offer. During the twenty-eight days that follow Gwen painfully begins to re-examine her own life, and slowly confronts the reality of her situation. When she returns home Jasper humours her resolution to change: "I'll buy running shoes. We'll take up yoga or jogging. You know, we'll be organised. Pay our bills, floss our teeth ... I'll buy a goldfish, and we'll be like normal people." But it soon becomes clear that he envisages life continuing as before. Gwen comes to a crossroad. A life of addiction with Jasper, or launching out alone by making a radical turnaround. It is a watershed moment; she must decide who she is and what she truly wants. Such moments confront us all on our journey of faith. They are akin to a death experience, but, in the words of Bonhoeffer, "When Christ calls a man, he bids him come and die."[187]

---

[187] Dietrich Bonhoeffer, *The Cost of Discipleship*, SCM Press, London, Third Impression, 2004, p. 44.

SECOND SUNDAY IN ORDINARY TIME

(YEAR A)

Look, there is the lamb of God that takes away the sin of the world.
(Jn 1:29)

The ministry of Jesus, as recorded in John's gospel, begins and ends with the image of the lamb. When John the Baptist saw Jesus coming towards him he said, 'Look, there is the lamb of God.' The Lamb of God! Why a lamb? It seems such an effete metaphor. Why not the lion of God, or at the very least why not the ram of God? Well, if we want to understand that text, let's examine the context. What would a lamb have symbolised to a Jewish audience? Lambs were sacrificed in the temple as expiation for certain kinds of sin, but the reference here is almost certainly to the Passover lamb. At the Lord's command, Moses approached Pharaoh, the king of Egypt: "Let my people go!" But Pharaoh refused, so the Lord sent a series of plagues upon the land of Egypt — plagues of frogs, mosquitoes, boils, hail, locusts, darkness. But Pharaoh was a stubborn and obstinate man and still refused to set the Jewish people free. And so the Lord said to Moses: 'I shall inflict one more plague on Pharaoh. At midnight, all the firstborn in Egypt will die, people and livestock alike, from the greatest in the land to the lowliest.' But the Lord promised to pass over any house where the blood of a lamb had been splashed on the lintels.

The Jewish people were therefore saved from destruction by the blood of a lamb. Each year since then, the Jewish people have commemorated the Passover, on the first full moon of spring in the northern hemisphere. And even to this very day a shank bone is placed on the Seder table during the annual Passover meal, a symbolic link with their enslaved ancestors. The book of Exodus tells us that when the lamb was being prepared for the celebration of Passover not one of its bones was to be broken (Ex 12:46; Nb 9:12). John's gospel alone tells us when Jesus was crucified the Jews asked Pilate that the legs of the condemned be broken (to hasten death), but when the soldiers came to Jesus and saw that he was already dead, they did not break his legs.

So, that is the context of calling Jesus the lamb of God. But it goes even further than that. John's gospel tells us that Jesus was crucified on Preparation Day. People prepared for the feast of Passover on Preparation Day. The lambs to be eaten during the Passover meal were slaughtered in the Temple on Preparation Day. It was a rather gruesome business. Each person slaughtered their own lamb, but the priests caught the blood of the slaughtered lamb in a basin. A row of priests formed a line from the place of slaughter to the altar of the temple, and the bowl of blood was passed along the line from one priest to another. The priest standing nearest to the altar tossed the blood against the base of the altar. Blood is a symbol of life, and all life belongs to God, symbolised by casting the blood of the slain lamb against the altar. And how many lambs were slain on Preparation Day? The Roman governor Cestius recorded that on one particular year during the reign of the Emperor Nero 256,500 lambs were slaughtered.[188] Endless slaughter and streams of blood flowing against the base of the altar.

While all of that was taking place in the Temple, Jesus, the Lamb of God, was dying on Calvary, just outside the walls of the city. What a stark contrast. Endless slaughter in the Temple, one perfect and unrepeatable sacrifice on Calvary. Just as the Jewish people in Egypt were saved by the blood of the lamb, we too are saved by the blood of a lamb — the blood of Jesus, the Lamb of God. This is where Christianity differs from other world religions. Jesus is a teacher and a prophet, but Buddha and Confucius were also revered teachers; Muslims call Mohammed a prophet. What makes Jesus any different? He is different because he heals and makes whole. By way of analogy, consider a person who consults his local doctor because he's worried about shortness of breath, palpitations, dizziness and fainting spells, general fatigue and chest pains. The doctor examines the patient and diagnoses a heart condition that requires radical surgery, maybe even a heart transplant. The doctor has accurately diagnosed the patient's symptoms, but doesn't have the skill or expertise to perform such complex surgery. The local doctor therefore refers the patient to a heart specialist. Jesus does more than diagnose the anguish and emptiness that gnaw away at the human heart. Many teachers and prophets before and after Jesus have diagnosed the human condition. Many of the Old Testament prophets denounced sin and called Israel to repentance. Jesus certainly called people to repentance, but he goes further. He bring healing and wholeness. He is the Lamb of God who takes away the sin of

---

[188] The governor Cestius reporting to the Emperor Nero. Josephus, *War of the Jews* 6.9.3. cf. William Barclay, *The Mind of Jesus*, SCM Press, London, 1960, pp. 10-11.

the world.

While the plural "sins" refers to sinful acts, the singular "sin" refers to a sinful condition.[189] St Paul experienced that condition as a civil war raging within. In his letter to the Romans (7:15-20) he writes: "I do not understand my own behaviour ... Though the will to do good is in me, the power to do it is not: the good thing I want to do, I never do; the evil thing which I do not want — that is what I do."

Lucy demonstrates this for Linus when she draws a picture of a heart, one side of which is shaded. "This, Linus, is a picture of the human heart! One side is filled with hate and the other side is filled with love. These are the two forces which are constantly at war with each other." "I think I know what you mean," replies Linus. "I can feel them fighting."[190] Although we acknowledge what is good and right, like St Paul we often find ourselves unable to do it. Charlie Brown confides in Lucy: "All it would take to make me happy is to have someone say he likes me." "Are you sure?" she replies. "Of course I'm sure!" "You mean you'd be happy if someone merely said he or she likes you? Do you mean to tell me that someone has it within his or her power to make you happy merely by doing such a simple thing?" Charlie is adamant. "Yes! That's exactly what I mean!" Lucy seems almost won over. "Well, I don't think that's asking too much ... I really don't. But you're sure now? All you want is to have someone say, 'I like you, Charlie Brown' and then you'll be happy?" "And then I'll be happy!" Lucy turns and walks away: "I can't do it!"[191]

Taking away the sin of the world is setting us free from the clutches of this illusory self and, in the words of St Paul to the Ephesians (3:16), enabling us "to grow firm in power with regard to (our) inner self."

---

[189] Raymond E. Brown, *The Gospel According to John*, I-XII, Doubleday & Company, New York, 1966, p. 56.

[190] Charles M. Schulz, *The Complete Peanuts, 1959 to 1960*, Fantagraphics Books, Seattle WA, 2006, p. 163.

[191] Ibid, p. 272.

THIRD SUNDAY IN ORDINARY TIME

(YEAR A)

Repent, for the kingdom of heaven is close at hand. (Mt 4:17)

Jesus began his public ministry, as Matthew tells the story, with two imperatives: "Repent" and "Follow me." Leaving his home town of Nazareth, Jesus settles in the lakeside village of Capernaum and begins his proclamation by echoing the message of John the Baptist: "Repent, for the kingdom of heaven is close at hand." Repentance is a translation of *metanoia*, a Greek word that means literally a change of mind or a change of heart. Repentance involves a new way of seeing or thinking. A story, now somewhat dated since the disintegration of the Soviet Union, tells of an occasion on which the ghostly figures of Stalin and Khrushchev returned to Earth to visit Brezhnev, who was then Premier of the USSR. Brezhnev invites his ghostly visitors to ride on the latest Soviet train, a symbol of Soviet technological excellence under his leadership. After a few minutes, the train grinds to a halt and the conductor tells his distinguished passengers that the engine has broken down. Stalin insists that he can deal with the situation, and making his way to the engine threatens the hapless driver: "Comrade driver, unless the train is moving in five minutes, I'll have you shot or exiled to the Gulag archipelago." The train remains stationary. Khrushchev then offers to handle the problem, and entices the engine driver with a flat in Moscow and as much Vodka as he can drink for the rest of his life if the train is moving within ten minutes. The train still doesn't move. Finally, Brezhnev takes control of the situation: "Comrades, that is not how we are doing things here nowadays." He then pulls the blinds down over each window in the carriage, sits back with a smile of contentment and relaxes: "You see, comrades, now we're moving … aren't we?"

There is more than a grain of truth in that story, and perhaps it helps to explain the demise of the Soviet empire. Any human endeavour that pulls down the blinds and refuses to see is doomed to failure. There is no greater blindness than self-deception.

Repentance is also a life-long process. After completing a 30-day retreat a Jesuit novice felt he had truly received the grace of repentance. The inner struggle had been intense, but with a deep sense of satisfaction he claimed victory over what St Paul calls "the sinful self". The Spiritual Exercises had transformed him, and to celebrate this newly-won grace of conversion he decided to bury, symbolically, his old self with its sinful ways. He fashioned a sign that read "Here rests the sinful self — R.I.P" and plunged it into the manure heap alongside the vegetable garden. This was the grave, so to speak, of his unreformed and sinful self. It was coincidental that the novice master happened to notice this rather edifying but theatrical gesture and decided to keep a close eye on the pious lad during the days that followed. Having observed his conduct for some time, the novice master made his way down to the manure heap where the sign still remained. He smiled at the epitaph: "Here lies the sinful self — R.I.P", and then with a felt pen added the words: "He is risen!"

Alan Jones, dean of Grace (Episcopal) Cathedral in San Francisco, makes a relevant observation: "It takes a long time for a life to be totally converted, and most of us want instant conversions and overnight transformations."[192]

The second imperative is "Come after me" or "Follow me." Anthony Bloom, the Russian Orthodox archbishop responsible for Great Britain and Ireland, once made the observation that "If we turn to God and come face to face with him, we must be prepared to pay the cost."[193] When asked if the surface culture of the modern English way of life made it difficult to communicate the Gospel, Archbishop Bloom replied, "Yes, because the Gospel must reach not only the intellect but the whole being. English people often say, 'That's interesting, let's talk about it, let's explore it as an idea,' but actually do nothing about it. To meet God means to enter into the 'cave of a tiger' — it is not a pussy cat you meet — it's a tiger. The realm of God is dangerous. You must enter into it and not just seek information about it."[194]

Following Jesus costs not just something, but everything. It demands all of us not just a part of us.[195] There are surely times when that seems too much and we take flight. The *Quo Vadis* story tells of St Peter's alleged flight from Rome during the emperor Nero's persecution. Perhaps Peter was afraid; perhaps he thought that as "the rock" he should be somewhere safe for the sake of the other disciples who relied upon his leadership. According to this ancient legend Peter is heading

---

[192] Alan Jones, *Soul Making*, pp. 167-8.
[193] Anthony Bloom, *School for Prayer*, A Libra Book, London, 1970, p. xiv.
[194] Ibid, pp. xv-xvi.
[195] cf George Weigel, *Letters to a Young Catholic*, Basic Books, New York, 2004, p. 28.

out from Rome along the Via Appia and meets Jesus who is walking into the city and the persecution. "Quo vadis, Domine," Peter asks. "Lord, where are you going?" "I am going to Rome to be crucified," Jesus answers, and then disappears. Peter turns back into the city to embrace martyrdom.[196] George Weigel finds it interesting that this legend has endured, quite possibly for the same reason that Peter's failures are included in all four Gospels. "Those stories could have been discretely edited out, airbrushed from history; they weren't. And that tells us something." It tells us that "weakness and failure have been part of the Catholic reality *from the beginning*."[197] One of the early crises that beset the early church revolved around the acceptance and forgiveness of those who had lapsed from the faith during a time of persecution. Rigorists (known as Donatists, after Donatus, bishop of Carthage in the early fourth century) refused to readmit those who had compromised their faith (*lapsi*, from the Latin for "lapsed ones"), and they held that sacraments celebrated by bishops or priests who had apostatised were invalidated by their personal unworthiness. This issue flared up again in the twelfth century with the Waldensians, and again in the fourteenth and fifteenth centuries, when John Wyclif and John Huss argued that sacraments administered by a sinful priest or bishop were not effective.[198] The church has always deemed such attitudes heretical because it is not an assembly of the perfect. George Weigel reminds us that weakness and failure, stupidity and cowardice are all "part of the grittiness of Catholicism" and "only the naive would expect it to be otherwise."[199] We who are members of the Church, including those who are our leaders, are earthen vessels, as St Paul reminds us in his second letter to the Corinthians (4:7). The apostles were very ordinary people; they were neither geniuses nor exceptionally gifted, but the grace of *metanoia* gradually transformed their lives. Jesus sees in each person, not only what that person is, but also what that person can become. Jesus chooses us, not only for who we are, but for who, with the grace of repentance, we are capable of becoming.[200]

---

[196] Ibid, p. 30.
[197] Ibid, p. 31.
[198] Gerald O'Collins and Maria Farrugia, *Catholicism*, Oxford University Press, 2003, p 241.
[199] George Weigel, p. 31.
[200] William Barclay, *Gospel of Matthew*, Volume 1, pp. 365-6.

FOURTH SUNDAY IN ORDINARY TIME

(YEAR A)

Jesus went up the hill. (Mt 5:1)

While Luke's gospel sets the beatitudes on a plain, Matthew has Jesus ascend a mountain. It's interesting to note that while the *Jerusalem Bible*, used in the lectionary, translates the Greek *oros* as "hill", the *New Jerusalem Bible* uses "mountain." The mountain is not a geographical place — there are no mountains in the countryside surrounding Capernaum — it is a theological setting. Writing for a predominantly Jewish-Christian community, Matthew creates an interesting parallel. Just as Moses received the Torah on Mount Sinai, Jesus reveals God's will on a mountain.[201] There are five book of the Torah, and Matthew presents the teaching of Jesus in five major speeches, the first of which is the so-called Sermon on the Mount, or Beatitudes.

Today's gospel contains the first twelve verses of Matthew's version of the beatitudes. The beatitude is a literary form "very much ensconced in the thought-world of OT wisdom, which saw a correlation between human behaviour and reward or punishment, all to be experienced in this present life. (For most of the OT, the idea of reward or punishment beyond the grave was simply not on the theological horizon.)." That rather simplistic view of life was increasingly challenged because it became "painfully obvious that the good did not always enjoy happiness in this life", and that led to a second type of beatitude — an apocalyptic beatitude that "kept the nexus between right living and happiness, but projected that happiness into a future beyond this present world."[202]

Who, then, are considered blessed, fortunate or happy? The first group are the "poor in spirit" and the "gentle" (or "meek" in some translations). The "poor in spirit" (Greek – *ptōchoi*) translates the Hebrew '*ănāwîm* (which carries more

---

[201] Matthew sets important events in Jesus; life on mountains: temptation (4:8-10; feeding of four thousand (15:29-39); transfiguration (17:1-9); arrest (26:30-35), and final commission (28: 16). Cf. Daniel J. Harrington, *The Gospel of Matthew*, The Liturgical Press, Collegeville, MN, 1991, p. 78.

[202] John P. Meier, *A Marginal Jew, Volume Two: Mentor, Message, and Miracles*, p. 324.

the idea of humble and meek), and the "gentle/meek" (Greek - *praeis*) translates the Hebrew '*ăniyyîm* (which carries more of the idea of afflicted and oppressed). These two beatitudes could be considered "functional equivalents."[203] They both refer to a destitution that leaves a person totally powerless and without any human resources, and therefore open to the need and desire for God.

Frank Sinatra's signature tune in his latter years was the Paul Anka song "I Did It My Way," and it is the ultimate expression of self-reliance: "I planned each charted course / Each careful step along the byway, / But more, much more than this, / I did it my way. / ... For what is a man, what has he got? / If not himself, then he has naught. / To say the things he truly feels; / And not the words of one who kneels, / The record shows I took the blows — / And did it my way!" Needless to say, this is not the theme song of the poor in spirit, but the siren voices of personal autonomy and self-sufficiency are alluring indeed. Consider the appeal of the super hero in popular culture. In the days before television, I remember rushing my homework so that I could listen to the serials on the wireless. Greenbottle, Sea Hound; Tarzan, King of the Apes; Hop Harrigan, Search for the Golden Boomerang, and then, best of all, at 5.30 pm on Radio Station 2GB, Superman. "Look up in the sky. It's a bird, it's a plane. No, it's Superman. Yes! Superman. Strange visitor from another planet, with powers far beyond those of mortal men. Faster than a bullet. More powerful than a speeding locomotive. Able to leap tall buildings in a single bound. And who, disguised as Clark Kent, mild mannered reporter for a great metropolitan newspaper, fights a never ending battle for truth, justice and the American way."

Superman began his life in comics, before progressing to radio, and finally graduating to television and the movies. A plethora of super heroes followed in his wake: Batman and Robin, Wonder Woman, Aqua Man, Spiderman, the Phantom — the list goes on and on! In one way or another, all of these characters followed the formula that Jerry Siegel popularised when he created Superman in 1934. And the formula is this: the Superhero has a double identity. The superhero's alter ego is almost his antithesis. Just contrast, for example, mild-mannered Clark Kent with Superman; the effete millionaire industrialist Bruce Wayne with Batman, the placid milk-drinking Kit Walker with the Phantom; the prim and proper secretary Diana Prince with Wonder Woman; the insecure Peter Parker with Spiderman; and the latest addition to the pantheon, Catwoman, with her mild-mannered alter ego, graphic artist Patience Phillips.

---

[203] Ibid, p. 334.

Why has this formula proved so successful? Why does it appeal to us? Perhaps it's because we all cherish the illusion that, deep down, beneath this mild mannered exterior, beneath our placid public persona, lurks a super hero. Given the right set of circumstances, the super hero can emerge and make all things well. It is interesting, though, that the various twelve step programmes, of which Alcoholics Anonymous is probably the best known, all begin with a surrender and an admission of powerlessness. The first step in A.A.'s programme puts it this way: "We admitted we are powerless over alcohol — that our lives had become unmanageable."[204] The psychiatrist Scott Peck writes of the blessing of alcoholism. "It is a blessing because it is a disease which visibly breaks people. Alcoholics are not any *more* broken than people who are not alcoholics. We all have our griefs and our terrors; we may not be conscious of them, but we all have them. We are all broken people, but alcoholics can't hide it any more, whereas the rest of us can hide behind our masks of composure."[205] The opening beatitudes of today's gospel offer advice that we ignore at our own peril: "Blessed are those who have realised their own utter helplessness, and who have put their whole trust in God."[206]

---

[204] "The Twelve Steps of A.A.", in *Twenty-Four Hours a Day*, Collins Dove, Melbourne, 1989, pages unnumbered.
[205] M.Scott Peck, *Further Along the Road Less Travelled*, p. 146.
[206] Cf. William Barclay, *Gospel of Matthew*, Volume 1, p. 86.

FIFTH SUNDAY IN ORDINARY TIME

(YEAR A)

You are the salt of the earth. (Mt 5:13)

Salt is one of the most effective and widely used food preservatives, but in recent years many people have reduced their intake because of a fear that salt causes high blood pressure. But the human body needs salt. Without enough of it our muscles won't contract, blood circulation is affected, we'll have difficulty with digestion, and our heart won't beat. The Romans had a saying — *Nil utilius sole et sale* — there is nothing more useful than sun and salt. Homer called salt a divine substance; Plato described it as especially dear to the gods. Salt has served as currency in various times and places. Roman soldiers were given an allowance of salt, a *salarium*, from which comes the English word "salary". In the ancient world salt served to confirm contracts and friendship. The covenant between Yahweh and Israel on Sinai was called a "covenant of salt" (Num 18:19). In pagan Rome a few grains of salt were placed on a baby's lips on the eighth day after birth to chase away demons, a custom that no doubt lay behind the now discontinued practice of placing a modicum of salt in the mouth of an infant during the rite of baptism.

Jesus tells his disciples they are the "salt of the earth," a famous phrase that first appeared in English in Tyndale's 1525 translation. Jesus also told his disciples that they are to be the "light of the world." In other words, they are to make a difference, just as salt flavours and preserves food. In an imaginary letter from the apostle Paul, Martin Luther King addresses American Christians: "I understand that there are many Christians in America who give their ultimate allegiance to man-made systems and customs. They are afraid to be different. Their great concern is to be accepted socially. They live by some such principle as this: 'Everybody is doing it, so it must be all right.' For so many of you morality merely reflects group consensus … You have unconsciously come to believe that what is right is determined by Gallup polls … You must be willing to challenge unjust mores, to champion unpopular causes, and to buck the status quo. You are called to be the salt of the earth. You are to be the light of the world."[207] And, indeed, Martin Luther King did challenge unjust mores, champion unpopular causes and buck the status quo, at great personal cost to himself and his family: "Due to my involvement in the struggle for the freedom of my people, I have known very few quiet days in the last few years. I have been imprisoned in Alabama and Georgia jails twelve times. My home has been bombed twice. A day seldom passes that my family and I are not the recipients of threats of death. I have been the victim of a near fatal stabbing. So in a real sense I have been battered by the storms of persecution. I must admit that at times I have felt that I could no longer bear such a heavy burden, and have been tempted to retreat to a more quiet and serene life. But every time such a temptation appeared, something came to strengthen and sustain my determination."[208] King was killed by an assassin's bullet in 1968.

Consider, also, the example of St Thomas More who refused to compromise firmly held beliefs to placate his monarch. When King Henry VIII put aside his wife, Catherine, to marry Anne Boleyn, he sought Thomas' seal of approval. Thomas' peers had sought to persuade him, and the threat of execution lurked in the background if he failed to support the king. In Robert Bolt's play, *A Man for all Seasons*, Henry attempts to coax Thomas to his point of view with all manner of arguments. Thomas tells the king, in so many words, that if his arguments are so compelling, why does he need his support? To which Henry replies, "Because you are honest. What's more to the purpose, you're known to be honest ... There are those like Norfolk who follow me because I wear the crown, and there are those like Master Cromwell who follow me because they are jackals with sharp teeth and I am their lion, and there is a mass that follows me because it follows anything that moves — and there is you."[209]

In April 1990, Michael Lapsley, an Anglican priest working in his adopted homeland of South Africa, was the target of a letter bomb, losing both of his hands and an eye. Nelson Mandela described Michael as "a foreigner who came to our country, and was transformed by what he saw of the injustices of apartheid. He could not remain aloof from the suffering of the people. In order to be true to himself, he had to participate in their struggle for liberation."[210] The starting point of Michael's theology is that "God is not neutral and the Church

---

[207] Martin Luther King, *Strength to Love*, Fontana Books, London, 1969, pp. 139-40.
[208] Ibid, p. 153.
[209] Robert Bolt, *A Man for all Seasons*, Heinemann, London, 1960, p. 32.
[210] From the Foreword in Michael Worsnip, *Priest and Partisan*, Ocean Press, Melbourne, Vic, 1996, p. 3.

of God cannot be neutral. Usually, when it thinks it is being neutral, it is simply sliding into ideological captivity, a captive to reactionary forces." In a foreword to Michael's book *Neutrality or Cooption?* Trevor Huddleston quotes Canaan Banana, the then President of Zimbabwe: "I refuse to accept the notion that Jesus assumed the role of honoured guest in the theatre of human slaughter and misery. He intervened in human affairs and challenged the principalities and powers that denied God's children their right to life and to fundamental human liberties."[211]

When Mother Teresa of Calcutta died on September 5, 1997 she had already been canonised in the popular imagination. She had won the Nobel Peace Prize in 1979, and was recognised and acclaimed world wide. In her writings Teresa described the call she heard from God: "Come, carry Me into the hovels of the poor. Come, be My light. I cannot go alone ... In your immolation, in your love for Me, they will see Me, know Me, want Me."[212]

St Thomas More, Martin Luther King, Michael Lapsley and Blessed Teresa of Calcutta are rather daunting examples for the average Christian. Must we imitate these heroes of the Christian faith if we are to be the salt of the earth and a light to the world? The answer, of course, is no! A handful of disciples are called to be salt and light on the world stage, but they are exceptions. When Agnes Gonxha Bojaxhiu joined the Institute of the Blessed Virgin she received the name Teresa after St Therese of Lisieux, a young Carmelite nun who had died from tuberculosis at the age of 24 a century earlier in 1897. Therese had lived a cloistered life of obscurity in the convent of Lisieux, France, since she was fifteen. Just a few weeks before she died, one of her community made this observation: "She's a sweet little Sister, but what will we be able to say about her after her death? She didn't do anything." In fact, Therese's sister, Mother Agnes, who knew her best, left the manuscript of her life unnoticed and unread for three months.[213] St Therese's "little way" is about being salt and light, but she remained truly hidden, forgetting herself in quiet acts of love. "In my little way," she wrote, "are only very ordinary things."

God calls a few of us to great things in far away and exotic places, but for most of us the call to be salt and light is to be lived out right where we are. One woman said that as a young Catholic she was inspired by the saints. "I had always wanted to do things like work with Mother Teresa in India, but most of my life has not

---

[211] Worship, op. cit., p. 103.
[212] Brian Kolodiejchuk, *The Soul of Mother Teresa: Hidden Aspects of her Interior Life*, quoted in George Pell, *Be Not Afraid*, Duffy & Snellgrove, Sydney, 2004, p. 128.
[213] James McCaffery, "A saint for our season," *The Tablet* (19 October 1996), p. 1351.

been so glamorous. After college I became a teacher in an elementary school. And then my mother had a stroke and I had to drop out of teaching and help her for two years: bathe her, care for her bedsores, cook, pay the bills, run the house. At times I wanted to complete these responsibilities and get back to my spiritual life. Then one morning it dawned on me — I was doing the work of Mother Teresa, and I was doing it in my own home."[214]

---

[214] Jack Kornfield, *After the Ecstasy, the Laundry*, p. 229.

SIXTH SUNDAY IN ORDINARY TIME

(YEAR A)

Do not imagine that I have come to abolish the Law or the Prophets.
(Mt 5: 17).

Chapter five of Matthew's gospel forms part of that discourse popularly known as the Sermon on the Mount. Matthew is presenting Jesus as the new Moses – the new law giver, and in today's gospel we gain an important insight into Jesus' understanding of the Law. But first of all, let us clarify what we mean by the Law in this context. The Hebrew word is *Torah*, but it's inadequately translated into English as "law". Torah in its most restrictive meaning refers to the first five books of the Bible – Genesis, Exodus, Leviticus, Numbers and Deuteronomy. It is the heart and soul of God's revelation of Israel, and a copy of the Torah is found in the ark of every synagogue, just as the Blessed Sacrament is reserved in the tabernacle in Catholic churches.

The first five books of the Bible, also known as the Pentateuch (coming from the Greek word *penta* which means five) certainly include a legal code, but the word Torah can't be reduced to a list of do's and don'ts. Admittedly, there are a lot of do's and don'ts in the Torah – 613 to be precise – 365 prohibitions and 248 prescriptions. These laws cover almost every aspect of being human – issues relating to birth, death, sex, gender, health, economics, jurisprudence, social relations, hygiene, marriage and ethnicity. The purity laws in chapters 11 to 16 of the book of Leviticus specify in minute detail what you can and can't eat. There are laws regarding bodily discharges, agricultural guidelines about planting seeds and mating animals, decrees about lawful sexual relationships, and laws about keeping the sabbath.[215]

The word Torah comes from the root *yarah*, meaning "to shoot" (such as at a target). When you shoot at a target you're trying to direct the arrow. So the image behind the word is "correct direction."[216] In other words, the Torah will

---

[215] Cf. Daniel B. Clendenin, *Journey With Jesus*, Sunday, August 30, 2009, at http://www.journeywithjesus.net/
[216] Benjamin Blech, *The Complete Idiot's Guide to Understanding Judaism*, Alpha Books, New York, 1999, p. 67.

help us find the right direction on life's journey. Torah should be liberating and life-giving, not oppressive and deadening. Moses tells the people in today's first reading from the book of Deuteronomy, "take notice of the laws and customs that I teach you today, and observe them, that you may have life …".

Alongside the Torah there was a large body of oral tradition, that is, additional laws that were passed on by word of mouth. This oral tradition, of human not divine origin, was eventually set down in writing about 200 years after Jesus. It is known as the Mishnah and it contains six main divisions. Later Jewish tradition compiled commentaries on the Mishnah, and these are known as the Talmud.

Consider, for example, the tractate in the Mishnah on the Sabbath. Well, the Torah says "Remember the Sabbath day and keep it holy" (Deut 20:8). That sounds a little vague, so the oral law steps in to help clarify the meaning of the written law. How do we keep the Sabbath day holy, remembering that the Hebrew word for "holy" is *qadesh*, meaning to be separate or set apart? If the Sabbath is holy, we must keep it separate. How? Well, by not working on that day. But how do you define work? The Mishnah lists 39 human activities that are defined as work, and orthodox Jews today try to follow these laws diligently. It is forbidden to kindle a fire, and for that reason devout Jews will not drive a car on the Sabbath – because ignition causes a spark. It has also been extended to include turning on a light.

In modern Israel there is an institute that addresses itself to finding solutions to problems arising from modern technology. The Institute for Science and Halakhah has produced a 200 page study on lifts. What is called the "Sabbath lift" automatically stops at all floors in a building, so there is no need to press buttons. But there's another more subtle problem with lifts. When an elevator descends it creates energy which is usually channelled for use elsewhere in the building. That would mean that Jews might benefit from electricity that has been generated on the Sabbath. Engineers from the Institute have come up with a new system to prevent that energy from being fed back into the grid. [217] Writing is defined as a form of work because it is forbidden to make a permanent mark on the Sabbath. The Sabbath pen conforms to requirements because the ink disappears after two days.

In three places the Torah forbids boiling a kid in its mother's milk (Ex 23:19; 34:26; Deut 14:21). Jewish tradition interprets this to mean that meat and dairy products cannot be eaten together. This separation includes not only the food itself,

---

[217] *New Zealand Herald*, 5 December, 1992.

but also the utensils, pots and pans that are used to cook meat and dairy products, and the sinks or dishwashers used to clean the cooking implements, and the towels used to dry them. A kosher kitchen will therefore always have two sinks – one for washing up cooking utensils used to cook meat, and the other for utensils used for dairy products. Do you also need two dishwashers? Well, you certainly can't wash implements used in the preparation of meat and dairy products in the same cycle. Google "kosher and dishwasher" and you'll become immersed in detailed discussions about what to do if you only have one dishwasher.

All of this reflects a rigid and literal adherence to the exact letter of the Law. But Judaism doesn't have a monopoly on legalism. Consider the rules and regulations that once surrounded the eucharistic fast. I recall an incident that took place in the 1950s when I was a young altar server. In those days Catholics were required to fast from food and drink from midnight if they wished to receive Holy Communion. A few minutes before Mass was about to commence, there was a timid knock on the sacristy door. "See who it is," the parish priest said as he completed vesting. Two young girls, boarders from the local convent school, asked if they could speak with Father. They sought his counsel about a delicate yet serious moral dilemma. One of them had gone to bed the previous night while still chewing gum. When she woke up the gum was still in her mouth. Did that constitute a violation of the eucharistic fast? Could she receive Communion at this morning's Mass? Like King Solomon of old, the parish priest gave the matter serious thought. "Yes" he decided, "you can receive Communion." He reasoned that the sugar coating on the chewing gum would surely have dissolved prior to midnight, and consequently the young girl would not have eaten anything since then!

Fr Edmund Campion has called Irish Catholicism, as practised in Australia last century, a religion of law. "Catholicism was a system of law," he writes, "and obedience was a prime virtue." Irish bishops sent to Australia made laws about everything: "laws about women wearing hats in church and laws about fasting; laws about Lenten observance and laws about receiving Communion at Eastertime; laws about who could wash the altar linen and who could not; laws forbidding priests to stay out late at night; laws forbidding them to frequent theatres or racecourses or prize fights; laws forbidding them to join political parties, or read uncatholic papers, or become guardians or tutors; and laws ordering what they must wear."[218]

---

[218] Edmund Campion, *Rockchoppers*, p. 60.

Several years ago, I came across a letter to the editor in the London *Times*. It read thus: "Sir, As a civil servant in a large Government department, one of my colleagues asked me the other day for some red tape (for a label making machine). It may surprise and delight your readers, in this age of the vilification of civil servants, to learn that we hadn't got any ..."[219]

Jesus had little time for "red tape". The Law was given not to entangle us but to set us free. In some ways, though, it sounds as if Jesus is making observance of the law more difficult; he seems to be tightening the screws. For example, he says: "You have heard how it was said to our ancestors: You must not kill ... But I say this to you: anyone who is angry with his brother will answer for it before the court ..." And again, "You have learnt how it was said: You must not commit adultery. But I say this to you, if a man looks at a woman lustfully, he has already committed adultery with her in his heart." And finally, there is Jesus' injunction against taking oaths, "All you need say is 'Yes' if you mean yes, 'No' if you mean no...".

Now on the face of it, it does sound as though Jesus is making observance of the Law much more difficult. In each of these three cases, though, Jesus is reaching beyond the letter of the Law and affirming the value that the Law is seeking to protect. We haven't killed our brother or sister, but have we harboured festering thoughts and attitudes of hatred and revenge? Have we killed our brother or sister in a hundred ways, apart from literally taking their life? His injunction against taking oaths is an injunction against equivocation – ways in which we might actually use the letter of the law to avoid the truth. The Sermon on the Mount releases the hidden potential of the Law and, in the words of the *Catechism of the Catholic Church*, "reveals their entire divine and human truth."[220] The basic principle seems to be this: the Law is given to protect and enshrine certain important values. It is given, not to enslave us in fear but to liberate us in love. As the *Catechism* states, "The New Law is a law of love, a law of grace, a law of freedom."[221]

---

[219] *The Times*, March 7, 1980.
[220] *Catechism of the Catholic Church*, Doubleday, New York, 1995, n. 1968.
[221] *Catechism*, n. 1985.

SEVENTH SUNDAY IN ORDINARY TIME

(YEAR A)

But I say this to you: love your enemies and pray for those who persecute you. (Mt 5:44)

The patron saint of Lawyers is, I believe, St Yves of Brittany, who lived in the thirteenth century. However, during his own lifetime the legal profession was without a patron saint. And so Yves and a group of fellow lawyers petitioned the Pope to grant them a patron. The Holy Father was a little nonplussed because no saint readily sprang to mind. He therefore suggested that Yves and his companions should go to the Cathedral of St John Lateran, the Cathedral church of the diocese of Rome. There Yves was to be blindfolded, spun around until he was totally disoriented, and then set to wander about the cathedral. The saint whose statue Yves first touched would be nominated as the patron saint of lawyers. And so, having been blindfolded, spun around and totally disoriented, Yves began groping his way around the walls of the ancient Cathedral. At last he came upon a statue, and excitedly cast off his blindfold. Which saint would it be? How delighted he was to find that the statue before him was that of Our Lady herself. What an honour! Our Lady would become the patron saint of Lawyers! But then he looked a little closer at the place on the statue where his hand rested. To his dismay he realised that his hand lay not upon Our Lady herself, but upon a small figure crushed beneath the foot of Mary: the figure of the serpent.

Whoever it was that first told that totally apocryphal story obviously had little time for lawyers and the law. The law both civil and religious can indeed become a tyrant when the letter of the law suffocates the spirit of the law. In this section of Matthew's gospel which we've been listening to over the past few weeks, we have heard the attitude of Jesus towards the Law. Law, in this context, is a translation of the Hebrew word *Torah*, which could also be translated as "teaching" or "doctrine". In Judaism the word *Torah* has at least three distinct yet overlapping meanings. It may refer to the Pentateuch, the first five books of the Bible. It could also refer to the entire Old Testament, or the *Tanakh* as it is called by Jews. It may also mean both the written and the oral Torah, which includes the Talmud.

In today's gospel Jesus quotes one of humanity's oldest laws: Eye for eye and tooth for tooth. Known as the *lex talionis*, it appears in the Code of Hammurabi, created in ancient Babylon about 1790 BC. One nearly complete copy of the Code survives today on a diorite stele now on display in the Louvre. The *lex talionis*, as found in the Code, is stated thus: "If a man puts out the eye of an equal, his eye shall be put out. If a man knocks the teeth out of another man, his own teeth will be knocked out."[222] Eye for eye and tooth for tooth may sound like a mandate for vengeance. In fact, this particular Old Testament law (cf. Ex 21:24; Lev 24:20 and Deut 19:21) sought to make the punishment commensurate with the offence, to restrict the vengeance one might exact. *Only* an eye for an eye, *only* a tooth for a tooth; you cannot exact any retribution beyond that. But Jesus really brushes aside the letter of that particular law and exhorts his disciples to exact no vengeance, no retribution whatsoever. As Martin Luther King pointed out, "The old law about 'an eye for an eye' leaves everybody blind."[223] What Jesus does is "to prohibit any court action to obtain retribution or compensation." This really subverts all legal systems "which are necessarily based on a need to balance rights and redress injuries." Here the "otherness" of God's kingdom and its justice could not be made clearer.[224] There may be an element of hyperbole in what Jesus says, but "it challenges disciples to value the kingdom above anything the world can take from them."[225]

Jesus goes on to say: "If anyone hits you on the right cheek, offer him the other as well." A hit on the right cheek is a backhanded blow, not intended to shatter teeth but to insult. It was a severe public affront to a person's dignity. Again, Jesus warns the offended disciple not to retaliate and to freely offer the other cheek. Such a gesture demonstrates an indifference to human honour. Jesus goes further: "You have heard how it was said, 'Love your neighbour, hate your enemies' But I say love your enemies." The Torah enjoins a love of one's neighbour (Lev19:18), but it does not teach a hatred of one's enemy. However, "the obligation of loving one's neighbour (i.e., a fellow member of Israel's cultic community) was naturally interpreted as permission not to love the 'non-neighbour'." Jesus rejects all

---

[222] http://en.wikipedia.org/wiki/Code_of_Hammurabi
[223] Quoted in Mark Link, *Vision 2000*, p. 239.
[224] John P. Meier, *Matthew*, Liturgical Press, Collegeville, MN, 1980, p. 54.
[225] Craig S. Keener, *The Gospel of Matthew*, William B. Eerdmans Publishing Company, Grand Rapids, Michigan, 2009, p. 199.

limitations on love.[226] Some people were scandalised when they heard Abraham Lincoln speak kindly of the Confederate soldiers during the American civil war. One woman berated him, saying, "I think we'd be better advised to focus on destroying our enemies, rather than befriending them." To which Lincoln replied, "Madam, we destroy our enemies when we befriend them."[227]

We may not be guilty of smashing teeth or plucking out another's eye, but we can harbour thoughts of anger and revenge that are just as virulent. John Cassian (c. 360 – 435), the monk who brought the teachings and practices of Eastern monasticism to the Latin West, called anger a "deadly poison ... that must be totally uprooted." Drawing on the scriptures he demonstrates the harm that can come to a person who is angry, destroying right judgement and wisdom.[228] Abbot Christopher Jamison writes: "As a monk, I find it better to be clearly against anger of all kinds and to support zeal for justice as something quite distinct. Nelson Mandela is a good example of somebody who combined zeal for justice with a lack of personal anger. He was zealous in bringing apartheid to an end in South Africa but still has friendly relations with his white former jailer. Getting angry about a problem rarely improves the situation; what is needed is a zealous determination to over come it."[229]

Some time ago, I celebrated a marriage between a couple who had encountered great opposition from the bride's parents leading up to the marriage. The bride's parents were very strict Protestants, and they were deeply distressed when their daughter made the decision to become a Catholic before the marriage. The parents told the couple quite bluntly, "We will not be present at the wedding!" However, as the date of the wedding drew closer, they relented and agreed to attend, but the father refused to walk his daughter down the isle in a Catholic church. The wedding ceremony and the reception were charged with tension, and it was so obvious that his hostile atmosphere had drained the occasion of so much joy and happiness. This couple could easily have become embittered at the way they had been treated and refused to have any further contact with the bride's parents. But they didn't. Instead, they prayed together that the rift would be healed and harmony restored.

When they returned from their honeymoon late on a Sunday afternoon, and were preparing to leave for Mass, the front doorbell rang. Who should be there to greet the couple but the bride's parents. They had brought a huge pizza and bottles of wine. It was a gesture of reconciliation. They had come to apologise.

---

[226] John P. Meier, op. cit., p. 54.
[227] Cf. Mark Link, *Vision 2000*, p. 239.
[228] Christopher Jamison, *Finding Happiness*, Weidenfeld & Nicolson, London, 2008, p. 132.
[229] Ibid, pp. 136-7.

But wait a minute! What does Canon Law have to say about attending Mass on Sunday? Canon 1247 says that "On Sundays and other holy days of obligation, the faithful are obliged to assist at Mass." So what are the couple to do? "Sorry Mum and Dad, we can't eat with you now because the law of the Roman Catholic Church says we have to go to Mass. See you Protestants later!" You'll be happy to know that the couple missed Mass that Sunday. They invited the parents in, and over the meal a great healing took place. The law of love was surely fulfilled, even if the letter of Canon 1247 wasn't!

EIGHTH SUNDAY IN ORDINARY TIME

(YEAR A)

No one can be the slave of two masters. (Mt 6:24)

The 2008 movie *The Bucket List* starring Jack Nicholson and Morgan Freeman is a story about two terminally ill men, Edward Cole and Carter Chambers, who share the same hospital room. They become friends and decide to draw up a bucket list, an agenda of things they'd like to do before they "kick the bucket". Because Cole is an extremely wealthy man they can do it. In one scene from the movie the two men are admiring the pyramids and Carter, a walking encyclopedia, tells Cole that the ancient Egyptians had a beautiful belief about death. "When souls got to the entrance of heaven the guards asked two questions. Their answer determined whether they were admitted or not." The two questions were: "Have you found joy in your life?" and "Has your life brought joy to others?"

How do we find joy in life? Today's gospel assures us that joy is ultimately a matter of the heart, the inner core of the person, and we don't achieve it by amassing wealth or by worrying about possessions. The cartoonist Michael Leunig reminds us that "There is more stuff in the world than ever before. Stuff you can touch. Stuff you can think. Stuff you can use and consume. Stuff you can know with all of your senses. The growth of stuff is out of control. It is now being created by means of an unstoppable, exponential chain reaction. Stuff has become a major threat to freedom and happiness. It destroys nature and peace. It steals time and space. It fouls beauty. It is relentless, virulent, invasive and addictive. Stuff makes us exhausted and mad. There is too much stuff. The following common statements can be taken very seriously: 'I'm stuffed.' and 'The world is stuffed.'"[230]

According to Paul Hamilton, Director of the Australia Institute, a public interest think tank, "some psychologists argue that our actions are driven by a desire for "self-completion."[231] That is to say, there is a gap between my here-and-now self and my ideal self, however that is defined. In his masterful analysis of story, *The*

---

[230] Michael Leunig, *Goatperson and Other Tales*, Penguin Books, Camberwell, Vic, 1999.
[231] Clive Hamilton and Richard Denniss, *Affluenza*, Allen & Unwin, Crows Nest NSW, 2005, p. 13

Writer's Journey, Christopher Vogler makes the observation that the hero's journey is a process of becoming a complete, integrated human being.[232] How, then, do I bridge the gap, how do I complete myself? Well, one temptation is to acquire more "stuff" to compensate for my shortcomings. Paul Barry's biography of James Packer, *Who Wants to be a Billionaire?*, quotes Packer's oft-repeated motto to friends, girlfriends and fellow executives: "Whoever dies with the most toys wins." One of the first treats James Packer allowed himself after the death of his father was a new boat. His new super-yacht at cruising speed burns 400 litres of fuel every 10 kilometres, and filling the 40,000-litre tank costs about $100,000. Six weeks after his father's death he bought a $60 million jet that seated up to 18 passengers. Almost as big as a Beoing 737, it was described by its manufacturer as "the most luxurious, most accomplished business jet" ever built.[233] This addiction to "stuff" has been named "affluenza", a condition described by Clive Hamilton as a confusion "about what it takes to live a worthwhile life."[234] It is the "bloated, sluggish and unfulfilled feeling that results from efforts to keep up with the Joneses."[235] Australia is one of the richest countries in the world, and our real income today is three times higher than it was in 1950. But, I ask myself, am I three times happier and more contented than my parents? According to Hamilton, Australians today feel they suffer from a chronic lack of 'stuff', and people in affluent countries are more obsessed than ever about money and material acquisition.[236] Rich societies appear to be "in the grip of a collective psychological disorder. We react with alarm and sympathy when we come across an anorexic who is convinced she is fat, whose view of reality is so obviously distorted. Yet, as a society surrounded by affluence, we indulge in the illusion that we are deprived."[237]

Our addiction to "stuff" is ultimately self defeating. American psychologist Tim Kasser summarises a decade of research into the relationship between materialistic values and psychological health: "When people and nations make progress in their materialistic ambitions, they may experience some temporary improvement of mood, but it is likely to be short-lived and superficial. Materialistic values of wealth, status and image work against close interpersonal relationships and connection to

---

[232] Christopher Vogler, *The Writer's Journey* (Third Edition), Michael Wiese Productions, Studio City, CA, 2007, p. 29.
[233] Paul Barry, "Whoever dies with the most toys wins", in *Good Weekend*, October 10, 2009, p. 16.
[234] Clive Hamilton and Richard Denniss, p. 7.
[235] Ibid, p. 3.
[236] Ibid, pp. 4,5.
[237] Ibid, p. 6.

others, two hallmarks of psychological health and high quality of life."[238] When President Franklin D. Roosevelt was asked what book he could give the Soviets to teach them about the advantages of American society, he pointed to the Sears catalogue.[239] One anonymous commentator describes our obsession with status in these words: "In rich countries today, consumption consists of people spending money they don't have to buy goods they don't need to impress people they don't like."

Jesus tells us that we cannot be the slave of two masters. Jewish law envisaged the uncommon situation in which a person was half-slave and half-free or jointly owned by two people.[240] Jesus draws the obvious conclusion: the slave will naturally prefer one master to the other. We cannot be the slave both of God and of money. This is not to say "that we should build humpies and live in self-satisified deprivation ... It is not money and material possessions that are the root of the problem: it is our *attachment* to them and the way they condition our thinking, give us our self-definition and rule our lives. The problem is not that people own things: the problem is that things own people. It is not consuming but consumerism ... not affluence but affluenza."[241] We need to cultivate detachment, a non-grasping stance towards life, and that isn't easy. "In our insecurity and neediness, we think attachment secures our happiness. We want what is ours, and we want it totally and completely. As children we are loath to share, because if we do, we think that somehow we have less, which, of course, we do – physically. But paradoxically, sharing produces its own abundance in a magnanimity of spirit that trumps anything our hands can hold. In the end we have more."[242] In the Zen tradition there is a story about two monks on a pilgrimage who come to the ford of a river. There they saw a girl dressed in all her finery who was unable to cross to the other side because the river was high and she didn't want to spoil her clothes. Without hesitation one of the monks lifted her onto his back and carried her across. He put her down on the other side and bade her farewell as the monks continued on their way. But it wasn't long before the other monk began to complain: "Surely it is not right to touch a woman; it is against the commandments to have close contact with

---

[238] Tim Kasser, *The High Price of Materialism*, MIT Press, Cambridge MA, 2002. Quoted in Hamilton, p. 14.
[239] Alain de Botton, *Anxiety Status*, Penguin Books, Camberwell, Vic., 2004, p. 40.
[240] Craig S. Keener, *The Gospel of Matthew*, William B. Eerdmans Publishing Company, Grand Rapids, Michigan, 2009, p. 223.
[241] Clive Hamilton and Richard Denniss, pp. 16-17.
[242] Edward L. Beck, *Soul Provider*, Doubleday, New York, 2007, p. 18.

women; how can you go against the rules for monks!" His tirade went on and on in a steady stream. The monk who had carried the girl walked along silently, but finally remarked: "I set her down by the river. But you are still carrying her."[243]

In the words of St Gregory of Nyssa, a fourth century Father of the Church: "As soon as a man satisfies his desire by obtaining what he wants, he starts to desire something else and finds himself empty again; and if he satisfies his desire with this, he becomes empty once again and ready for still another. And this never stops until we depart from this material world ... the soul should fix its eye on its true good and not be immersed in the illusion of the present life."[244]

---

[243] Adapted from Irmgard Schloegl, *The Wisdom of the Zen Masters*, Sheldon Press, London, 1975, p. 39.
[244] Quoted in Edward L. Beck, op. cit., pp. 19-20.

NINTH SUNDAY IN ORDINARY TIME

(YEAR A)

Therefore, everyone who listens to these words of mine and acts on them will be like a sensible man who built his house on rock. (Mt 7:24)

Some time ago I participated in a group simulation exercise designed to teach the basics of problem-solving. A group of eight of us had to imagine that we were passengers aboard a twin engine plane that had crash-landed in central Australia, killing the pilot and co-pilot. We survivors, badly shaken but relatively unharmed, scrambled from the wreck before it burst into flames. The pilot was unable to notify anyone of our position before the crash, but as the plane slowly descended some of the passengers noticed a small mining town below us in the distance, perhaps some fifty or sixty kilometres to the south-west. The eight of us were stranded in the desert where the temperature soars to over 50 degrees celsius during the day. All that could be salvaged from the plane were the following items: a magnetic compass; a large, light-blue canvas; a book, Animals of the Desert; a rearview mirror; one flashlight; one jacket per person; an accurate map of the area; a loaded .38-calibre pistol; a bottle of 1,000 salt tablets; four two-litre bottles of water.

The problem-solving exercise ahead of us was this: as a group we had to rank these items in the order of their importance for our survival. This entailed two fundamental decisions. Firstly, should we try to walk out, or should we stay close to the wreck of the burnt-out plane? And secondly, should we try to hunt for food? Let me tell you, it was a heated discussion, with some members of the group insisting that we should stay put, and others wanting to head off in the general direction of the mining camp. The decision that we made would dramatically affect the ranking that we gave to the items retrieved from the plane.

Survival experts tell us that we must always stay put in such a situation. The vital problem for the group is dehydration – from exposure to the sun, from bodily activity causing perspiration, and from the hot, dry air circulating next to the skin. The most important item for survival is the mirror. In sunlight a simple mirror can generate five to seven million candlepower, which can be seen even beyond the horizon. By using the mirror to signal our presence, the group has an 80 percent chance of being rescued within twenty-four hours. The basic problem is slowing down dehydration, and for that reason the jackets will prevent the hot and dry desert air from circulating next to the skin.

Move out and die; stay put and survive. If the group had decided to walk out, even walking only at night, everyone would probably be dead by the second day. Today's gospel, which rounds off what we know as the Sermon on the Mount, is also about living with the decisions that we make. If we build on rock our dwelling stands firm; if we build on sand it collapses. Needless to say, Jesus is not giving us a lesson in house-building; he is talking about how we build our lives.

What are the foundational values of my life; who and what are truly important to me? I'm sure that I could rattle off an impressive list, but is the answer I give reflected in the way I actually live my life? Or am I like the people that Jesus describes – big on talk but short on action? "It is not those who say to me, 'Lord, Lord', who will enter the kingdom of heaven, but the person who does the will of my Father in heaven."

The *Devil Wears Prada* is a story about Andrea "Andy" Sachs, an aspiring journalist fresh out of university, who lands the magazine job a million girls would kill for: junior personal assistant to the imperious editor-in-chief Miranda Priestly, who dominates the fashion world from her perch atop Runway magazine. In the world of fashion, hers is the only opinion that matters. Andy puts up with Miranda's eccentric and demeaning requests because, she is told, if she lasts a year in the position she will get her pick of other jobs, perhaps even the journalistic position she truly craves.

At first, Andy fits in poorly among the gossipy fashionistas who make up the magazine staff. Although an attractive woman, she is like a fish out of water in the superficial world of fashion and glamour, where outward appearance is all that really matters. Her lack of style or fashion knowledge make her an object of scorn around the office. Gradually, though, with the help of art director Nigel, Andrea adjusts to the position and its many perks, including free designer clothing and other choice accessories. She begins to dress more stylishly and do her job competently. But all of this comes at a price. Slowly she begins to change, and the Andy her friends knew has become a different person. As one of her close girlfriends, Lily, says, "For the last sixteen years I've known everything about that Andy, but this person, this glamazon ... I don't get her."

Miranda becomes increasingly demanding, expecting Andrea to be at her beck and call at any time, night or day. This obviously strains the relationship with her boyfriend, Nate, and things come to a head just prior to her departure on a business trip to Paris with Miranda. She justifies the trip to Nate, "I didn't have a choice." To which he replies, "That's your answer for everything lately, 'I didn't have a choice.' Like this job was forced on you, that you don't make these decisions yourself ... You used to say this was just a job. You used to make fun of the Runway girls. What happened? Now you've become one of them." To which Andy replies, "That's absurd." But Nate persists: "That's OK; that's fine. Just own up to it. Then we can stop pretending that we have anything in common anymore." Taken aback, Andy replies: "You don't mean that." But, of course, he does. Andy is startled. "Well, maybe this trip is coming at a good time. Maybe we should take a break." As Nate walks away, Andy calls his name. He turns, and as they look at each other in silence, her mobile rings. It's Miranda, of course! Here is the moment of truth. Who is more important to her? We can sense her inner turmoil, but the mobile wins out. Before walking off, Nate's parting words are: "You know, in case you were wondering, the person whose calls you always take, that's the relationship you're in. I hope you two are very happy together."

Get the movie out on DVD if you'd like to see how things turn out. Tempted by the "devil" wearing Prada, Andy has to comes to terms with who and what is truly important in her own life. In the course of the movie she changes dwellings – from a house built upon rock to an office block perched precariously upon the shifting sands of glamour and fashion. It was a move that occurred incrementally, without her being fully conscious of the effect it was having upon her. And that's how it usually happens – imperceptibly. For that reason we must, from time to time, call in the building inspector to check our own foundations. Rock or sand?

TENTH SUNDAY IN ORDINARY TIME

(YEAR A)

Follow me (Mt 9:9)

Let's consider the dramatis personae of today's gospel – the who's who! Firstly, we have tax collectors. Such people, *telonai*, appear at transport and commercial centres such as Jericho and Capernaum and they collected indirect taxes, especially on the transport of goods. *Telonai* were universally despised, and this is reflected in secular literature, the New Testament and in rabbinic writings. In Roman and Hellenistic literature tax collectors are lumped together with beggars, thieves and robbers. In the New Testament they are paired with sinners and with "immoral people", and they are likened to Gentiles. Rabbinic literature (which, although not committed to writing until the third century AD, undoubtedly incorporates earlier oral traditions) links tax collectors with robbers, murderers and sinners.[245] The Pharisees considered tax collectors to be ritually impure, and a tax collector's entry into a house rendered it unclean. Their association with Gentiles, who were deemed to be impure, and their direct contact with Roman coins, some of which bore the idolatrous image of the Roman emperor, were further reasons why they were considered unclean.[246] Despite the fact that Matthew is collecting taxes in Galilee, which was not under direct Roman rule, and the taxes supported Herod Antipas, nevertheless tax collectors were suspected of overcharging and being in the employ of the Romans.[247]

Secondly, we have the Pharisees. The word "Pharisee" comes from the Hebrew word *perushim*, which means literally "the separate ones." The Pharisees were obsessed with purity laws, ultimately as an effective means of protecting Jewish identity against the political and cultural influence of foreigners. In other words, if you don't want your own belief system to become contaminated or compromised, separate yourself from all people with contrary ideas. They arose around the middle

---

[245] John R. Donahue, "Tax Collector", in David Noel Freedman (Ed), *The Anchor Bible Dictionary, Volume 6*, Doubleday, New York, 1992, p. 337.
[246] Joel Marcus, *Mark 1-8*, Doubleday, New York, 2000, pp. 225-6.
[247] John P. Meier, *A Marginal Jew, Volume III: Companions and Competitors*, p. 330.

of the second century BC as one response to the radical Hellenisation unleashed by Antiochus IV and his Jewish supporters. According to John P. Meier, the Pharisees "emphasised the zealous and detailed study and practice of the Mosaic Law" and they "possessed a normative body of traditions – the traditions of the fathers (or the elders) – which went beyond the written Mosaic Law."[248]

Every society is governed by what sociologists call purity laws. A purity system is "a cultural map which indicates 'a place for everything and everything in its place'."[249] For example, soil in the garden or even in a pot is in its correct place. But if I were to tip some soil from a pot onto the floor of the church, it is no longer in its correct place. Purity laws establish boundaries around people and indicate permissible degrees of interaction. In some societies those boundaries are rigid and inflexible; in others they are porous – but, however subtly, they are present in every society. Apartheid (meaning "separateness" in Afrikaans) is an obvious example of purity laws in action. In places where apartheid or segregation was enforced, people were discriminated against on the basis of their racial origin or the colour of their skin. The caste system in India is another example of discrimination. Members of the upper castes consider the lowest castes to be ritually unclean. Today, caste barriers have largely broken down in the large cities and "untouchability" has been abolished by law. However, loyalty to a caste is much harder to eliminate and it still provides a sense of community and belonging, particularly in country areas. Though inter-caste marriages are now relatively common in India, caste remains a criterion for matrimonial choices for some. Many Indian matrimonial websites and matrimonial columns in Indian newspapers contain caste-based categories and matrimonial advertisements frequently state the caste as a criterion of choice.

In this country the White Australia policy restricted non-white immigration from 1901 until 1973. It was only in 1975 that the Australian Government passed the Racial Discrimination Act which made racially based selection criteria illegal. Within Australia there were also more subtle forms of discrimination. In 1908, for example, the Committee of the Royal Sydney Golf Club recognised that "the feeling of the Club is adverse to the admission of Jews," and no Jew became a member of the Club for the next 75 to 80 years.[250] Virulent sectarianism within the Australian Catholic Church of the late nineteenth century continued well into the twentieth century. The plenary council of bishops convened by Cardinal Moran

---

[248] John P. Meier, *A Marginal Jew, Volume III: Companions and Competitors*, p. 330.

[249] Jerome Neyrey, *The Social World of Luke-Acts*, Hendrickson, Peabody, MA, 1991, p. 275.

[250] Les Kausman, *What's Golf? The First 50 Years of the Cranbourne Golf Club*, p. 12. You can find the text of this book if you Google the author's name and the name of the Club.

in 1885 laid down that parents who sent their children to a state school without cause or permission were to be denied absolution in the confessional. The bishops also determined that a Catholic who got married before a non-Catholic minister or a civil registrar was automatically excommunicated.[251] You might be relieved to know that neither of those provisions remains in force today!

Jesus' choice of someone ritually unclean and a social outcast like Matthew would have been anathema to the Pharisees, but as he makes clear when he calls Matthew, "I came to call not the upright, but sinners" (Mt 9:13). Such a choice has been called an "acted parable" of his message of God's mercy to sinners, and "anticipatory sitting at table in the kingdom of God."[252] The table has become a parable of the Kingdom. Pope John XXIII (1881-1963) was one of thirteen children and his family was very poor. Looking back on his childhood, he recalls that there was always room for the stranger at their table: "We were poor, but happy with our lot and confident in the help of Providence. There was never any bread on our table, only polenta; no wine for the children and young people; only at Christmas and Easter did we have a slice of home-made cake. Clothes, and shoes for going to church, had to last for years and years ... And yet when a beggar appeared at the door of our kitchen, when the children – twenty of them were waiting impatiently for their bowl of minestra (vegetable soup), there was always room for him, and my mother would hasten to seat this stranger alongside us."[253] The future pope certainly inherited his parents' marvellous spirit of generosity and welcome. In the words of his successor, Pope Paul VI, "Perhaps never before in our time has a human word – the word of a master, a leader, a prophet, a pope – rung out so loudly and won such affection throughout the whole world."[254] John XXIII's ministry as Bishop of Rome became an extension of the family table at Bergamo.

Over thirty years ago Franciscan Telecommunications produced a series of television advertisements promoting the Gospel message. One of these advertisements showed a white woman walking stridently to church on a Sunday morning with a missal tucked securely under her arm. She is warmly greeted by a couple walking in the opposite direction towards a nearby Protestant church. With an air of self-righteousness she totally ignores them. A little further onwards a beggar approaches her for some small change to buy a cup of coffee. Her disgust is obvious

---

[251] Edmund Campion, *Australian Catholics*, p. 65.
[252] John R.Donahue, op. cit., p. 338.
[253] Loris Capovilla (ed) *Giovanni XXIII, Lettere ai familiari,* I, p. 8, in Peter Hebblethwaite, *John XXIII,* Geoffrey Chapman, London, 1984, p. 8.
[254] Hebblethwaite, p. 503.

as she brushes the man aside. As she approaches the front door of the church a black family smiles and wishes her a good morning. She snubs them, obviously indignant at their impertinence. Just as she reaches out to grasp the handle of the church door the frame freezes and a voice-over says, "If you can't find God out there, you won't find him in here!" The religion of the Pharisees crushed rather than liberated; excluded rather than welcomed. They had failed to learn the lesson of Hosea 6:6, (today's first reading): "I desire love, not sacrifice."

ELEVENTH SUNDAY IN ORDINARY TIME

(YEAR A)

He summoned his twelve disciples. (Mt 10:1)

The American writer Joseph Campbell has written extensively on the subject of myth. One of his most popular works is entitled *The Hero With a Thousand Faces*. The significance of the title is the realisation that the heroic figure in many of the great stories of humanity embarks upon what is essentially the same journey of discovery. Whether the story be Homer's Illiad or Odyssey, or the story of King Arthur in Camelot, Robin Hood in Sherwood Forest, Wyatt Earp in the American West, Tarzan in the jungles of Africa, Luke Skywalker in a distant galaxy, or even Bilbo the Hobbit deep in the Lonely Mountain – we are essentially hearing the same story. Only the "face" of the hero and the setting of the story change. And ultimately, the story of the hero is our own story writ large! The great stories of humanity "carry the keys that open the whole realm of the desired and feared adventure of the discovery of the self."[255]

Campbell outlines a number of key stages in the journey of the hero, beginning with the Call to Adventure. This involves crossing a threshold, and here we encounter what Campbell calls the Guardian of the Threshold. The Guardian symbolises those intimidating forces, from both within and without, that discourage us from embarking upon the Adventure: the fear of failure, the loss of safety and security, the fear of leaping into the unknown, and the fear of risking danger and hostility.

Jesus has summoned the Twelve, but they have a daunting task ahead of them. "The harvest is rich but the labourers are few." And so Jesus exhorts them to pray to "the Lord of the harvest to send labourers to his harvest." That is a prayer that resonates down through the ages, and today the harvest is greater than ever. But the Guardian of the Threshold is working overtime to ensure that nothing much is done. Indifference and apathy and the fear of making a commitment seem to be his weapons of choice.

Elie Wiesel is a Jewish writer and political activist. When he was awarded the

---

[255] Joseph Campbell, *The Hero With a Thousand Faces*, Fontana Press, London, 1993, p. 8.

Nobel Peace Prize in 1986 the Norwegian Nobel Committee recognised him as one of the most important spiritual leaders and guides in an age when violence, repression and racism continue to characterise the world. "Wiesel is a messenger to mankind; his message is one of peace, atonement and human dignity."[256] Wiesel's 1962 autobiographical novel *The Town Beyond the Wall* tells the story of Michael, a young Holocaust survivor who returns to his Hungarian hometown to satisfy his curiosity. In one sense he could understand the brutality of the prison guards and executioners. What he could not understand was the man whom he calls the spectator, an individual who lived not far from the synagogue and peered through his window day after day as thousands of Jews were herded into the death trains. His face "was gazing out, reflecting no pity, no pleasure, no shock, not even anger or interest. Impassive, cold, impersonal. The face was indifferent to the spectacle. 'What, men are going to die? That is not my fault, is it?' ... The face is neither Jewish nor anti-Jewish. A simple spectator, that's what it is.[257] This is what had troubled Michael ever since the end of the war. "Nothing else. How a human being can remain indifferent."[258] The brutal executioner and the victim belong to the same universe, Michael thought, but that is not true of the spectator. "The spectator is entirely beyond us. He sees without being seen. He is there but unnoticed."[259]

The Town Beyond the Wall is a true story, although the novel was written before Wiesel had actually returned to his hometown. Ironically, the novel became the script for his own return journey years later. Like the fictional character Michael, Wiesel also wanted to return to see the man at the window. Speaking over a year ago at the University of California, Wiesel talked about his reasons for returning: "At one point I realised why I wanted to go back – to see that man. A man who was indifferent. He saw us in the courtyard, already gathered by the enemy to be sent off to death. And there he was, indifferent. And I wanted to see him, to confront him."[260]

The man at the window, a spectator looking down at the tragedy unfolding before his eyes, but remaining impassive, cold and impersonal – that man could be any one of us, indifferent to the world's tragedies played out right beneath our window. It is this indifference that has haunted Elie Wiesel and motivated his

---

[256] http://nobelprize.org/nobel_prizes/peace/laureates/1986/press.html
[257] Elie Wiesel, *The Town Beyond the Wall*, Schocken Books, New York, 1964, p. 150.
[258] Ibid, p. 149.
[259] Ibid, p. 151
[260] See the talk on Youtube: http://au.youtube.com/watch?v=kC5MbVsyFh8

activity for years. "I began fighting indifference. I wrote about it. I spoke about it. The Millennium Lecture that I gave at the White House for the President was on the perils of indifference ... The opposite of love is not hate, but indifference; the opposite of education is not ignorance, but indifference; the opposite of art is not ugliness, but indifference; the opposite of life is not death, but indifference."

The mantra of Anita Roddick, founder of the Body Shop, was "I am an activist." This passionate woman, who died recently, travelled among the destitute, the oppressed, the exploited and the condemned, but she never lost hope or stamina, because she knew that there was joy and possibility in creating new, imaginative ways to make things better. She had little patience for those who said they were too busy to be activists. She knew that doing any small thing to improve a life, to right a wrong, brings joy to those who do as well as to those who benefit.[261] In her own words, "I am not an activist in pursuit of recognition or fame. I am not an activist so that strangers will think I am a good person. I am not an activist because it's good for business (although more often than not, it is). I am an activist because being an activist makes me feel alive."[262]

People like Anita Roddick intimidate me. She was an activist in the areas of human rights, trade justice, peace and conflict resolution, homelessness and poverty, health equality, women's issues, the environment and media. She had a certain clout and people listened when she spoke. She made a difference. My immediate reaction is, "What can I do?" Because I can't do anything that will make the slightest bit of difference, I'm tempted to put Anita's catalogue of worthwhile causes into the "too hard" basket. Let's leave it to the government to do something. By way of response, Anita quotes Betty Reese: "If you think you are too small to be effective, you have never been in bed with a mosquito." May the Lord of the harvest shake us out of our indifference and help us to make Anita's words our own: "I wake up every morning thinking ... this is my last day. And I jam everything into it. There's no time for mediocrity. This is no damned dress rehearsal. You've got one life, so just lead it. And try to be remarkable."

---

[261] Taken from the booklet, *I Am An Activist*, a PDF file you can download from http://www.iamanactivist.org/
[262] Ibid.

TWELFTH SUNDAY IN ORDINARY TIME

(YEAR A)

Do not be afraid. (Mt 10:26)

"**Do not be afraid of those who kill the body** but cannot kill the soul; fear him rather who can destroy both body and soul in hell." These words of Jesus are about counting the cost. Is it worth sacrificing our integrity and violating our conscience – or, in the words of Jesus, destroying our soul, simply for the sake of a quiet, untroubled life?

Towards the end of the last millennium, the world's media tried to pick the most inspiring leader of the 20th century. One name that invariably appeared close to the top of all such lists was that of Nelson Mandela. Although Mandela's opponents imprisoned his body for twenty-seven years, they were unable to crush his spirit. On February 11, 1990, Nelson Mandela was finally set free at the age of 71, having served ten thousand days in prison.[263] In Mandela's autobiography, *Long Walk to Freedom*, he writes that solitary confinement was the most forbidding aspect of prison life. "There was no end and no beginning; there is only one's own mind, which can begin to play tricks. Was that a dream or did it really happen? One begins to question everything. Did I make the right decision, was my sacrifice worth it? In solitary, there is no distraction from these haunting questions … I have found that one can bear the unbearable if one can keep one's spirits strong even when one's body is being tested. Strong convictions are the secret of surviving deprivation; your spirit can be full even when your stomach is empty."[264]

Another great leader of past century must surely be the civil rights leader, Martin Luther King. King was buffeted relentlessly from all sides. "He faced death threats from segregationists as well as the FBI. A bomb went off in his home … His volunteers were being threatened, beaten and jailed, and some of them were dying. Often his southern Christian Leadership Conference had no money to pay the wages bill," and President Kennedy had demanded that he dismiss his

---
[263] Nelson Mandela, *Long Walk to Freedom*, Abacus, London, 1994, p. 673.
[264] Mandela, 494.

most effective fund-raiser.[265] In the wake of Rosa Parks courageous stand against segregation in local busses, the black community organised a bus boycott. At the age of twenty-six King was chosen to lead the movement, and as soon as his leadership was announced threats from the Ku Klux Klan began. "Nigger, we are tired of you and your mess now. And if you aren't out of this town in three days, we're going to blow your brains out, and blow up your house."[266] King was tempted to step aside from the civil rights movement and resume a quiet life of scholarship. As he sat drinking a cup of coffee his wife Coretta and their newborn daughter Yolanda lay asleep in the next room. O for a peaceful family life! It was at that moment that he felt God's call. "I discovered then that religion had to become real to me, and I had to know God for myself. And I bowed down over that cup of coffee. I never will forget it … I prayed a prayer, and I prayed out loud that night. I said, 'Lord, I'm down here trying to do what's right. But Lord, I must confess that I'm weak now. I'm faltering. I'm losing my courage.' … and it seemed at that moment that I could hear an inner voice saying to me, 'Martin Luther, stand up for righteousness. Stand up for justice. Stand up for truth. And lo I will be with you, even until the end of the world.' … I heard the voice of Jesus saying still to fight on. He promised never to leave me, never to leave me alone."[267] Martin Luther King was killed by an assassin's bullet in 1968.

Nelson Mandela and Martin Luther King are larger than life figures. The suffering and the sacrifices they made were courageous by any standard. Both men embodied the words of today's gospel, "Do not be afraid of those who kill the body but cannot kill the soul." But what do those same gospel words say to us? King and Mandela paid a great price for the values that were important to them. Many of us are also prepared to pay a great price for values that are dear to us, but so often we mistakenly confuse the means with the end. The end we seek is a life of love and happiness, but we choose the wrong means to achieve our goal. Let me offer an example. A few years ago I celebrated the marriage of a young couple who wanted to move into their dream home as soon as they were married. Unfortunately, their dream home was way beyond their budget, and they each worked two jobs to service a voracious home loan. As a result, they seldom saw each other, and when they did they were tired, tense and irritable. They were not happy, and it wasn't long before the marriage began to flounder. The price

---

[265] Philip Yancey, *Soul Survivor*, Hodder & Stoughton, London, 2001, p. 18.
[266] Ibid, pp. 19-20.
[267] Ibid, p. 20.

they had paid for what they thought they wanted was slowly killing both body and soul.

The story does have a happy ending. A marriage counsellor helped them to realise what was truly important to them, and that was their love for each other, and not the dream home which had turned their life into a nightmare. The modest house they now own is filled with love and laughter, happiness and peace, which is what they really wanted in the first place. All too frequently people pay too high a price in a vain attempt to achieve the values they cherish so dearly. Consider a contemporary parable. An investment banker from the United States was standing on a wharf located in a coastal Mexican village. He watched a small boat dock at the wharf, and cast an eye over the day's modest catch of just a few large yellow-fin tuna. The banker complimented the fisherman on the quality of the fish he'd caught and asked how long it had taken to catch the fish. "Only a little while" replied the Mexican. The banker asked why he didn't stay out longer and catch more fish. The Mexican replied that the fish he'd caught that day would be enough to supply his family's immediate needs.

The banker then asked, "But what do you do with the rest of your time?" The Mexican fisherman said, "I sleep late, fish a little, play with my children, take a siesta with my wife, and stroll into the village each evening where I sip wine and play my guitar with my friends. I have a full and busy life." The investment banker scoffed: "You should spend more time fishing. You'd catch more fish, and therefore you'd make more money. With the proceeds you could buy a bigger boat. With the proceeds from the bigger boat you could buy several more boats. Eventually you'd have a fleet of fishing boats and a huge catch of fish each day. Instead of selling your catch to a middleman you could sell directly to the processor, and in time you could open your own cannery. Of course, as the business expanded you'd need to leave this small village and move to Mexico City, then to Los Angles, and eventually to New York, from where you'd run your expanding business." The Mexican fisherman asked, "But how long would all of that take?" The banker replied, "15 to 20 years." "But what then?" the fisherman asked. The banker laughed and said, "That's the best part. When the time is right you'd float your company on the stock market, sell your stock to the public and become very, very rich. You would make millions of dollars." "Millions … then what?" The investment banker took the fisherman aside and whispered confidentially. "Your dreams will all come true. You can then retire and move to a small coastal fishing village. There you'd be able to sleep late, fish a little, play with your kids, take a siesta with your wife, stroll to the village in the evenings where you could sip wine and play your guitar with your friends."[268]

---

[268] Adapted from *The Tablet*, 22 May, 1999, p. 703.

THIRTEENTH SUNDAY IN ORDINARY TIME (YEAR A)

Anyone who welcomes a prophet because he is a prophet will have a prophet's reward. (Mt 10:41)

Today's gospel concludes Jesus' missionary instruction to the Twelve. They have been warned that the call to discipleship must take precedence over every other relationship in their lives, including family loyalty. They have been warned that the way of discipleship is the way of the cross; they will be persecuted and betrayed. They are, however, not to fear, for the Father knows them intimately, and if they lose their life for Jesus' sake, they will find it. The three sayings of today's gospel speak of the reward granted to anyone who welcomes the disciples. Given the selection of today's first reading from the book of Kings, our attention is directed to the second of these three sayings: "Anyone who welcomes a prophet because he is a prophet will have a prophet's reward." Who, then, is a prophet? The popular notion of the prophet is someone who foretells the future. However, the essential role of the prophet is to be an inspired spokesperson for God, to forth-tell rather than foretell. Nor are prophets venerable and aged figures who graced the pages of the Old and New Testaments, people whose day has long since passed. God calls prophets in every age, including our own.

Jesus is a prophet, despised only in his own country (Mt 13: 57), a motif that resonates in the lives of many prophets. It certainly resonated in the life of Archbishop Oscar Romero who was shot dead twenty-five years ago on March 24, 1980 while celebrating Mass in the chapel of Divine Providence Hospital. Romero had been appointed archbishop of San Salvador just over three years earlier on February 22, 1977, at a time of growing civil unrest in El Salvador. The country was controlled by an oligarchy of fourteen families and their allies, and the military ruthlessly suppressed dissent. The legislature and judiciary were at the service of this powerful elite, and there was an enormous gulf between rich and poor. Less than one per cent of the population owned ninety per cent of the country's wealth.

In 1968 the Council of Latin American Bishops met in the Columbian city of Medellin and made a radical declaration for a preferential option for the poor. Jon Sobrino makes the observation that well before the church in El Savador had made an option for the poor, the poor had made an option for the church. "They had found no one else to defend them, not in the government, not in the armed forces, not in the political parties, and not in private enterprise."[269] At the time of his appointment Romero was staunchly conservative and opposed priests and bishops who supported the Medellin Conclusions. The ruling junta welcomed the appointment of a prelate who was obviously going to be a pliable ecclesiastical puppet.

A significant turning point in Romero's life was the death of a close Jesuit friend, Fr Rutilo Grande. Fr Grande had denounced the unjust treatment of 30,000 peasants working in local sugar cane farms and defended their right to organise co-operatives. He was shot dead in his jeep, almost certainly by government death squads, together with an elderly peasant and a 16-year-old boy. The archbishop was summoned to view the bodies, presumably as a warning against meddlesome priests. Romero's response was dramatic. He cancelled all Sunday Masses in the archdiocese and celebrated a single Mass to which all the faithful were invited. People responded in their thousands and were left in no doubt about their archbishop's commitment to justice.

Romero became a prophet, proclaiming God's word with great courage. He spoke of a "prophetic awakening" in his archdiocese: "I have never felt I was a prophet in the sense of being the only prophet of the people. I know that you and I, the people of God, together, compose the prophetic people. I am happy to say, thank God, there is a prophetic awakening in our archdiocese: in the base church community, in prayer and study groups, and in this critical awareness that is developing in our Christianity, which will be a Christianity of the herd no longer; now it means to be a Christianity of awareness."[270] He called for "a genuine Christian conversion (that) must discover the social mechanisms that make marginalised persons of the worker or *campesino*."[271] He denounced "the outrages of arbitrary arrest, disappearances, and torture."[272] On the day before his death Romero appealed to the military: "In the name of God, then, and in the

---

[269] Jon Sobrino, *Archbishop Romero: Memories and Reflections* Orbis Books, Maryknoll, NY, 1990, pp. 12-13. Quotes from Archbishop Romero are all taken from Sobrino.
[270] July 8, 1979.
[271] December 16, 1979.
[272] June 24, 1979.

name of this suffering people, whose screams and cries mount to heaven, and daily grow louder, I beg you, I entreat you, I order you in the name of God: Stop the repression!"[273]

Romero encountered growing opposition, not only from the ruling junta, but also from within the church. In response to complaints the Vatican sent three apostolic visitors with the course of a year and a half, much to the astonishment of Salvadorans "who wondered when even one apostolic visitor would be sent to another diocese that had drawn up no pastoral plan, or whose bishop had publicly endorsed the acts of a criminal army."[274] A fellow bishop told certain journalists that Archbishop Romero was acting irresponsibly and endangering the entire church by bringing it into confrontation with the government. His actions were motivated by vanity.[275] Then there were those people whose faith had not developed since school days: "I am saddened to think that there are individuals who do not develop. They remember their boarding-school days, and would like a static Christianity, like a museum piece. But this is not what Christianity and the gospel are about."[276] Just as the prophet Amos denounced the rich – "lying on ivory beds and sprawling on their divans" (6:4) – who cared nothing for the poor, Romero confronted the ruling elite of El Salvador because "peoples are toyed with, elections are toyed with, human dignity is toyed with."[277] And just as the prophets of Israel denounced religion that was little more than liturgical niceties, Romero had no time for religion that was only "particular liturgical traditions, clerical and religious dress, and particular ways of praying." These, he argued, were merely human traditions. Instead, he said, "let us seek what is more pleasing to God – some greater manifestation of a religion that lives amidst the people. Let us 'look after orphans and widows in their distress and keep ourselves unspotted by the world (cf. James 1:27). This is true religion."[278]

Jesus warned his disciples that they would be persecuted, a warning that Oscar Romero fully understood. His sole comfort was that Christ "was misunderstood, was called a rebel, and was condemned to death, as I have received death threats these past days."[279] Archbishop Romero, the prophet of God's word, said on the

---

[273] March 23, 1980.
[274] Sobrino, 21.
[275] Sobrino, 21.
[276] June 21, 1979.
[277] March 11, 1979.
[278] June 21, 1979 and September 2, 1979.
[279] June 3, 1979.

day before he died, "If they kill me, I shall rise again in the Salvadoran people."[280] He was truly prepared to lose his life that he might find it. Just minutes before his death he reminded his congregation of the parable of the grain of wheat. "Those who surrender to the service of the poor through love of Christ, will live like the grain of wheat that dies. It only apparently dies. If it were not to die, it would remain a solitary grain. The harvest comes because of the grain that dies ... We know that every effort to improve society, above all when society is so full of injustice and sin, is an effort that God blesses; that God wants; that God demands of us."[281]

---

[280] March 23, 1980.
[281] This final quotation is from the on-line magazine of St Peter's Church, Nottingham, England. http://www.stpetersnottingham.org/saints/romero.html

FOURTEENTH SUNDAY IN ORDINARY TIME

(YEAR A)

No one knows the Father except the Son and those to whom the Son chooses to reveal him. (Mt 11:27)

We have an unequivocal claim in today's gospel: "no one knows the Son except the Father, just as no one knows the Father except the Son and those to whom the Son chooses to reveal him." If Christians, therefore, have such a privileged insight into God, what could they learn by entering into dialogue with non-Christian religions? What can they possibly teach us? The Indian Jesuit Fr Anthony de Mello (1931–87) received a posthumous rebuke from the Congregation for the Doctrine of the Faith in 1998 because allegedly he considered Jesus "a master alongside others." He is accused of teaching that the only difference between Jesus and other spiritual masters is that "Jesus is 'awake' and fully free, while others are not".[282] Fr de Mello's collections of stories from different religious traditions have inspired many Catholic teachers and preachers, and my own homilies have often benefited from his wisdom. But are we walking through a field of landmines when we dabble with the wisdom and insights of non-Christian religions?

The Second Vatican Council's *Declaration on non-Christian Religions* acknowledged that "The Catholic Church rejects nothing which is true and holy in these religions."[283] Any study of non-Christian religions, particularly religions of the East, is not a denial of our faith in Jesus, who is the unique revelation of the Father. It is rather an acknowledgment that our faith in the eternal Word of God is always communicated in human words, and therefore limited, constricted and hedged in by language and culture. Fr John Main, the founder of the World Community for Christian Meditation, was introduced to meditation by a Hindu monk while working as a colonial officer in Malaya. When he asked Swami Satyananda if he, as a Christian, could learn to meditate, the swami laughed and

---

[282] Congregation for the Doctrine of the Faith; *Notification concerning the writings of Father Anthony De Mello, SJ*, June 24, 1998.
[283] Declaration on the Relationship of the Church to Non-Christian Religions, n. 2, in Walter M. Abbott, *The Documents of Vatican II*, Geoffrey Chapman, London, 1966, p. 662.

replied that, of course, it would only make him a better Christian.[284] Ironically, when John returned to England and joined the Benedictine Order, his novice master at Ealing monastery considered that meditation was a foreign import and alien to the Christian tradition. He was told to give up the meditation that had not only become the foundation of his spiritual life but had also led him to become a monk.[285] In time John Main discovered that the method of meditation he had learnt from Swami Satyananda was also an ancient form of Christian prayer used by the ancient desert fathers and mothers and documented by John Cassian (c.400 AD).

The English Benedictine monk Fr Bede Griffiths sought to build a bridge between East and West. He joined the Benedictine Order shortly after his reception into the Catholic Church in 1933, and lived in English monasteries for twenty years before receiving permission to live in India. In 1955 he joined an ashram founded in 1950 by two French monks. This particular ashram was an attempt to found a Christian community in India that followed the customs of a Hindu ashram and adapted itself to Hindu ways of life and thought. Fr Bede sought that which is fundamental to all religions: the search for the absolute that transcends all human limitations. He therefore emphasised the unity between all religions. His hope for the future was that all religions would discover their own depths. He believed that as long as the various world religions remained on the surface they would always be divided and in conflict. When they plumbed their depth they would approach unity. To illustrate this point Fr Bede used the spread out fingers of his right hand. "Here", he said, pointing in turn to the tip of each finger, "you have Buddhism, here Hinduism, here Islam, here Judaism, and here Christianity." Demonstrating how far the tip of the thumb is from the tip of his little finger, he continued. "Buddhism is miles from Christianity, and all of the world's religions are divided." He then joined the fingers of both hands together, still spread out, and slowly drew the fingers of his left hand down along the fingers of his right hand, until they converged in the centre of his right palm. "But as you go deep into any religion, you converge on the centre – you converge on the Divine Mystery at the heart of all religions."[286] Fr Bede's analogy cannot be interpreted naively as saying that all religions are ultimately the same once you delve beneath the

---

[284] Laurence Freeman, *John Main: Essential Writings*, Orbis Books, Maryknoll, NY, , 2002, p. 18.
[285] Ibid, p. 21.
[286] *A Human Search: The Life of Father Bede Griffiths* (Video), More Than Illusion Films, 1993.

superficial differences. At the heart of the Christian faith is our belief that in the life and ministry of Jesus we have a privileged insight into the mystery of God. But that does not mean that Christianity has a monopoly on truth and holiness.

Fr Bede remained in his ashram for thirty-seven years, seeking "the other half" of his soul. He writes of his quest in one of his books, *The Marriage of East and West*: "I want to discover the other half of my soul. I had begun to find that there was something lacking not only in the Western world, but in the Western church. We were living from one half of our soul, from the conscious, rational level, and we needed to discover the other half, the unconscious, intuitive level. I wanted to experience in my life the marriage of these two dimensions of human existence: the rational and intuitive, the conscious and the unconscious, the masculine and the feminine. I wanted to find the way to the marriage of East and West."[287] The Christian churches of the West, by looking to the religions of the East, may find help in liberating God's word from the violent, aggressive, empirical and rational mindset of Western culture.

I recall seeing a cartoon years ago that had a small chapel fenced around by a high barbed wire fence. A warning sign cautioned passers by: "Beware of the god." God cannot be "fenced in" by human words and concepts, and least of all by the "harsh distorting microscope of sceptical Western rationality."[288] In the words of Fr John Main, "We know that God is intimately with us and we also know that he is infinitely beyond us."[289]

---

[287] Bede Griffiths, *The Marriage of East and West*, Fount Paperbacks, London, 1983, pp. 7-8.
[288] A phrase used by William Dalrymple in *From the Holy Mountain*, Harper Perennial, London, 1997, p. 60.
[289] Quoted in Freeman, op.cit., p. 63.

FIFTEENTH SUNDAY IN ORDINARY TIME

(YEAR A)

Imagine a sower going out to sow. (Mt 13:4)

When Pope John Paul II's simple pine coffin was set down before the altar in St Peter's Square, an open copy of the book of the gospels was placed upon it. This was a powerful and poignant statement about his life as a Christian and his ministry as the Bishop of Rome – a life lived under the word of God. Now in death he lay quite literally beneath the word of God.

The prophet Isaiah likens God's word to rain and snow that moisten the soil and make it fertile. Likewise, the Lord says, "the word that goes from my mouth does not return to me empty, without carrying out my will and succeeding in what it was sent to do" (Is 55:10-11). Jesus qualifies that a little. God's word is not a battering ram, smashing asunder the door to our heart. As the risen Lord says in the book of Revelation, "Look, I am standing at the door, knocking. If one of you hears me calling and opens the door, I will come in to share a meal at that person's side" (3:20). Like the sower's seed, God's word can fall on the edge of the path and be eaten by birds; it can also fall on shallow soil and wither under the scorching sun; and it can fall among thorns and be choked. But when God's word falls on fertile ground, it indeed yields a rich harvest.

Let us reflect on God's word. I think it's true to say that many Catholics who had left school before the Second Vatican Council do not know the bible very well. From the first to the last year of my life at school I never once had a "hands on" experience of the Bible, and I think that was typical of my generation. I'm not saying that I wasn't familiar with the gospels. I assiduously followed the readings at Mass from my *St Joseph's Daily Missal* while the priest read them in Latin, and religion classes at school certainly acquainted us with the life of Jesus. Every night my family prayed the rosary, and so we meditated daily upon the mysteries of our faith. But I couldn't have navigated my way through the Bible. When, as a seminarian, I went to confession for the first time, the priest gave me one of the psalms to say as a penance. I had no idea where to find the book of psalms.

Until comparatively recent times most people were illiterate, and until the invention of the printing press in the fifteenth century, the cost of owning a book would have been prohibitive to all except the very wealthy. Moreover, there were very few vernacular translations of the Bible in the Middle Ages, and the most available version at the time, the Latin Vulgate, would have been accessible only to scholars. For those reasons relatively few medieval Christians were familiar with the Bible *as a book*. The Christian message was passed on in other ways – through the liturgy certainly, but also through art and sculpture, and through Mystery, Miracle and Morality plays, performed outdoors before large crowds from the tenth until the sixteenth centuries. Mystery plays were dramatic enactments of biblical stories, and Miracle plays reenacted events from the lives of the saints. Morality plays, common throughout medieval Europe, sought to teach their audience lessons about the moral life.

When, on midday of October 31, 1517, a Catholic priest, an Augustinian friar by the name of Martin Luther, fastened a piece of paper to the door of the castle church of Wittenberg, he triggered what we now know as the Protestant Reformation. At this stage Luther had no intention of breaking away from the Catholic Church and beginning a new movement; he sought only to debate certain abuses and theological issues that disturbed him deeply. He aimed at "purifying the Catholic Church and preserving its truth."[290] But ultimately his so-called Ninety-Five Theses were condemned by Rome, and on June 15, 1520, Pope Leo X issued the bull *Exsurge Domine*, condemning Luther as a heretic.

One of the fundamental themes of Luther's reform was the Bible as the ultimate foundation of all Christian belief and practice.[291] "*Sola scriptura*", the scriptures alone, was to become his catch-cry. "Unless I am convicted by Scripture and plain reason," he said, "I do not accept the authority of popes and councils ... my conscience is captive to the Word of God ... Here I stand, I cannot do otherwise. God help me. Amen."[292] Here we have the essence of Protestantism. William Chillingworth, a seventeenth century English theologian, expressed it thus: "The Bible, the Bible alone, is the religion of Protestants."[293] The Anglical Thirty-nine Articles, formulated in 1571, set out this position with classic precision in article 8: "Holy Scripture containeth all things necessary to salvation: so that whatsoever

---

[290] Owen Chadwick, *The Reformation*, Penguin Books, Harmondsworth, Reprinted 1973, p. 51.
[291] Alister McGrath, Christianity's Dangerous Idea, HarperOne, New York, 2007, p. 56.
[292] Quoted in McGrath, p. 55
[293] Quoted in McGrath, p. 199.

is not read therein, nor may be proved thereby, is not to be required of any man, that it should be believed as an article of the faith, or be thought requisite or necessary to salvation."[294]

Such a position could lead to chaos, and that perhaps explains why there is not one but thousands of Protestant churches. To suggest that scripture is clear enough for the ordinary Christian to understand and apply without any assistance whatsoever is like wanting to play a game of football without an umpire. That is why the Catholic Church has always insisted that the Bible must be read and interpreted within the living tradition from which it emerged. By way of analogy I remember a story told by a Franciscan who studied for the priesthood in Melbourne during the Second World War. The students' daily timetable included an hour of sport, usually cricket in summer and football in winter. Some students became a little bored with cricket and suggested baseball as an alternative. None of the students had ever played baseball before, nor had anyone else in the seminary community. However, they eventually obtained a rule book, and from that they worked out how the game was played. When the chaplain from a visiting US warship joined the community for lunch the students were anxious to impress him with their prowess at baseball. And so, from a verandah in the common room the chaplain watched their game. He chuckled, because the antics he saw played out on the makeshift diamond below were almost a parody of baseball. Sure, he recognised the basics, but it was played in a totally different spirit to anything that he'd ever experienced in the United States. The rule book alone, it seems, wasn't enough. The true spirit of baseball resides within the living tradition of the game.

So it is with the Bible. The Bible didn't fall from heaven as a neatly bound volume. It's not as if someone stumbled across the Bible and decided to establish a community based upon the teachings it contained. Both the Old and New Testaments emerged from faith communities. The Old Testament, for example, "took shape slowly, over a period of more than 1,000 years, and many inspired writers, editors, scribes and others were involved in its making. First, stories ... were passed on by word of mouth. Later, ... these stories began to be set down in writing and other stories, laws, prophecies and poetry were added to them. Over the centuries, these writings, which describe God's involvement in human history, were revised and combined and slowly took on the form they

---

[294] Quoted in McGrath, p. 203.

have today."[295] It was a process of gradual and prayerful discernment. The New Testament, written over a much shorter span of time, contains twenty-seven books written by fifteen or sixteen different authors between 50 AD and possibly as late as 120 AD. But the New Testament did not emerge as a single collection of books immediately. Different groups of early Christians had different collections of sacred books, and there were heated debates about which of these writings were true to Jesus' own teachings. [296] There were many gospels available to early Christians, not just the four that were eventually included in the New Testament. The New Testament canon, those writings considered to be the inspired word of God, emerged as a result of ongoing discernment by the Christian community, a process that continued for almost two and a half centuries after the last New Testament book was written.[297] Debates over the contour of the canon (i.e. the collection of sacred texts) were "long, hard, and sometimes harsh."[298] Some works, such as the *Gospel of Peter* or the *Gospel of Philip*, were deemed heretical and didn't make it into the canon of Scripture. In other words, the Christian community did not accept these works as authentic or authoritative expressions of the teachings of Jesus. If, therefore, the Bible emerged from the faith of a living community, surely it must be read, interpreted and lived with the tradition of that same community.

Let us also remember that the Bible is the word of God, but in human words. The sacred writers were not stenographers, copying, verbatim, words and phrases dictated by God. Scripture is our experience of God's multiple attempts to communicate with humanity, to get through to us. But no experience remains unexplained for very long. In order to explain or talk about any experience, it has to be expressed in human thoughts and words. And those thoughts and words inevitably reflect the limitations of the time, language and culture in which they were expressed. All words and thoughts inevitably reflect the value system, the prejudices, the world view and culture of the people using those words — even if they are not aware of it themselves. And so the Scriptures are a record of our wrestling with God, of our fumbling attempts to express the ineffable in human

---

[295] Stephen M. Miller & Robert V. Huber, *The Bible: A History*, A Lion Book, Oxford, 2003, p. 10.
[296] Bart D. Ehrman, *The New Testament: A Historical Introduction to the Early Christian Writings*, 4th Edition, Oxford University Press, 2008, p. 11.
[297] It was not until the year 367 AD that any Christian of record named our current twenty-seven books as the authoritative canon of Scripture. The author of this list was Athnasisus, the bishop of Alexandria in Egypt. See Ehrman, op. cit., p. 12.
[298] Bart D. Ehrman, *Lost Scriptures*, Oxford University Press, 2003, p. 1.

words and concepts. And that is why we grow into the word of God, slowly, over a lifetime. But the struggle is worth it because, if we are receptive and persevere, it yields a harvest and produces now a hundredfold, now sixty, now thirty. So, let us scrutinise ourselves to discover how open and receptive we are to the word of God. "Is our openness superficial, like the rocky ground? Is it fickle, like the thorny ground? Or are we really receptive to the word of God, like the ground that produces? And finally, are we as productive as we might be?"[299]

---

[299] Dianne Bergant with Richard Fragomeni, *Preaching the New Lectionary, Year A*, p. 294.

SIXTEENTH SUNDAY IN ORDINARY TIME

(YEAR A)

Some enemy has done this. (Mt 13:28)

Today's gospel comes from chapter thirteen of Matthew's gospel which is devoted to a series of parables about the kingdom of God (or kingdom of Heaven, as Matthew would have it). The kingdom is likened to a seed, a treasure, a pearl of great price and a catch of fish.

The parable of the wheat and weeds tells of a farmer who sows wheat in his field, but during the night an enemy sows a noxious weed, called zizanion in the Greek text and usually referred to in English as darnel, or tares in the King James Version. It is a poisonous rye-grass that closely resembles wheat until the heads appear. By the time the darnel is identified its root system has become so intertwined with the wheat that to uproot the weed would destroy the wheat as well.

I would like to highlight two points from this parable. Firstly, the parable raises the question of disappointment or disillusionment. All of the farmer's hard work has been subverted by an enemy. What should have been a perfect crop is instead a field of weeds and wheat, and the two can't be separated. Amidst the euphoria surrounding World Youth Day in Sydney in 2008 the news media gave extensive coverage to the events of the past week, but they have also covered another issue that we would rather not think about – clerical sexual abuse. The media berated Cardinal Pell for the way in which he dealt with allegations of sexual abuse by a Sydney priest. And the front page of the *Sydney Morning Herald* carried the story of a Melbourne man and his wife who have travelled from London to confront Cardinal Pell and Pope Benedict over the repeated rape of two of their daughters by a Melbourne priest. It is a tragic story. One of the girls committed suicide, aged twenty-six, after a long struggle with drugs. The other sister, who turned to drink, was hit by a car in 1999 and left physically and mentally disabled.[300] The church, like the farmer's field, includes both the good and the bad. "Despite all the dedicated work that goes into the establishment of the kingdom of God,

---
[300] Joel Gibson, Jano Gibson and Erik Jensen, "A cranky father tells the church: the wounds are still raw and open," *The Sydney Morning Herald*, Thursday, July 16, 2008.

there will not be a perfect yield."[301] Wheat and weeds, the good and the bad, are intertwined not only within the church, but also within our own hearts. In his opening World Youth Day address to young people at Barangaroo, Pope Benedict observed that "in our personal lives and in our communities, we can encounter a hostility, something dangerous; a poison which threatens to corrode what is good, reshape who we are, and distort the purpose for which we have been created."[302]

We can easily be disappointed or disillusioned when we encounter that poison, either within the church or within ourselves. We have a tendency to desire a perfect, flawless situation – a field of wheat alone. But sooner or later the bubble bursts and we are confronted by the stark reality of a world which is a mixture of positives and negatives, of good and bad, dark and light, and in time the dark and imperfect become apparent. Life is a field of wheat and weeds. Today's parable states the plain truth: we are not in paradise and reality is a lot messier than we'd like. We must apreciate that neither others nor ourselves are 'goodies' or 'baddies', but a complex mixture of both and more.[303] It also reminds us that there may be right and wrong, good and evil. But don't be so sure, don't be so certain that you have all the answers. Be cautious, the gospel warns, about claiming a monopoly of truth and goodness and right. When *The Times* asked a number of writers for essays on the topic, "What's wrong with the world?" Chesterton sent in the shortest reply:

Dear Sirs,

I am.

Sincerely yours,

G.K. Chesterton.[304]

That leads me to the second point that I would like to make about the parable of the wheat and the weeds. Why doesn't God intervene and eradicate evil immediately? Because "the struggle within the human heart is so subtle, so delicate, that the attempt to root out the evil may also destroy the good. Like the farmer in the parable, God is patient, prepared to tolerate evil along with the good, until the time for the harvest has come."[305] Moreover, this parable also counsels caution because it's not always easy to distinguish between good and evil.

---

[301] Dianne Bergant, *Preaching the New Lectionary, Year A*, p. 298.
[302] The full text of the Pope's address can be found at http://www.vatican.va/holy_father/benedict_xvi/speeches/2008/july/documents/hf
[303] Peter A. O'Connor, *Looking Inwards*, Penguin Books, Camberwell, Vic, pp. 75-78.
[304] Philip Yancey, *Soul Survivor*, p. 56.
[305] Brendan Byrne, *Lifting the Burden*, p.111.

On February 13, 2008, the Prime Minister of Australia, Kevin Rudd, said "sorry" in the National Parliament to the indigenous peoples of this land for their past mistreatment, and in particular to the stolen generation. The Prime Minister apologised for the indignity, degradation and injustice that "inflicted profound grief, suffering and loss" on our fellow Australians. It is now time, Mr Rudd said, "to turn a new page in Australia's history by righting the wrongs of the past and so moving forward with confidence to the future."[306]

Today, no fair minded Australian can deny that the Aboriginal people were treated with indignity and degradation, but not everyone saw it that way at the time. Sadly, when successive parliaments and governments enacted legislation that today seems so unjust and inhumane, they thought they were acting in the best interest of Aborigines and Torres Strait Islanders. The Leader of the Opposition, Brendan Nelson, alluded to this in his speech of reply when he said that in some cases "government policies evolved from the belief that the Aboriginal race would not survive and should be assimilated." And there were some people who believed "that half-caste children in particular should, for their own protection, be removed to government and church-run institutions where conditions reflected the standards of the day." Mr Nelson argued that what was done "in many, but not all cases, (was done with) the best of intentions," and with "inherent humanity and decency." In this context he made the observation that "no one should bring a sense of moral superiority to this debate in seeking to diminish the view that good was being sought to be done."[307]

It may have been insensitive of Brendan Nelson to make this point on that particular occasion, but there is truth in what he says. Policies that caused profound upheaval and suffering to Aboriginal people were often carried out by humane and decent people acting with the best of intentions. In terms of today's gospel, people thought they were pulling out weeds. Maybe they were, but the wheat crop was also devastated. With hindsight we acknowledge how ill-advised those policies were, and Kevin Rudd's "sorry" speech was long overdue.

Reconciliation was also one of the themes of the pontificate of Pope John Paul II: a recognition that the Church has sometimes uprooted the darnel and thereby destroyed the wheat. On December 17, 1999, the Pope offered an apology for the Catholic Church's treatment of the 15th-century Czech priest and theologian

---

[306] A copy of Kevin Rudd's speech may be found at http://www.smh.com.au/articles/2008/02/13/1202760379056.html
[307] A copy of Brendan Nelson's speech may be found at http://www.smh.com.au/news/national/brendan-nelsons-sorry-speech/2008/02

John Hus, who was burned at the stake in 1415 after being condemned as a heretic at the Council of Constance. "Today, on the eve of the great jubilee, I feel the need to express deep regret for the cruel death inflicted on John Hus and for the consequent wound of conflict and division which was thus imposed on the minds and hearts of the Bohemian people," he said.[308]

In 1633 the Holy Office tried Galileo for heresy. He was found guilty of holding "doctrine which is false and contrary to the Sacred and Divine Scriptures, that the Sun is the centre of the world and does not move from east to west and that the Earth moves and is not the centre of the world." He was condemned to "formal imprisonment in this Holy Office" and forbidden to "hold, defend (or) teach in any manner whatever, either orally or in writing, the said false doctrine."[309] The year following his election Pope John Paul II called upon theologians, scholars and historians to re-examine Galileo's case. "We cannot deny that Galileo suffered greatly at the hands of churchmen," the pope admitted.[310] The outcome of a review of the trail by the Pontifical Academy of Sciences resulted in a Vatican statement in 1984 that "Church officials had erred in condemning Galileo," and the Pope John Paul II subsequently acknowledged that the church had "imprudently opposed" Galileo.[311]

The parable of the wheat and the darnel assures us that God will separate the just and the unjust at the final judgment. But in the meantime let us be patient and tolerant, because the church has erred so often in the past in discerning between right and wrong, just and unjust. A story from the Islamic tradition offers an interesting way of reading the parable. Mulla Nasrudin decided to start a flower garden. He prepared the soil and planted the seeds of many beautiful flowers. But when they came up, his garden was filled not just with his chosen flowers but also overrun by dandelions. He sought advice from gardeners near and far, and tried every known method to get rid of them, but to no avail. Finally he sought out the royal gardener at the sheik's palace. This wise old man had counselled many gardeners before and suggested a variety of remedies to expel the dandelions, but Nasrudin had tried them all. They sat together in silence for some time before the royal gardener looked at Nasrudin and said, "Well, then, I suggest you learn to live with dandelions!"[312]

---

[308] *America*, 182:1, January 1, 2000.
[309] Dava Sobel, Galileo's Daughter, Fourth Estate, London, 1999, p. 288-90.
[310] Michael Walsh, John Paul II: A Biography, HarperCollins, London, 1994, p. 259.
[311] Encyclopaedia Britannica CD Rom, "Theological Contributions (from John Paul II)."
[312] Slightly adapted from Christina Feldman and Jack Kornfield, Stories of the Spirit, Stories of the Heart, HarperSan Francisco, 1991, pp. 141-2.

SEVENTEENTH SUNDAY IN ORDINARY TIME

(YEAR A)

The kingdom of heaven is like ... (Mt13:44)

The three brief parables in today's gospel are about the kingdom of heaven. Let's deal with the third parable first, the dragnet cast into the sea that brings in a haul of all kinds. There are close parallels between this parable and last Sunday's story about the wheat and tares. The dragnet gathers many kinds of fish, some of which were of no use to the fishermen. But the separation of the good ones from those that are of no use will take place later, when the fishermen reach shore. Likewise, in God's kingdom there will always be a mixture. I'm always amused at the accusation constantly levelled against the Church, that it has so many sinful people in its midst. "The plain implication of this parable is that it cannot be any other way because the net as it sweeps the sea gathers all kinds of things into itself."[313]

Let us now consider the first two parables, the treasure hidden in a field and the pearl of great price. John Dominic Crossan argues that there are three elements in these parables that provide a key to understanding all the other parables of Jesus. Those three elements are "advent", "reversal", and "action." By "advent" he means the coming of the kingdom, with its new world and new possibilities. It's important to remember that the kingdom of heaven is not a way of talking about life after death – going to heaven. While the gospels of Mark and Luke talk about the kingdom of *God*, Matthew prefers to speak of the kingdom of *heaven* because he is writing for a predominantly Jewish audience. Teachers who are examiniers for the Higher School Certificate Studies in Religion course tell me that the examination papers of Orthodox Jewish students stand out because they invariably write "G-d" instead of "God". Like Matthew's use of "heaven" rather than "God", this is simply a way of acknowledging the transcendence (the holiness or otherness) of God. The kingdom of God (or heaven) does not refer to a specific territory or place that God rules or will rule. It is a way of describing

---

[313] William Barclay, *And Jesus Said*, The Saint Andrew Press, Edinburgh, Republished 1970, p. 50.

God's kingship or sovereign and saving rule, and for Jesus the coming of God's kingdom "did not belong to a moment but constituted a series of events that would cover a period of time."[314]

"Reversal" means the undoing of the past and all its values. The advent of God's kingdom involves a profound upheaval in our lives. These two parables are about a person finding something they would dearly love to possess – treasure in a field and a pearl of great price; they are prepared to sacrifice everything they possess to obtain it. In first century Palestine finding treasure buried in a field is not as improbable or contrived as it might sound to us. Before there were financial institutions such as banks, the only way to keep large sums of money or valuables safe was to bury them. The Rabbis had a proverbial saying, "There is only one safe repository for money – the earth."[315] A sudden death or the ravages of war could result in such treasures remaining hidden for ages.[316] Commentators have long discussed whether the man who discovered the treasure had acted immorally or unlawfully when he covered it up and devised a way of keeping it for himself. Such discussions are probably a distraction from the main point of the parable because we don't really know enough about the situation to evaluate the legal or moral implications of the man's actions.[317] Nevertheless, the Talmud, a record of rabbinic discussions that pertained to Jewish law, ethics, customs and history, stated quite unambiguously that "if a man finds scattered fruit or scattered money, these belong to the finder."[318]

There is, however, no moral ambiguity about the merchant's purchase of the pearl of great price. He is probably a professional trader of pearls, and his trained eye would recognise the value that another might overlook.[319] These two parables are making essentially the same point. "When the truth is encountered, a choice has to be made, a decision, and it must be acted on immediately, whole-heartedly. And a price must be paid, amounting to all that one has."[320]

"Action" refers to all the new possibilities that are brought about by the coming

---

[314] W.D. Davies and D.C. Allison, *Matthew 1-7*, p. 390.
[315] William Barclay, *And Jesus Said*, p. 67
[316] Brendan Byrne, *Lifting the Burden*, p. 114.
[317] W.D. Davies and D.C. Allison, *Matthew 8-18*, p. 436.
[318] William Barclay, *And Jesus Said*, p. 68. Although the Talmud was not committed to writing until 200 AD it almost certainly contains much earlier material that had been transmitted orally.
[319] Dianne Bergant, *Preaching the New Lectionary, Year A*, pp. 303-4.
[320] G. Vermes, quoted in W.D Davies and D.C. Allison, *Matthew 8-18*, p. 437.

of the kingdom.³²¹ But that crucial moment must be seized at once, however unexpectedly it may come. Shakespeare put it this way in *Julius Caesar*:

There is a tide in the affairs of men,
Which, taken at the flood, leads on to fortune;
Omitted, all the voyage of their life
Is bound in shallows and in miseries. (Act 4, Scene 3).

There is another important point to make about these two parables. Both men discovered their treasure while about their daily business, one by chance, the other after a long search. Although it is not stated explicitly, we may assume that the man who discovered the treasure hidden in the field wasn't a prospector; he was ploughing or digging in the field, and the pearl merchant was also about his usual business. For most of us, the in-breaking of God's kingdom – finding the treasure in the field or the pearl of great price – does not occur in faraway and exotic places; it is to be found here and now. In other words, the kingdom of God is present though unperceived.³²² Take the case of Johann Sebastian Bach. Bach's job required him to instruct the students of the Thomasschule in singing and to provide new compositions every Sunday for services at the two main churches in Leipzig, St. Thomas' and St Nicholas's. These compositions were never published; "they were simply written, sung and piled into a cupboard to grow old and dusty and forgotten. Priceless music – *Sheep may safely graze* and *Jesu, joy of man's desiring*, all kinds of things – was written, used and piled away."³²³ These musical masterpieces were all created as part of a day's work!

In the aftermath of World Youth Day in 2008 I was asked about the highlights of the week for me personally. There were so many moments of grace throughout the week that it's difficult to single out one. I attended both the opening and closing Masses, and watched highlights of the week on television, including the Stations of the Cross dramatically reenacted at spectacular venues throughout the city. I also sat in on some of the catechesis sessions held in my own parish church, even though they were in French. During that week Catholics were able to celebrate and share their faith openly, surrounded by joyful pilgrims. I felt we had here a foretaste of the kingdom fully realised. But for me personally, the

---

³²¹ John Dominic Crossan, *Parables*, 26-36, quoted in W.D. Davies and D.C.Allison, *Matthew 8-18*, p. 438.
³²² Dianne Bergant, p. 303.
³²³ William Barclay, pp. 70-71.

highlight of the week was something that only a handful of people will ever know about. One of the French pilgrims billeted at our parish school was a severely disabled twenty-eight-year-old man, Philippe. Although very intelligent, in fact he is completing a sociology degree at university, Philippe has no control of his body: he can neither talk nor feed himself. He is confined to a wheelchair and totally dependent upon his carers to look after his every need. His carers were two young men in their early twenties who had volunteered to accompany Philippe on the WYD pilgrimage. And they fulfilled this task with great fidelity, even though it severely restricted their own participation in World Youth Day activities. They fed and showered him, saw to his toiletry needs, stayed by his side day and night, and took him to all the events he wanted to attend. Communication with Philippe was a slow process. Sometimes the boys could guess what he wanted, but on other occasions they had to get him to spell out, quite literally, what he wanted — by going through the alphabet letter by letter and having him jerk his head at the right letter. I never once saw either of these two lads grow impatient or annoyed with Philippe, nor were they resentful at missing out on all the fun in the city following the celebrations. Here, during World Youth Day, I found the pearl of great price, the treasure buried in a field.

EIGHTEENTH SUNDAY IN ORDINARY TIME

(YEAR A)

Give them something to eat yourselves. (Mt 14:16)

The author Robert Fulghum relates the following story carried in a tabloid newspaper: "A small-town emergency squad was summoned to a house where smoke was pouring from an upstairs window. The crew broke in and found a man in a smouldering bed. After the man was rescued and the mattress doused, the obvious question was asked: 'How did this happen?' 'I don't know', the man replied. 'It was on fire when I lay down on it.'"[324]

If the story is at all amusing it is surely because of the total absurdity of the man's response. Why would anyone knowingly lie down on a smouldering mattress? Was he drunk, on drugs, ill, blind, or just suicidal? We instinctively seek an explanation for such bizarre behaviour. What does it mean?

Caroline Jones' highly acclaimed radio program *The Search for Meaning* was developed on the presumption "that all people have within them an innate concern for meaning and coherence."[325] The dominant theme of her program turned out to be "the struggle which is common to all people to find some meaning to the things that happen in this life."[326] Pope John Paul II's 1998 Encyclical, *Fides et Ratio*, speaks of the "quest for meaning which has always compelled the human heart." [327]

This relentless and instinctive quest for meaning is satirised in a story from Bryce Courtenay's novel, *The Power of One*. A cobbler in a Jewish village in Russia was spreading honey on a piece of bread when the bread fell to the floor. To his amazement, the bread fell the right side up. "How can this be?" he said, and with the slice of bread in his hand he ran to consult the rabbi and the village elders. "We are Jews in Russia, how can it be that I spread honey on my bread and

---

[324] Robert Fulghum, *It was on Fire when I Lay Down on It*, Grafton Books, London, 1990, p. 5.
[325] David Millikan, in the Preface to Caroline Jones, *The Search for Meaning*, Sydney, ABC and Collins Dove, Crows Nest, NSW, 1989, p. 3.
[326] Ibid, p. 4.
[327] John Paul II, *Fides et Ratio*, St Pauls Publications, Strathfield, 1998, p. 10.

when it fell to the floor it landed right side up? Since when did luck such as this come to a Jew?" The rabbis and the elders pondered the point for several days, consulting the Torah frequently. Finally, they called the little cobbler into the synagogue. The rabbi pronounced the verdict, "The answer my boy is quite clear, you honeyed your bread on the wrong side."[328]

The Austrian psychiatrist, Viktor Frankl, argues that the human search for meaning is a "primary motivational force" in each of us. He has coined the term *logotherapy* to describe his school of psychotherapy. *Logos*, he explains, is a Greek word denoting "meaning", and so logotherapy focuses on "the meaning of human existence" and on each individual's search for such a meaning.[329] Logotherapy grew out of Frankl's experience as a prisoner in concentration camps during the Second World War. His entire family, except his sister, perished in these camps, and he lost all his possessions.

Some 1500 captives arrived at Auschwitz with Frankl, and upon arrival everyone was ordered to file past a senior SS officer. With the casual wave of his finger the officer directed some prisoners to his left, others to the right. Almost 90 per cent of the prisoners were directed to the left. These prisoners were marched into a building that had the word "bath" written over its doors in several European languages. It was in fact a crematorium, and for 90 per cent of the prisoners who arrived with Frankl it meant death.[330]

Prisoners slept in beds constructed in tiers, and nine men were forced to share each tier, usually no wider than six-and-a-half to eight feet, lying directly on the boards and sharing only two blankets despite the bitter cold.[331] The daily food ration was "absolutely inadequate" to sustain prisoners forced to undertake heavy manual labour in a bitterly cold climate with only scant clothing. Frankl describes the appearance of the prisoners as death approached: "When the last layers of subcutaneous fat had vanished, and we looked like skeletons disguised with skin and rags, we could watch our bodies beginning to devour themselves. The organism digested its own protein, and the muscles disappeared. Then the body had no powers of resistance left. One after another the members of the little community in our hut died. Each of us could calculate with fair accuracy whose

---

[328] Bryce Courtenay, *The Power of One*, Mandarin, Port Melbourne, 1992, p. 473.
[329] Viktor E. Frankl, *Man's Search for Meaning*, Hodder and Stoughton, London, 1964, pp. 98-99.
[330] Ibid, p. 10.
[331] Ibid, p. 15.

turn would be next, and when his own would come."[332]

Amidst such unrelenting horror and hopelessness, it was only natural that prisoners entertained the thought of suicide, however fleetingly. The most popular method of suicide was to touch the electrically charged barbed-wire fence that surrounded the camp, to "run into the wire".[333] Only one person in 20 survived Auschwitz, but Frankl discovered that chances of survival depended more upon the will to meaning than on physical fitness.

Frankl adopted the words of the German philosopher Friedrich Nietzsche (1844–1900) as the guiding motto for survival in the concentration camp: "He who has a *why* to live for can bear with almost any *how*."[334] In other words, those people who had discovered a meaning in their own life could endure almost any hardship. Australian psychotherapist Peter O'Connor argues that we need to believe. "We find it very difficult to sustain ourselves in a state of uncertainty. Believing in something, in anything, is necessary for psychological survival; otherwise we are subject to the most profound feelings of despair." [335]

For those who have eyes to see, the feeding of the multitude is much more than an act of compassion towards the large crowd that had followed Jesus into a lonely place. It is indeed a sign. There is food in abundance, not only to satisfy hungry bodies, but food for the deepest yearning and longings of the human heart. St Augustine once wrote, "You have made us for yourself, and our heart is restless until it rests in you."[336]

---

[332] Ibid, p. 29
[333] Ibid, p. 16.
[334] Ibid, p. 76.
[335] Peter O'Connor, in John Marsden (ed) *This I Believe*, Random House, Sydney, 1996, p. 253.
[336] St Augustine, *Confessions*, Book I, Chapter 1.

NINETEENTH SUNDAY IN ORDINARY TIME

(YEAR A)

Courage! It is I! Do not be afraid. (Mt 14: 27)

Now here's a simple Bible quiz. Which command is repeated most often in the Bible? "Repent", perhaps, or "Do not judge"? What about "Love one another" or "Take up your cross and follow me"? Or maybe "Be compassionate" or "Forgive one another" or "Do not doubt but believe"? They're all important but, according to Tom Wright, a Scripture scholar and the Anglican bishop of Durham, they don't occur as often as "Do not be afraid."[337] The disciples needed that assurance because Jesus had already given them plenty of reasons to be afraid. He has warned them that they will be persecuted and universally hated, handed over to sanhedrins and scourged, and brought before governors and kings. They will even be betrayed by members of their own family (Mt 10:17-23).

There are two faces of the human emotion of fear. On the one hand, fear alerts us to danger. In Herman Melville's epic saga on whaling, *Moby Dick*, Starbuck says that the only men he wants in his boat are men who are afraid of whales. Those who are afraid truly know the power and awesome strength of their adversary, and are not likely to be foolhardy. But fear can also be debilitating. We hear of people being paralysed with fear. In his book *Let Go of Fear*, the Spanish Jesuit Carlos Valles tells a story about the paralysing effects of fear. When he worked as a missionary in India he recalls riding his bicycle along a track when he was brought to a halt by the sight of a cobra only a few metres ahead. The snake wasn't paying any attention to him. Its gaze was firmly fixed on the branch of a nearby tree where a small bird sat paralysed by the cobra's gaze. He had heard that snakes could have that effect on birds, but he had never seen it before. The bird was motionless. It had a voice, but it couldn't sing; wings but it couldn't fly. Carlos jumped off his bike and did all he could to distract the snake. After a few moments the snake slithered off into the grass, and the bird flew away. This is what fear does to us; it paralyses us, keeping us from moving forward in our lives.[338]

---

[337] Tom Wright, *Matthew for Everyone*, Part 1, p. 118.
[338] Cf. Edward L. Beck, *Soul Provider*, Image Books, New York, 2007, pp. 194-5.

When Linus comes to consult Lucy he admits that he's in a bad way. "My life is full of fear and anxiety." Lucy suggests that they try to pinpoint his fears. "If we can find out what it is you're afraid of, we can label it." Lucy then runs through a number of possibilities: "Are you afraid of responsibility? If you are, then you have hypengyophobia!" Linus doesn't hink that's quite it, so Lucy goes through a litany of other possibilities: ailurophobia (fear of cats), climacophobia (fear of staircases), thalassophobia (fear of the ocean or gephyrophobia (fear of crossing bridges). Linus is not sure, so Lucy suggests that he might have pantophobia. "What's pantophobia?" asks Linus. Lucy explains: "The fear of everything." Linus lights up: "THAT'S IT!!!"[339]

Clint Eastwood's 1985 Western, *Pale Rider*, is a saga about a mysterious stranger who arrives, seemingly out of nowhere, at a gold mining camp in the mountains. This small community of simple and struggling panning miners is in grave danger from a powerful and ruthless landowner, Coy LaHood. LaHood runs a successful hydraulic mining operation and, with the support of the local sheriff, intends to drive the miners off their land. In the movie's opening scene LaHood's ruffians terrorise the miners, causing havoc as they ride through the camp shooting indiscriminately, killing livestock and destroying property. Soon afterwards, one of the panners foolishly heads into town to buy supplies, and is set upon by a band of the same thugs. A drifter (Clint Eastwood) suddenly appears and defends the miner with unexpected skill wielding an axe handle. When he later arrives at the panners' camp the drifter surprises everyone by removing his coat to reveal a minister's collar. And so he acquires the name Preacher, but as you'd expect, he's not your average preacher. When asked if he "imbibed", he replies "Only after nine in the morning."

There are heavy-handed supernatural overtones in the portrayal of the Preacher. He rides into the miners' settlement on a pale horse just as a young girl is reading a passage from the book of Revelation about the fourth horseman, Death, riding on a pale horse (Rev 6:8). At one point in the movie we see six bullet wounds on his back, wounds that no ordinary person could have survived. And when LaHood describes the Preacher to Marshal Stockburn, the lawman acknowledges that he sounds familiar, but the person he's thinking of is already dead. *Pale Rider* is a story based upon a perennial theme. Fearful and powerless people are overwhelmed by adversity and oppressed by forces beyond their control. But

---

[339] Charles Schulz, *The Complete Peanuts, 1961 to 1962*, Fantagraphics Books, Seattle, WA, 2006, p. 67.

things change with the appearance of the Preacher. As the arch-villain LaHood tells Stockburn: "For a while I had them buffaloed. Then this preacher come along, shot them full of sass."

The gospel offers a paradigm of faith and discipleship in the face of fear. The disciples are struggling in the boat on Lake Gennesaret (also known as the Sea of Galilee). The lake was and is notorious for the sudden and violent storms that arise on it. As they battle heavy seas, the disciples are symbolic of the Church weathering storms of persecution. Where, we may ask, do we place our faith — in the terrifying power of the storm or in the divine presence? Like the impetuous Peter, we can at first brave difficulties, only to falter when lashed by the fury of the storm.

The 19th century French poet, playwright and novelist Victor Hugo is perhaps best known for his novels *Les Misérables* and *Notre-Dame de Paris* (known in English as *The Hunchback of Notre Dame*). His final novel, *Quatrevingt-treize* (Ninety-Three), was published in 1874. It is a story set during the French Revolution, and in one memorable scene the Marquis de Lantenac, leader of a monarchist insurrection, is returning to France by ship. The vessel is battered from without by storm, but assailed from within by a far more insidious danger — a loose cannon below deck. "A gun that breaks its moorings becomes suddenly some indescribable supernatural beast. It is a machine which transforms itself into a monster."[340] Thanks to the heroic efforts of the ship's gunner the monster is secured and the ship saved from destruction. That scene is itself a parable. We too are assailed from without by stormy seas and buffeted by violent winds; but we are also overwhelmed from within by fear and trepidation. When fear overcomes faith we begin to sink, placing our faith in the wind and the waves rather than in the power of God. But like Peter, we of little faith can reach out for the strong hand of the Lord to rescue us from the depths. Peter "models the mixture of boldness and fear, strength and weakness" that is characteristic of all believers.[341]

---

[340] *The Works of Victor Hugo, Volume VII, Ninety-Three*, (The Jefferson Press), p. 27. The novel may be downloaded as a PDF file from http://www.archive.org/details/worksofvictorhur07hugouoft
[341] Brendan Byrne, *Lifting the Burden*, p. 120.

TWENTIETH SUNDAY IN ORDINARY TIME

(YEAR A)

Woman, you have great faith. (Mt 15:28)

When I attended the final Mass for World Youth Day my pass indicated that I was cleared to enter the area designated "Back of House" in the Southern Cross Precinct. During all of the World Youth Day celebrations there were unrestricted areas where the general public was welcome, there were designated areas for registered pilgrims, and there were secure, restricted areas where only authorised people were admitted. Needless to say, relatively few people had access to the papal area. The Southern Cross region was arranged like a series of concentric circles: all were admitted to the outer circle, only a handful of people could access the inner circle (the sanctuary area).

Ancient Israel was structured along similar lines — there were "insiders" and there were "outsiders". The Jewish view of the world was one in which there were concentric rings of holiness. At the very centre of these concentric circles of holiness was the Holy of Holies (known as the *Devir*) in the Temple. God was especially present in this holy place. Only one person, the high priest, was allowed to enter the Holy of Holies, and then only briefly once a year on *Yom Kippur* (the Day of Atonement). Then came the *Hekhal*; the space around the Altar; the court of the priests; the court of the Israelites (men); the court of the women; the Temple Mount; the walled city of Jerusalem; the walled cities of the land of Israel; the land of Israel. Each level of holiness was more sacred than the last, and as the worshipper ascended towards the Holy of Holies, the groups of people who were permitted to enter were progressively reduced.[342] Only the high priest could enter the Holy of Holies, once a year, on the day of atonement. Philo of Alexandria (20 BC – 50 AD) explains that "any Jewish intruder, even a priest, faced 'death without appeal' if found in the innermost Holy of Holies of the sanctuary."[343]

Beyond Israel were the lands of the *goyim*, outsiders, pejoratively called

---

[342] Karen Armstrong, *Jerusalem*, Ballentine Books, New York, 1996, pp. 168-9.
[343] Geza Vermes, *The Passion*, Penguin Books, London, 2005, p. 105.

"dogs" in today's gospel. Although gentiles could enter the outer court of the Temple, known as the Court of the Gentiles, they were not permitted to enter the Temple precincts. A wall of approximately 1.5 metres, called the Wall of Partition, surrounded the Sanctuary, and they were forbidden to pass beyond that wall, on pain of death. A notice to this effect was discovered in Jerusalem in 1872 by Charles Clermont-Ganneau. Engraved on a block of limestone the notice reads: "No foreigner is to enter within the balustrade and the embankment around the sanctuary. Whoever is caught will have himself to blame for his ensuing death."[344] In today's first reading the prophet Isaiah presents a bold and unsettling vision for insiders. God intends to welcome outsiders "to my holy mountain … for my house will be called a house of prayer for all the peoples."

Today's gospel story is set "outside", in the region of Tyre and Sidon. Jesus has crossed a boundary; he is now in unclean gentile territory. The Canaanite woman is not Jewish, and yet she begs Jesus to take pity on her because her daughter is tormented by a devil. Jesus totally ignores her. She persists and the disciples ask Jesus to give her what she wants, if only to keep her quiet. Another rejection follows: "I was sent only to the lost sheep of the House of Israel." This feisty woman will not be deterred: "Lord, help me." Seemingly cold and insensitive to the woman's predicament, Jesus rebuffs her yet again using the heartless image of not throwing the children's food to dogs. Giving as good as she gets, the Canaanite woman throws Jesus' image back at him. Jesus is outwitted and gives in, agreeing to her request and praising her greatness of faith. This non-Jewish woman had prevailed upon Jesus to think beyond the narrow understanding of his mission reflected by his earlier responses. "This unnamed woman, surely one of the great heroes of the gospel tradition, drags the Jewish Messiah from an understanding that his powers were solely for the benefit of his own people to one in which he uses them for a representative of the Gentile world."[345]

This story must have made a deep impression upon Matthew's congregation. They were Jews, struggling with a fundamental question: Is there a place for non-Jews in our community? If so, do they have to observe *Torah*, the Jewish Law, in all its rigour? This story reflects the arguments that raged within Matthew's community. And the conclusion? Despite his initial reluctance, Jesus heard the outsider and responded to her pleas. The Christian community must therefore do likewise.

---

[344] Ibid, p. 106.
[345] Brendan Byrne, *Lifting the Burden*, p. 124.

Racial identity has emerged as a significant moral and cultural issue over the last hundred years. People were horrified when they learnt that the Nazis had killed six million people, merely because they were Jews. International pressure mounted against South Africa because of the apartheid system which discriminated against people because of the colour of their skin. In the 1990s the term "ethnic cleansing" slipped into our vocabulary as a euphemism for the persecution, imprisonment, expulsion and killing of members of an ethnic minority by a majority to achieve ethnic homogeneity in majority-controlled territory. The White Australia Policy, a raft of government policies and legislation that operated from 1901 until 1973, discriminated against "non-white" immigration to this country. The Canaanite woman challenges us to pay more than lip service to the belief "that all humans are equal, irrespective of race and colour, and to make this work within actual societies, where people from very different backgrounds can live together in peace and harmony."[346]

The South African novelist Alan Paton (1903-1988) has written nearly a dozen books supporting the struggle for racial equality during the era of apartheid. His 1981 novel *Ah, But Your Land Is Beautiful* is set in the 1950s and revolves around the everyday experiences of a group of men and women whose lives reflect the human cost of maintaining a racially divided society. When the Afrikaner Nationalist Party comes to power in 1958 strict apartheid measures are imposed and activists opposed to apartheid are arrested. This novel traces the careers of several white leaders, in particular Robert Mansfield, a respectable upper-middle-class headmaster and former soccer star, who is ultimately driven to emigrate to Australia by the fierce hatred he encountered because of his opposition to a segregated society.

When, as headmaster of a school for white students, Mansfield arranged games of cricket and hockey between black and white students the department of education intervened and forbade it. He resigned in protest. Shortly afterwards Emmanuel Nene, a leader in the black community, came to meet him. He said, "I've come to see a man who resigns his job because he doesn't wish to obey an order that will prevent children from playing with one another." To which Mansfield replies, "I resigned because I think it is time to go out and fight everything that separates people from one another ...". Nene warns him that he is going to get wounded. "I expect that may happen," he replies. "Well, Nene says, "you expect correctly. People don't like what you are doing, but I am thinking of joining with you in the

---

[346] Tom Wright, *Matthew for Everyone, Part 1*, p. 199.

battle ... Yes, and I'm going to get wounded, too. Not only by the government, but also by my own people as well." Mansfield then asks, "Aren't you worried about the wounds?" "I don't worry about the wounds," Nene replies. "When I get up there, which is my intention, the Big Judge will say to me, 'Where are your wounds?' and if I say, 'I haven't any,' he will say, 'Was there nothing to fight for?' I couldn't face that question."[347]

---

[347] Alan Paton, *Ah, But Your Land is Beautiful*, Scribner Book Company, 1996. The dialogue between Robert Mansfield and Emmanuel Nene is taken from William Bausch, *Once Upon a Gospel*, Twenty-Third Publications, Mystic, CT, 2008, pp. 262-2.

TWENTY-FIRST SUNDAY IN ORDINARY TIME

(YEAR A)

Who do you say I am? (Mt 16:15)

During the Sundays of Ordinary Time the first reading from the Old Testament is chosen because in some way or another it complements a theme present in the gospel. The image of the key is the obvious link between the two readings this Sunday. The first reading from the prophet Isaiah is set in the eighth century BC during the reign of King Hezekiah. Hezekiah's prime minister (master of the palace), the self-serving Shebna, is dismissed and replaced in office by Eliakim. Eliakim will be invested with robe and sash, and the key of the house of David (symbolising his authority over the entire royal palace) will be placed on his shoulder — doubtless a reference to one of the rituals of the investiture ceremony.

In today's gospel Jesus promises Peter the "keys to the kingdom of heaven", a text that has undoubtedly given rise to the popular perception of Peter as the gatekeeper of heaven. Jesus is giving Peter the power to bind and loose. In the rabbinic tradition the power to "bind" and "loose" related to authoritative halakic decisions.[348] In other words, the disciples are entrusted with the authority to declare what is permitted and what is prohibited.[349] The Church "is being provided with a teaching authority for the time when Jesus will not be physically present to interpret the Torah authoritatively."[350] This commission assures the Church of divine guidance, particularly through the ministry of Peter, the rock, or what Catholics refer to as the Petrine office. The Petrine office, located according to Catholic tradition in the ministry of the Bishop of Rome, is important

---

[348] In Judaism, Halakah refers to the totality of laws and ordinances that have evolved since biblical times to regulate religious observances and the daily life and conduct of the Jewish people. Quite distinct from the Law of the Pentateuch, Halakhah purports to preserve and represent oral traditions stemming from the revelation on Mount Sinai or evolved on the basis of it.

[349] Joel Marcus, "The Gates of Hades and the Keys of the Kingdom (Matt 16:18-19)", in *Catholic Biblical Quarterly*, 50:3, p. 452.

[350] Brendan Byrne, *Lifting the Burden*, p. 130.

because without it "the Church lacks the capacity flexibly, creatively, and also *authoritatively* to adapt Jesus' interpretations of the Torah to the ever-changing conditions of human life."[351]

At Caesarea Philippi Jesus asks his disciples, "Who do people say the Son of Man is?" The setting of this story — Caesarea Philippi — is significant. The district of Caesarea Philippi is forty kilometres north of the Sea of Galilee. It was gentile territory, and a number of temples dedicated to the god Baal were scattered throughout the region. The Jewish historian Josephus wrote that certain springs welling up from a deep cavern in the region were the source of the River Jordan. It was also an area associated with the nature god Pan, and the town's original name was Panias. Herod the Great had built a magnificent marble temple there and dedicated it to the Roman emperor. His son Phillip subsequently enlarged the town and renamed it in honour of Augustus (Caesar) and himself. In the words of William Barclay, "No one could look at Caesarea Philippi, even from the distance, without seeing that pile of glistening marble, and thinking of the might and of the divinity of Rome."[352] Against this backdrop Peter's acknowledgement of Jesus as "the son of the living God" was provocative. An inscription on Roman coins during the reign of Tiberius (42 BC – 37 AD) acclaimed the emperor as "son of the divine Augustus."[353] To affirm that Jesus is the Son of God is to challenge the pretentious claims of Caesar.

"Who do people say the Son of Man is?" This is a timeless question that rolls down the centuries, but we must be aware that our response to the question will always be conditioned by our personal and cultural imagination. Laurence Freeman offers the example of a beautiful mosaic in a fourth-century Roman villa in Dorset. At first glance it appears to be a typical portrait of the young god Apollo, but a closer inspection reveals the chi-rho symbol that identifies it as one of the earliest representations of Jesus.[354] We, too, portray Christ as someone who looks like us. None of the representations of Jesus in most parish churches look at all like a first century Galilean Jew born of humble origins.

Abraham Biderman is a Polish-born Jew whose immediate family perished in Nazi concentration camps. Biderman himself was liberated from Bergen-Belsen

---

[351] Ibid, p. 131.
[352] William Barclay, *Gospel of Matthew, Volume 2*, p. 149.
[353] The wording on a coin from the time of the Emperor Tiberius (42BC – 37AD) reads: Tiberius CAESAR DIVI AVGusti Filius AVGVSTVS (Tiberius Caesar Augustus, son of the Divine Augustus).
[354] Laurence Freeman, *Jesus, the Teacher Within*, Continuum, New York, 2000, p. 22. Chi and rho are the first two Greek letters of the word "Christos" (Christ).

by the British army on 15 April 1945 and eventually made his way to Melbourne where he now lives. In his memoir, *The World of My Past*, Biderman tells of an occasion on which his parents invited a neighbour's son to dinner while he was on leave from the Polish army. The neighbour's son, Berish Staszewski, was a gifted painter who had been commissioned by his Colonel to paint a portrait of Christ. The Colonel almost became apoplectic when he saw the completed painting: "'What is this? What have you painted?' he demanded. 'Is this supposed to be Jesus Christ?'

"Berish, standing to attention, answered. 'Yes, sir, this is my Jesus Christ.'

"'But you have painted a Jew, a typical Jew!' the Colonel replied angrily. 'Are you making fun of me?'

"Berish replied, 'Sir, this is my Jesus Christ. This is how I imagine he looked. This is the way I understand he must have looked at that time when he lived amongst the poor people. He himself was poor.'

"At the end of his tether, the colonel burst out: 'But he looks like a rotten Jew!'"[355]

An amusing but sad example of the obvious truth that our perception of Jesus (and of his physical appearance) is culturally conditioned. Mark Driscoll, an American evangelist, recently toured Australia exhorting Christians to "burn your plastic Jesus — the really nice respectable guy — and discover the authentic Jesus of the New Testament." He goes on to identify what he believes are a number of false perceptions of Jesus that people have. "There is 'prosperity Jesus' — that if you worship Jesus he'll make you rich; there's a tolerant Jesus - that whatever you do, he's OK with it. I think there's a 'religious Jesus', where people say Jesus is all about rules and regulations."[356] Reflecting on the portrayal of Jesus in recent theological writings, Pope Benedict XVI makes the observation: "If you read a number of these reconstructions one after the other, you see at once that far from uncovering an icon that has become obscured over time, they are much more like photographs of their authors and the ideals they hold."[357]

"Who do people say the Son of Man is?" In the fourth century the emperor Constantine sought to make Christianity the glue that held the vast Roman empire together. He therefore summoned a council of bishops from all over the

---

[355] Abraham H. Biderman, *The World of My Past*, Random House, Sydney, 1995, pp. 100-101.

[356] Linda Morris, "God's motormouth looks to set us straight," *The Sydney Morning Herald*, August 23-24, 2008.

[357] Joseph Ratzinger (Pope Benedict XVI), *Jesus of Nazareth*, Doubleday, New York, 2007, p. xii.

empire when a theological controversy threatened the stability of both church and empire. This council, held in 325 at Nicea in modern day Turkey, responded to the teaching of a presbyter in Alexandria named Arius (256-336). Arius sought to defend God's absolute uniqueness and transcendence. He argued "that God's essence *(ousia)* could not be shared, for such sharing in nature would imply a division in God. The Word of God cannot therefore be fully God, but must be a creature that the Father formed, and as a creature, then the Word had a beginning and was subject to change." [358] The creed that we recite together on Sunday — the Nicean creed — was the outcome of that Council. After several months of debate it was approved almost unanimously on 19 June 325 by the 318 bishops gathered at Nicea. This creed did not come as a bolt from the blue. The Nicean creed "had very much in common with the creeds that had developed in a natural and organic way over time."[359]

If Arius and his followers had difficulty in accepting the divinity of Christ, others had difficulty in accepting his humanity. This heresy was called docetism, coming from the Greek word "to seem" or "to appear." In other words, the divine Jesus only appeared to be human, but he wasn't really. Consider, by way of example, what St Clement of Alexandria (c.150 – c.215) had to say about Jesus: "For he (Jesus) ate, not for the sake of the body, which was kept together by a holy energy, but in order that it might not enter the minds of those who were with him to entertain a different opinion of him ... he was entirely impassible, inaccessible to any movement of feeling, either pleasure or pain."[360] Over a century later St Basil the Great (c.330 – 79) wrote: "He (Jesus) ate and drank in a manner peculiar to Himself; He did not even pass his food, so great was the power of self-control in Him."[361] Writing over forty years ago, the Anglican bishop John Robinson argued that "Popular Christology has always been dominantly docetic. That is to say, Christ only appeared to be a man or looked like a man: 'underneath' he was God. ... The traditional ... way of describing the Incarnation almost invariably suggests that Jesus was really God almighty walking about on earth, dressed up as a man."[362] The Catholic theologian Cardinal Walter Kasper would agree: "It is undeniable that in generally current ideas of Christianity, Jesus Christ is often

---

[358] Luke Timothy Johnson, *The Creed*, Darton, Longman & Todd, London, 2003, p. 33.
[359] Ibid, p. 34.
[360] Quoted in J. M. Carmody and T.E. Clarke (Eds), *Word and Redeemer*, Paulist Press, New York, 1966, p. 27.
[361] Basil the Great, *Letter to the Young Men*, 14; Epist. 366, PG 32, 1109–1112.
[362] J.A.T. Robinson, *Honest To God,* Macmillan, New York, 1965, pp. 65-6.

thought of more or less as a God descending to earth whose humanity is basically only a kind of clothing behind which God himself speaks and acts. Extreme notions of that kind see God dressed as a Father Christmas, or slipping into human nature like someone putting on dungarees in order to repair the world after a breakdown. The biblical and Church doctrine that Jesus was a true and complete man with a human intellect and human freedom, does not seem to prevail in the average Christian head."[363]

"Who do people say the Son of Man is?" Jesus then asks a second question: "Who do you say I am?" Note that the question isn't "Who am I?" Councils and creeds have addressed that question, and theologians of all ages have wrestled with it. "Who do *you* say I am?" is an intimately personal question, and "if we do not feel its intimacy as disturbing — even intrusive — we have not listened to it. It is not twisting our arm however. Its authority is not violent but vulnerable, not forceful but humble. To ask a person who they really think you are is a declaration of love."[364] It is a question that "summons a response from a silent depth within the heart itself."[365]

---

[363] Walter Kasper, *Jesus the Christ*, Paulist Press, New York, 1976, p. 199.
[364] Laurence Freeman, *Jesus, the Teacher Within* p. 33.
[365] Ibid, p. 30.

TWENTY-SECOND SUNDAY IN ORDINARY TIME

(YEAR A)

If anyone wants to be a follower of mine, let him renounce himself and take up his cross and follow me. (Mt 16:24)

The prophet Jeremiah lived in the 6th century BC at a time when Babylon was the superpower in the Near East. Judah was a vassal state of Babylon, but Jehoiachim, king of Judah (605 – 598 BC), foolishly attempted to throw off his allegiance to Babylon by seeking an alliance with Egypt. The Babylonian king Nebuchadnezzar was not amused and set out to punish the rebellious Judaeans. As the Babylonian army marched towards Judah, Jehoiachim died and his son Jehoiachin assumed the throne. After a siege that lasted three months, Jerusalem, the capital of Judah, capitulated in 597 BC. The Temple was plundered and the Judaean leadership was deported to Babylon. Nebuchadnezzar placed Jehoiachin's uncle, Zedekiah, on the throne. Zedekiah, however, had not learnt the lesson and he, too, rebelled. A second time the might of Babylon taught Judah a lesson. This time the Babylonians showed no mercy. After a siege that lasted eighteen months the walls of Jerusalem were finally breached in August 586 BC, and Zedekiah was forced to watch as his sons were executed in his presence. He was blinded and carried off to Babylon in chains. Jerusalem was then systematically destroyed; the Temple of Solomon was burned and the city was left a pile of rubble. More Judaeans were deported to Babylon.

Today's first reading from the prophet Jeremiah is set during the reign of Jehoiachim. Jeremiah could see that rebellion against Babylon was sheer folly and would inevitably lead to violence and ruin. That, alas, was a message that neither the king nor his subjects wanted to hear. Jeremiah became a daily laughing-stock, insulted and derided, but unable to remain silent. The Lord's message seemed like a fire burning in his heart, and the effort to restrain it wearied him.

The bridge between the first reading and the gospel is surely that of persecution and suffering. "If anyone wants to be a follower of mine," Jesus said, "let him renounce himself and take up his cross and follow me." What exactly did he mean? Is this an invitation to masochism? Is it a command to embark upon severe forms of penance? In Dan Brown's best seller *The Da Vinci Code* we're told that it's a "fact" that an organisation within the Catholic Church known as Opus Dei uses "a dangerous practice known as 'corporal mortification'." One of the villains of the novel is Silas, a member of Opus Dei. He's described as an albino "monk", although Opus Dei is not a monastic order and its members are not monks. As a form of mortification Silas wears a spiked *cilice* belt clamped around his thigh. The narrator informs us that "All true followers of *The Way* wore this device — a leather strap, studded with sharp metal barbs that cut into the flesh as a perpetual reminder of Christ's suffering." As an act of expiation for the murder he has just committed Silas not only undertakes to wear the *cilice* longer than the requisite two hours, but he "clinched it one notch tighter, wincing as the barbs dug deeper into his flesh. Exhaling slowly, he savoured the cleansing ritual of his pain."[366]

I have no idea whether or not members of Opus Dei wear the *cilice*, but it is certainly true that Christians down through the ages have mortified the body by, for example, fasting or giving up something for Lent. That is hardly a "dangerous practice", but is it the kind of behaviour that Jesus had in mind when he said, "If anyone wants to be a follower of mine, let him renounce himself and take up his cross and follow me"? Is the church saying, "Look here everybody, if you really want to be a Christian you need to suffer; pain, humiliation, repression and guilt are the way to heaven; if you're enjoying yourself, it can't be right"? Who in their right mind would want to join an organisation like that? This is surely not what Jesus had in mind when he told his disciples that they must take up their cross and follow him.

The image of the cross had been part of Jesus' life since his youth. When he was about eleven years of age a series of peasant revolts erupted throughout the country. This civil unrest was a desperate and spontaneous expression of frustration at constant hardship and harsh taxation. Judas, son of the bandit leader Ezekias, raided the royal armoury in Sepphoris, the capital city and administrative centre of Galilee. Sepphoris was built on a mountain top only a few kilometres from the neighbouring village of Nazareth. The Roman response was swift and brutal. The Roman general Varus burnt the city to the ground and enslaved its inhabitants. Two thousand of the rebels were crucified along the roadside as a warning. Smoke from the burning city wafted into the sky above, easily visible

---

[366] Dan Brown, *The Da Vinci Code*, Corgi Books, London, 2003, p. 29.

from Nazareth. Peasants who sought relief from oppression paid with their lives — a slow and painful death, the price one paid for defying the imperial might of Rome. Although never mentioned in the gospels, this gruesome spectacle must surely have warned the young Jesus that it was dangerous to upset the status quo.

A cross is made up of two intersecting beams. It is therefore a symbol of decision; standing at the crossroads you can go one way or the other. We are at a point of crisis, a word that comes from the Greek *krinein*, meaning to judge or decide. Dietrich Bonhoeffer, the German Lutheran theologian who was executed by the Gestapo days before the close of World War II, asked a fundamental question in *The Cost of Discipleship*: "And if we answer the call to discipleship, where will it lead us? What decisions and partings will it demand?"[367] So, "take up your cross and follow me" is talking about making choices that are authentic, liberating and life-giving; choices based upon love and integrity. At the crossroad we make a radical and deeply challenging choice to follow Jesus and turn away from selfishness and self-centredness; we resolve to leave behind our compulsions, addictions, fears and insecurity, to move out of the prison of the ego. This is a death experience, but, in the words of Bonhoeffer, "When Christ calls a man, he bids him come and die."[368]

Bonhoeffer wrote about "cheap grace". Cheap grace seeks all the consolations of the faith without commitment or conversion. Costly grace, on the other hand, "is the treasure hidden in the field; for the sake of it a man will gladly go and sell all that he has. It is the pearl of great price to buy which the merchant will sell all his goods. It is the kingly rule of Christ, for whose sake a man will pluck out the eye which causes him to stumble, it is the call of Jesus Christ at which the disciple leaves his nets and follows him."[369] To follow Jesus is to leave self behind by placing God's will above all else. As Bonhoeffer put it, "It is costly because it costs a man his life, and it is grace because it gives a man the only true life."[370] The lives of Jeremiah and Jesus reveal the cost of choosing a true and authentic life. Amy Carmichael writes:

---

[367] Dietrich Bonhoeffer, *The Cost of Discipleship*, SCM Press, London, Third Impression, 2004, p. xxxiv.
[368] Ibid, p. 44.
[369] Ibid, p. 4.
[370] Ibid, p. 5.

No wound? No scar?
Yes, as the master shall the servant be,
And pierced are the feet that follow me;
But thine are whole. Can he have followed far
Who has no wound? No scar?[371]

---

[371] Amy Carmichael in Roger Pooley and Philip Seddon (Eds), *The Lord of the Journey*, Collins, 1986, p. 333, quoted in Alan Jones, *Passion for Pilgrimage*, p. 141.

TWENTY-THIRD SUNDAY IN ORDINARY TIME

(YEAR A)

If your brother does something wrong ... (Mt 18:15)

The Habsburgs were once Europe's most powerful and influential royal family. In the course of history members of the House of Habsburg had been emperors of the Holy Roman Empire, kings of Spain, Portugal, Hungary and the Austro-Hungarian empire. However, by the end of the First World War their influence had come to an end and the Austro-Hungarian monarchy was dissolved in 1919. The last Habsburg emperor, Charles, died in 1922, but his wife, Zita, lived to the age of 96, dying in 1989. She had married in 1911, was crowned empress in 1916, and exiled in 1918. It was only in 1982, after celebrating her 90th birthday, that she was allowed to return to Austria. Her four-and-a-half hour funeral, celebrated in Vienna's St Stephen's Cathedral, was watched by millions on Austrian State television. Following Requiem Mass in the Cathedral, the ornate imperial catafalque, drawn by six black horses, made its way to the imperial burial vault in the Kapuzinerkirche, the Capuchin church of St Mary of the Angels. When the procession arrived at the church, the doors were locked. Following an ancient ritual, the chamberlain hammers on the door. From inside, a friar asks: Wer ist da? Who is there? The chamberlain reels off the titles of the deceased: Empress of Austria, Apostolic Queen of Hungary, Princess of Bohemia, Grand Duchess of Lodomeria, and so on. A voice behind the closed doors cries out: Ich kenne sie nicht! I know you not! The chamberlain knocks on the door a second time, and again the question: Who is there? "Empress Zita" was the more simple reply. But the doors remained shut. A third time the chamberlain knocks, and again the question: "Who is there?" And the answer this time, "Zita, a poor sinner." The doors opened.

When each of us enters the church we come, like Zita, as a poor sinner. We have not come together to celebrate Mass because we are perfect. Far from it. The Anglican *Book of Common Prayer* has the priest say what is known as the Prayer of Humble Access on behalf of all present: "We do not presume to come to this thy Table, O merciful Lord, trusting in our own righteousness, but in thy manifold and great mercies. We are not worthy so much as to gather up the crumbs under thy Table ...".

Today's gospel offers guidelines for dealing with sinful members of the community. At some time or another every community has to deal with members who misbehave. The Church, like any community, "cannot simply turn a blind eye to one or more members who consistently, either knowingly or unknowingly, act or live contrary to the values central to its identity." Nor can the Church "simply paper over serious disagreements and resentments among its members without serious detriment to communal wellbeing."[372] Disagreements within the Church can lead to schism, such as happened between Rome and Constantinople at the end of the first millennium, or during the Reformation in the sixteenth century.

One way to deal with dissent within a community is simply to walk out. Rabbi Lionel Blue tells of a Jewish man who was shipwrecked on a desert island. Years pass before a passing ship notices the man's flag tied to a palm tree and sends a rescue party. The man couldn't stop talking as he showed the sailors around. "Is that the house you built to live in?" asked one sailor politely, pointing to a beautifully made hut on a hill. "Oh no," said the man proudly, "that's the synagogue I go to pray in." The sailors are impressed. "Is that the home you built to live in?" asked another, pointing to a lovely hut on a nearby hill. "Oh no," said the man dismissively, "that's the synagogue I wouldn't be seen dead in!"[373]

So, we can walk out and go to another synagogue, parish or club. Or, uncomfortable and distressing as it may be, we can live amidst the chaos of dissension. A young rabbi was completely dismayed to find serious division and quarrelling among the members of his new congregation. During the Friday evening service half of the congregation would stand during part of the service and the other half would sit. Members of each group insisted that theirs was the correct tradition, and arguments back and forth became heated. The young rabbi took a representative from each of the two factions and went to visit the synagogue's founder, a ninety-year-old rabbi now living in a nursing home.

"Rabbi, isn't it true that tradition was always with the people who stand at this point of the service?" inquired the representative from the faction that insisted upon standing. "No, that was not the tradition," the elderly rabbi replied. The representative from the faction that insisted upon sitting seemed complacent as he asked, "So, we're right to stay seated?"

---

[372] Brendan Byrne, *Lifting the Burden*, pp. 141-2.
[373] Lionel Blue, "I don't think I did theology. Intermarriage, mysticism, kosher chicken, yes", *The Tablet*, 11 June 2005, p. 14.

"No," the rabbi said, "that was not the tradition either." The young rabbi seemed exasperated. "But Rabbi, what we have now is complete chaos. Half the people stand and shout, while the others sit and scream."

"Aha," said the old man, "*that* was the tradition!"[374]

Communities must discover appropriate methods to resolve conflict because complete chaos is not a life-giving environment. Today's gospel lays down a three-step procedure to be followed in dealing with "a brother (or sister) who does something wrong." Firstly, the person who has been offended should go privately to the person who has committed the offence and attempt to resolve the situation. If this proves fruitless, the person offended should approach the person who has committed the offence in the company of one or two members of the community. If nothing comes of this, the matter should be reported to the entire community. If the person who has committed the offence remains obdurate then he or she is to be treated "like a pagan or a tax collector." Pagans and tax collectors are singled out because they are "symbolic of those people who have been disdainful toward the message of the gospel. Any community member who remains adamant throughout this process of reconciliation demonstrates the same kind of disdain and should thus be treated with the same kind of separation."[375]

Today's second reading from St Paul's letter to the Romans offers the only enduring solution to conflict resolution: "You must love your neighbour as yourself. Love is the one thing that cannot hurt your neighbour; that is why it is the answer to every one of the commandments." Such love has a transformative power. The transformative power of love is beautifully portrayed in a scene from Victor Hugo's novel *Les Miserables*. Jean Valjean is arrested for stealing a loaf of bread to feed his sister's family during a very hard winter. He is sentenced to five years in the galleys, but as a consequence of several abortive attempts to escape, his sentence is extended for a further fourteen years. After nineteen years in the galleys he is at last set free, but rejected at every turn. At the suggestion of a kindly woman he knocks on the door of the local bishop, unaware of who lives in the house. Valjean is forthright in explaining his predicament: "Jean Valjean, discharged convict ... has been nineteen years in the galleys: five years for housebreaking and burglary; fourteen years for having attempted to escape on four occasions. He is a very dangerous man. There! Every one has cast me out. Are you willing to receive me? Is this an inn? Will you give me something to eat and

---

[374] Adapted slightly from William J. Bausch, *A World of Stories*, Twenty-third Publications, Mystic, CT, 1998, p. 357.

[375] Dianne Bergant, with Richard Fragomeni, *Preaching the New Lectionary, Year A*, p. 341.

a bed? Have you a stable?" To Valjean's utter amazement the bishop is gracious in his welcome. Even after the bishop has revealed his identity Valjean remains wary of such generous and unconditional hospitality.

The bishop, seated at his side, laid a hand gently on his arm. "You need have told me nothing. This house is not mine but Christ's. It does not ask a man his name but whether he is in need. You are in trouble, you are hungry and thirsty, and so you are welcome. You need not thank me for receiving you in my house. No one is at home here except those seeking shelter. Let me assure you, passer-by though you are, that this is more your home than mine. Everything in it is yours. Why should I ask your name? In any case I knew it before you told me." Valjean looked up with startled eyes. "You know my name?" To which the bishop replied, "Of course. Your name is brother." Valjean exclaims, "Monsieur le cure, I was famished when I came in here. Now I scarcely know what I feel. Everything has changed."[376]

---

[376] Victor Hugo, *Les Miserables*, tr Norman Denny, Penguin Classics, 1987, p. 79.

TWENTY-FOURTH SUNDAY IN ORDINARY TIME

(YEAR A)

Lord, how often must I forgive my brother if he wrongs me? (Mt 18:21)

Peter obviously thought he was being very fair-minded and compassionate by suggesting that he should forgive seven times. Numbers are often symbolic in the Bible, and the number "seven" symbolises totality, fullness, or completeness.[377] Peter is therefore asking if we should always forgive those who offend us. The question wasn't as obvious as it might seem. There was a Rabbinic saying that gave the following guidelines on extending forgiveness: "If a man transgresses once, forgive him; if a second time, forgive him; if a third time, forgive him; if a fourth time, do not forgive him."[378]

When Jesus replied, "Not seven, I tell you, but seventy-seven times" he meant, "Yes, always!" Forgiveness must be "uncalculating, limitless."[379] A monk who sat meditating on the banks of a river saw a scorpion fall into the water before him, and he scooped it out, only to have it sting him. The scorpion fell into the river a second time. Again the monk saved the creature from drowning, and again it stung him. This occurred twice more, much to the amazement of a bystander, who was compelled to ask, "Why do you keep rescuing the scorpion when the only gratitude it shows is to sting you?" The monk replied, "It is the nature of scorpions to sting, but it is the nature of a Christian to forgive."[380]

The disciple of Jesus must always forgive, and to illustrate the point Jesus told the story of the unforgiving debtor. A king is owed ten thousand talents, but the debtor had no means of paying. The king therefore gave orders to sell the man, together with his family and all his possessions, to meet the debt. The servant's

---

[377] John L. McKenzie, *Dictionary of the Bible*, Geoffrey Chapman, Lodon, 1968, p. 794; J.-J. von Allmen, *Vocabulary of the Bible*, Lutterworth Press, London, Ninth Impression, 1967, p. 309.

[378] Cf. William Barclay, *And Jesus Said*, The Saint Andrew Press, Edinburgh, Republished 1970, p. 86.

[379] Brendan Byrne, *Lifting the Burden*, p. 143.

[380] Adapted from a story in Huston Smith, *The Religions of Man*, Harper and Row, New York, 1958, p. 49.

appeal for mercy moved the king so much that he remitted the entire debt. We can imagine how joyful the man felt as he left the king's presence. In the midst of his euphoria he came across a fellow-servant who owed him one hundred denarii. Because this fellow-servant was unable to repay the debt immediately, he was thrown into prison.

The astronomical contrast in the two amounts of money mentioned in this parable is disguised by the fact that they're stated in terms of talents and denarii. The word "talent", as used in this parable, refers to a weight, probably of silver. The value of one talent at today's price of silver is approximately $12,000, so ten thousand talents is an enormous amount of money.[381] To place it in perspective, the total revenue for the whole province of Galilee was only three hundred talents.[382] A denarius, by contrast, is a day's wage for a common labourer.[383] One hundred denarii, while not a trifle, is a pittance alongside ten thousand talents. The contrast is quite deliberate. The servant whose colossal debt was remitted in full has a fellow-servant imprisoned because he defaulted on a paltry sum. He who has been restored "through an overwhelming triumph of mercy over justice, now in a case against himself that a little mercy would swiftly resolve, withdraws from the sphere of mercy and reverts, with brutal effect, to a narrow application of justice."[384]

This parable dramatically illustrates two fundamental truths. Firstly, whether it is ten thousand talents or one hundred denarii, a king's ransom or a mere trifle, we all stand in need of mercy and forgiveness, however reluctant we may be to admit it. When Abba Macarius was informed of a self-confident monk whose counsel had depressed others, he decided to pay him a visit. When he was alone with him, Macarius asked, "How are things going with you?" The monk, whose name was Theopemptus, replied, "Thanks to your prayers, all is well." Macarius then asked, "Do you not have to battle with your fantasies?" He answered, "No, up to now all is well." He was afraid to admit anything. But Macarius said to him, "I have lived for many years as an ascetic and everyone sings my praises, but despite my age, I still have trouble with sexual fantasies." Theopemptus said, "Well, it is the same

---

[381] A talent is a weight, usually of silver, equivalent to 34.02 kgms. The price of silver varies daily, but at the time of writing 1 kgm is worth $354 AUD.

[382] William Barclay, *Gospel of Matthew*, Volume 2, The Saint Andrew Press, Edinburgh, Seventh Impression, 1969, p. 214.

[383] Daniel J. Harrington, SJ, *The Gospel of Matthew*, p. 270; David H. Stern, *Jewish New Testament Commentary*, Jewish New Testament Publications, Clarksville, Maryland, 1989, p. 59.

[384] Byrne, *Lifting the Burden*, p. 144.

with me, to tell the truth." And Macarius went on admitting, one by one, all the other fantasies that caused him to struggle, until he had brought Theopemptus to admit all of them himself."[385] Abba Joseph once asked Abba Poemen, "Tell me how to become a monk." He said, "If you want to find rest in this life and the next, say at every moment, 'Who am I?' and judge no one."[386]

Secondly, this parable reminds us that we must forgive, as we have been forgiven. When we pray the Lord's Prayer we say: "Forgive us our trespasses as we forgive those who trespass against us." In other words, to be forgiven we must be forgiving. "And this presents us with a truth so challenging and even so threatening that we are not surprised to find that (St John) Chrysostom tells us that in his day there were many who suppressed this clause of the Lord's Prayer altogether."[387] It was Robert Louis Stevenson's custom to have family worship each day, and to include in it the Lord's Prayer. "One day in the middle of the prayer he rose from his knees and left the room. His wife hurried after him thinking that he was ill. 'What is the matter?' she said. 'Are you ill?' 'No,' He answered, 'but I am not fit to pray the Lord's Prayer today.'"[388]

We will never be truly free unless we learn to forgive. In India hunters had a proven way of catching monkeys. A half coconut would be hollowed out and a hole made that was only large enough to allow a monkey's open hand to pass through. The coconut was placed over some tempting food, and then nailed to the ground. The only access to the food was through the small hole. A monkey would soon approach, intent on getting hold of the food beneath the coconut, but as soon as it grasped the food in its fist it was unable to pull its hand and the food free of the coconut. The monkey would stay imprisoned, caught by its own unwillingness to open its fist and let go of the food.[389] We, likewise, remain imprisoned unless we can let go of past hurts and grievances and forgive our brother and sister from the heart.

---

[385] Rowan Williams, *Silence and Honey Cakes*, Lion Publishing, Oxford, 2003, p. 27.
[386] Benedicta Ward (Tr), *The Desert Fathers: Sayings of the Early Christian Monks*, Penguin Books, London, 2003, p. 85.
[387] William Barclay, *The Plain Man Looks at the Lord's Prayer*, Fontana Books, London, 1964, p. 106.
[388] Ibid, 109.
[389] Christina Feldman and Jack Kornfield (Eds), *Stories of the Spirit, Stories of the Heart*, HarperCollins, New York, 1991, p. 345.

TWENTY-FIFTH SUNDAY IN ORDINARY TIME

(YEAR A)

Why be envious because I am generous? (Mt 20:15)

In a novel entitled *The Collector*,[390] John Fowles tells the story of an extremely shy and awkward young man named Frederick Clegg who is a clerk at the local post office. His hobby is collecting butterflies, which he then mounts in display cases. Frederick is totally smitten by a young art student whose name is Miranda Grey, but he is far too socially inept to introduce himself, and perhaps invite her out. He is hopelessly obsessed, but unable to do anything about it. Until, that is, he wins a fortune in the football pools. He buys a large house in a secluded and remote part of the countryside, and makes plans to kidnap Miranda.

He successfully kidnaps her, and takes her to his secret hideaway. Like his butterflies, Miranda is caught and locked away in a display case. She is imprisoned in a basement apartment, but with every luxury she could desire — everything, that is, except her freedom. It is Frederick's hope that she will eventually be overcome by his generosity, and come to love him. But, alas, Miranda will have none of it. "Do you think you'll make me love you by keeping me prisoner?" she asks.[391] And as the story unfolds, Miranda has nothing but the deepest contempt and loathing for him.[392] He who would be Miranda's Ferdinand has become Caliban.

This novel explores a number of themes, including the obvious one, that love cannot be bought, nor can it be given under coercion. Love is a gift. As King Solomon said long ago in the *Song of Songs*, "Were a man to offer all his family wealth to buy love, contempt is all that he would gain (8:7)."

Love cannot be bought; it is a gift freely given. Nor can we earn love. If, then, love cannot be bought or earned, what about salvation? Is salvation a gift or an earned reward? The parable of the labourers in the vineyard, unique to Matthew's gospel, offers a response to this question by likening the kingdom of heaven to

---

[390] John Fowles, *The Collector*, Pan Books, London, 7th Printing, 1972.
[391] Ibid, p. 38
[392] Ibid, p. 126.

a landowner going out to hire workers for his vineyard (a traditional symbol for Israel in the scriptures). September was the month when grapes were harvested in ancient Israel. But harvesting was not without its problems. September was also the month when the rainy season begins in Israel. If torrential rains came before the harvest, the entire crop could be ruined or severely damaged. And so harvesting the grapes often became a race against time.

We can imagine the scene behind this parable. The vineyard owner is waiting until the last minute to harvest his grapes. The riper the grape, the better its taste. One morning he wakes up and sees an overcast sky that threatens torrential rain. At 6 am, the beginning of the working day, he rushes to the market place to hire workers to pick his grapes. He offers them a denarius, the usual daily wage for a manual labourer. As the day progresses the threat of rain increases, and he returns to the market place several more times to hire workers — at the third hour (9 am), at the sixth hour (midday), and at the ninth hour (3 pm). The last group to be employed begins work at 5 pm, an hour before the end of the working day. It's frantic work, but the owner's efforts pay off, and he gets his grapes picked before the rain falls. He's so happy that he decides to celebrate, and he pays all the workers a full day's wage, even though some had only worked a few hours, some only one hour.[393]

It's important to realise that those workers who were employed at the eleventh hour were not what we might call dole-bludgers. They genuinely wanted to work, but nobody had hired them. They were in the market place because that was where day labourers gathered to seek employment. It was just like Sydney's "hungry mile", the docklands area where, during the Great Depression, workers would walk from wharf to wharf in search of a job. The atmosphere of that time and place are expressed in a 1930 poem by Ernest Antony: "They tramp there in their legions on the mornings dark and cold / To beg the right to slave for bread from Sydney's lords of gold; / They toil and sweat in slavery, 'twould make the devil smile, / To see the Sydney wharfies tramping down the hungry mile."[394]

When employers needed workers, they went to the marketplace, saw who was available, and chose those who appeared to be the fittest. It reminds me of high school days when we played cricket at lunchtime. Two captains would take it in turns to select a member for their team from all who wanted to play. As you would imagine, the best batsmen and bowlers were always chosen first; those

---

[393] Mark Link, *Illustrated Sunday Homilies, Year A, Series II*, Tabor Publishing, Allen, TX, 1990, p. 103; William Barclay, *Gospel of Matthew, Volume 2*, pp. 245-6.

[394] http://unionsong.com/u149.html

with little or no ability were picked last. By the eleventh hour, who was left at the marketplace? Nobody but the rejects and the left-over, the people whom nobody would employ. Here we come to the subversive part of the parable. The idea that any employer would come along and employ the rejects, if only for an hour, and then pay them the same wage as those who have done a full day's work — it's unthinkable. It's not fair! Imagine that you have been standing in a queue for hours, waiting to buy tickets for a concert or a sporting event. Wouldn't you feel indignant if an official appeared on the scene and gave away some free tickets to a person at the very end of the queue, someone who had only been waiting in line for five minutes? The official is free to give the tickets away to whomever he chooses, but it doesn't seem fair. Well, something similar is happening in this parable.

Why did Jesus tell this parable? What point was he trying to make? The workers employed at the eleventh hour represented the sinners and outcasts of his own day. The workers who were employed early in the morning, those who had laboured a full twelve hours, represent certain narrow-minded people who resented the fact that the invitation to God's kingdom was extended to people who hadn't put in the hard work.

This parable bears a striking resemblance to the parable of the prodigal son. Both parables are about unexpected generosity (to the younger son in one story, and to workers hired late in the day in the other); such generosity begets resentment and complaints of injustice (from the elder son and from the workers hired at daybreak); and both the father and the employer justify their extravagant generosity.[395] The resentment of those who have worked a full day reflects a small-mindedness that is extremely unattractive. And the presumption of such people is that God should govern the world in a similar way. The owner of the vineyard had not been unjust. He had been extraordinarily generous. It was this strange and unexpected generosity that created the problem.

The Pharisees assumed that God worked on a merit system. According to this system, you must earn God's favour by hard work. God will then give you a reward in direct proportion to your efforts. Nothing more, nothing less. And here is Jesus saying that God doesn't work on a commission system. Like love, God's gifts cannot be earned. They are freely given. No matter how hard Frederick tries, he cannot force Miranda to love him. In its original context, therefore, this

---

[395] W.D. Davies and D.C. Allison, *Matthew 19-28*, T & T Clark International, London, Reprinted 2006, p. 69.

parable "may have been used by Jesus to defend his reception of tax collectors and sinners against the objections of the scandalised Pharisees."[396] Jesus admitted the tax collectors and sinners to his fellowship, he ate and drank with them, and invited them into the kingdom, "because God who has sent him is generous with his forgiveness and mercy."[397] The parable is making the point that God's indiscriminate and abundant generosity is extended to everybody, even to those rejected, to the outcasts that nobody wants. God doesn't make contracts with us, "as if we could bargain or negotiate for a better deal. He makes covenants, in which he promises us everything and asks of us everything in return. When he keeps his promises, he is not rewarding us for effort, but doing what comes naturally to his overflowingly generous nature."[398] Or, as God says in today's first reading: "My thoughts are not your thoughts, my ways are not your ways."

---

[396] John P. Meier, *Matthew*, Liturgical Press, Collegeville, MN, 1980, p. 224
[397] J.C. Fenton, *Saint Matthew*, Penguin Books, Harmondsworth, 1963, p. 319.
[398] Tom Wright, *Matthew for Everyone*, Part 2, SPCK, London, 2002, p. 57.

TWENTY-SIXTH SUNDAY IN ORDINARY TIME

(YEAR A)

Tax collectors and prostitutes are making their way into the kingdom of God before you. (Mt 21:31)

An inner city parish had a serious problem with pigeons. Their droppings had disfigured the façade of the church and their nests constituted a fire hazard. The parish priest raised the matter at the local deanery meeting, eager to seek advice from his confreres. The pastor of an adjacent parish said that he had laid thin wires along every ledge of the church building to deter the birds from settling, and that had been moderately successful. Another priest admitted that he took pot shots at the pigeons with an air rifle. That sounded a little too dangerous and probably illegal! A third priest managed to lure the pigeons into a cage using decoy birds. Within a matter of weeks he had snared the entire flock and disposed of them. But it wasn't long before pigeons from elsewhere moved in. Finally, one priest announced that he had discovered a foolproof method of ridding his church of pigeons. "I simply baptised them all, and I haven't seen a pigeon anywhere near the church ever since."

Sadly, it is not only pigeons that disappear once they've been baptised! Many parents who present a child for baptism disappear off the ecclesial radar screen soon afterwards. Even more difficult to fathom are those people who have participated in the Rite of Christian Initiation of Adults, but fall by the wayside soon after baptism or reception into the church, despite months of preparation. It is so easy to say "Yes" like the second son in today's gospel, but to do nothing about it.

The devil Screwtape (in C.S. Lewis' *The Screwtape Letters*) is quite right to alert his nephew Wormwood to the difficulty that we humans have in making the transition from "dreaming aspiration to laborious doing." It's one thing for lovers to marry, but quite another thing to begin "the real task of learning to live together."[399] There is so often a yawning gap between profession and

---
[399] C.S. Lewis, *Screwtape Letters*, Fontana Books, London, 1955, p. 17.

practice. I'm reminded of a letter written by a young man, Oswald, to his beloved, Annabelle: "My dearest, sweetest, most adorable Annabelle, I would trek across desert wastelands, the Sahara, the Nullarbor, if I could but hold your hand. I would swim the oceans of the world, the Atlantic, the Pacific, if you would grace me with a single smile. I would climb Mount Everest a thousand times for a kiss from your ruby red lips. Your everlasting and devoted slave, Oswald. P.S. I'll be across to see you tonight, provided it doesn't rain!" Then there was the young man who told his beloved, "I love you passionately." "Would you die for me?" she replied. "No!" he said quite firmly. "My love is undying." This parable has a lesson for both of these young men: "promises can never take the place of performance, and fine words are never a substitute for fine deeds."[400]

The second son offers a perfect example of what Dietrich Bonhoeffer called "cheap grace." Cheap grace seeks the consolations of religion without taking seriously the call to discipleship. "Cheap grace," wrote Bonhoeffer, "is the preaching of forgiveness without requiring repentance, baptism without church discipline, Communion without confession, absolution without personal confession. Cheap grace is grace without discipleship, grace without the cross, grace without Jesus Christ, living and incarnate."[401]

Archbishop Anthony Bloom makes the observation that "If we turn to God and come face to face with him, we must be prepared to pay the cost."[402] When asked if the surface culture of the modern English way of life made it difficult to communicate the Gospel, Archbishop Bloom replied, "Yes, because the Gospel must reach not only the intellect but the whole being. English people often say, 'That's interesting, let's talk about it, let's explore it as an idea,' but actually do nothing about it. To meet God means to enter into the 'cave of a tiger' — it is not a pussy cat you meet — it's a tiger. The realm of God is dangerous. You must enter into it and not just seek information about it."[403]

In the Islamic tradition, there is a cycle of stories surrounding a legendary Turkish teacher, Nasreddin. Nasreddin, the wise fool, seldom lectured his disciples. Often he caught them off guard by subtly dramatising a simple yet profound lesson. One morning, amidst the hustle and bustle of a busy market

---
[400] William Barclay, *Gospel of Matthew, Volume 2*, p. 287.
[401] Dietrich Bonholeffer, *The Cost of Discipleship*, SCM Press, London, Third impression, 2004, p. 4.
[402] Anthony Bloom, *School for Prayer*, A Libra Book, London, 1970, p. xiv.
[403] Anthony Bloom, pp. xv-xvi.

place, Nasreddin got down on his hands and knees and began to search. Despite a multitude of people and animals going hither and yon Nasreddin began carefully searching every crack and crevice of the town square. Eventually, one of his disciples became so intrigued by the master's bizarre behaviour that he asked him what he was doing. "I am searching for the key that I lost," came the simple reply. So the disciple offered to help, and he, too, got down on his hands and knees and began to search. Five minutes, ten minutes, half an hour passed, but there was no sign of the key, and the disciple was becoming increasingly impatient with the search. "Master," he said respectfully, "are you sure that you lost your key out here?" Nasreddin replied, "Ah, no! I didn't lose my key out here. I lost my key inside." Understandably exasperated, the disciple asked, "Then why are we looking for the key out here?" Nasreddin explained, "Well, it's very simple. Outside it is light and bright, and easy to search. Inside, where I lost the key, it is dark and dingy, and difficult to find anything."

Some people simply enjoy the pose of being a searcher, but they are unwilling to make a surrender. Fr Ronald Rolheiser writes about the dichotomy between religion and spirituality. "A divorce is taking place between spirituality and ecclesiology, between those who understand themselves to be on a spiritual quest and those inside our churches." This is reflected today in "the person who wants faith but not the Church, the questions but not the answers, the religious but not the ecclesial, and the truth but not obedience."[404] In other words, they are reluctant to embark upon the arduous task of searching where it is dark and dingy.

The chief priests and elders in today's gospel, the Jewish leadership in Jerusalem, are the second son. By all outward appearances they were doing God's will, but they stubbornly resisted John the Baptist's preaching. The tax collectors and prostitutes are the first son. By all outward appearances their lives seemed to be saying "No" to God, but when John preached their lives changed, they repented. What this parable is saying is that "what God looks to is the final outcome in people's lives." We might say "No" a number of times along the way to a final and lasting "Yes."[405]

---

[404] Ronald Rolheiser, *Seeking Spirituality*, Hodder & Stoughton, London, 1998, pp. 32-33.
[405] Brendan Byrne, *Lifting the Burden*, p. 161.

TWENTY-SEVENTH SUNDAY IN ORDINARY TIME (YEAR A)

Come on, let us kill him and take over his inheritance. (Mt 21: 38)

Israel is likened to a vineyard in today's first reading from the prophet Isaiah and again in the Responsorial Psalm. Despite the best efforts of the friend who has a vineyard, the vines yield nothing but sour grapes. And so the hedge and walls are taken away, leaving the vineyard to be ravaged and devoured. It will languish, unpruned, undug and overgrown by the briar and the thorn. Sounding like a popular ballad, Isaiah's song of the vineyard laments God's judgment upon his people.

The gospel gives the metaphor of the vineyard a different slant, focusing instead on the murderous tenants rather than on choice vines and sour grapes. There are elements of allegory in the parable. The vineyard is Israel, and God is the landowner. The tenant farmers are the Jewish leaders and their allies. The servants sent to the tenants are the prophets, and the son whom the tenants kill and throw outside of the vineyard is Jesus. Here the image of the vineyard shifts from Israel to Jerusalem, and the reference is to Jesus crucified outside the city walls. The landowner will bring "those wretches to a wretched end", presumably a reference to the destruction of Jerusalem in 70 A.D . He then leases the vineyard to other tenant farmers, undoubtedly "a reconstituted Israel made up of Jewish and Gentile believers."[406]

Matthew's community lived during the early stages of Christianity's slow and painful separation from Judaism. At this stage they still considered themselves Jews and lived within the framework of Judaism, although in tension with other Jewish groups. Following the destruction of the Temple in 70 A.D, Matthew's community was one of several groups that "were laying out rival programs for reconstituting Judaism without Temple and land."[407] Against the background of this crisis that faced all Jews, Matthew's gospel attempts to show "how the Jewish

---

[406] Brendan Byrne, *Lifting the Burden*, p. 162.
[407] Ibid, p. 16.

tradition is best preserved in a Jewish-Christian context."[408] Ultimately rabbinical Judaism took a different path and those who acknowledged Jesus as Messiah were eventually expelled from the synagogue. Matthew's vitriolic denunciation of Israel's leaders reflects the anger and pain of this rejection. For that reason Matthew and his community "probably saw the events of A.D. 70 as a vindication of the claims made by Jesus' followers and the appropriate punishment for their opponents."[409]

It is important to read Matthew's gospel within its historical context. Daniel Harrington offers a salutary warning: "When taken out of its late first-century context within Judaism and read by Christians unaware of that context, Matthew can be interpreted as anti-Jewish ... Without attention to its historical setting Matthew becomes a dangerous text, capable of giving encouragement to anti-Semites."[410] A Christian reading Matthew in the twenty-first century must therefore break through the polemical intensity of the gospel's late first-century setting and ask what message it holds for us today.

Matthew presents Jesus as the authoritative interpreter of the Torah; he is the true and final revelation of God. The one factor that counted against the chief priests and the elders of the people was their refusal to change. They were so self-confident, so self-assured in their religious outlook that they failed to hear the invitation that God extended to them in the person, in the words, in the ministry of Jesus.

The Jewish leaders of the late first century are not the only ones who have failed to read the signs of the times. Christian leaders can be equally as resistant and intransigent. At the beginning of the sixteenth century, for example, "everyone that mattered in the Western Church was crying out for reformation. For a century and more Western Europe had sought for reform of the Church 'in head and members' and had failed to find it."[411] When Giovanni de' Medici was elected pope at the age of thirty-seven in 1513, taking the name Leo X, he is reputed to have said, "Now that God has given us the papacy, let us enjoy it."[412] In the wake of Luther's protest, Pope Leo X "was unaware of the issues and incapable of understanding the protest that had been developing for the century and a half since Wycliffe had repudiated priesthood as necessary to salvation, as well as

---

[408] Ibid, p. 17.
[409] Ibid, p.19.
[410] Daniel J. Harrington, S.J., *The Gospel of Matthew*, p. 22.
[411] Owen Chadwick, *The Reformation* Penguin Books, Harmondsworth, Reprinted 1973, p. 11.
[412] Barbara W. Tuchman, *The March of Folly*, Cardinal, London, 1984, p. 126.

the sacraments and the Papacy itself. Leo hardly noticed the fracas in Germany except as a heresy to be suppressed like any other."[413]

In 1984 Barbara Tuchman, American historian and two times winner of the Pulitzer Prize, published *The March of Folly*, a study of the persistent pursuit by governments of policies contrary to their own interests.

One example of such folly is that of the Renaissance popes whose extravagant lifestyles over a period of some sixty years eventually provoked the Protestant Reformation. These Renaissance popes of the fifteenth and sixteenth centuries were, Tuchman argues, "fixed in a refusal to change, almost stupidly stubborn in maintaining a corrupt existing system. They could not change the system because they were part of it, grew out of it, and depended on it."[414] When Pope Leo X died in 1521 he left the Church in the "lowest possible repute," wrote a contemporary historian Francesco Vettori, "because of the continued advance of the Lutheran sect."[415] We can only speculate on the course of Christian history had Leo been open and sympathetic to the calls for reform in head and members.

Tuchman then reflects upon the British loss of the American colonies in the 18th century. The British attitude towards the American colonists was a sense of superiority — "a sense of superiority so dense as to be impenetrable." The British remained defiant in the face of inevitable change.[416] The final scenario Tuchman examines in *The March of Folly* is the American presence in Vietnam. America, she argues, was locked in the trap of its own propaganda. Committed to a disastrous course of action, American policymakers became inflexible and intransigent. They adopted what Tuchman calls a "don't-confuse-me-with-the-facts" mentality.[417]

The medieval papacy, the government of King George III, American policy in Vietnam are cited as examples of the march of folly, as examples of human suffering that inevitably follows when influential people seek to maintain intact the ideas they started with. Such resistance to change is indeed fertile ground for folly, a folly responsible for a great deal of human suffering.

The eventual parting of Christianity and Judaism had catastrophic consequences for Jews once Christianity came into the ascendancy, and the fragmentation of the Christian church at the Reformation remains a gaping wound in the Body of

---

[413] Ibid, p. 141.
[414] Ibid, p. 153.
[415] Ibid, p. 142.
[416] Ibid, p. 286.
[417] Ibid, p. 472.

Christ. Daniel Harrington has written that historical study of Matthew "can give Jews and Christians today important insight into the context of and reasons for the eventual parting of the ways between them and their long history over against one another." The aim of such a study "is for both Jews and Christians to look at a turning point in the history of both movements and to ask themselves whether theological differences necessarily demand conflict and eventual separation. They did in the past. But do they have to in the future?" The same may also be said of the enduring division between Catholic and Protestants.

TWENTY-EIGHTH SUNDAY IN ORDINARY TIME

(YEAR A)

The kingdom of heaven may be compared to a king who gave a feast for his son's wedding. (Mt 22:2)

There is something inherently unfair in the gospel story about a king who gave a feast for his son's wedding. The king acts quite arbitrarily when he orders a guest to be bound, hand and foot, and cast out into the darkness because he wasn't suitably attired. After all, the man was only a passer-by, someone pounced upon by the king's servants with an invitation to attend a wedding feast — immediately! Did the king expect all of his subjects to go around carrying a suitcase filled with formal attire, just on the off-chance that they might be invited to a wedding?

You could argue that this man was really doing the king a favour by attending the wedding at all, given the fact that most people who had been invited had turned down the invitation. And on top of this, the gospel makes it clear that the king's servants went into the street and invited people indiscriminately — good and bad alike! And presumably, the well-attired and the poorly clothed alike. Why, then, should the king be so astonished to find a guest present without the appropriate clothing for a wedding?

The reason why the king's behaviour seems so irrational is because today's gospel contains two separate stories, probably used by the Lord on different occasions, each of them making a different point. It was Matthew, the gospel writer, who joined the two stories together, probably because they were both about weddings. But by doing this he's caused a good deal of confusion.

The first story was simply about a king holding a wedding feast for his son, but those invited were all too busy and sent their apologies. The king then sends his servants into the highways and the byways to invite anyone they can find. And so the banquet hall is filled with guests. End of story. This parable was a thinly veiled allegory of salvation history. Those first invited were the Jews. When they declined God's invitation extended to them through Jesus, a second round of invitations went out to Gentiles, and they accepted with enthusiasm.

The second story, originally independent of the first, tells of a person invited to a wedding banquet, but turning up inappropriately dressed. The king is not amused, and has him tossed out. Kings did sometimes invite their subjects to a banquet, regardless of status, and even provided suitable clothing for those unable to afford it. There was no excuse, therefore, for not wearing what the king had provided.[418] If this story stood on its own, the king's behaviour wouldn't seem so irrational. But the fact of the matter is that the stories have been fused together, and we have to deal with them as they are presented to us in the gospel.

So what can we make of the king's apparently irrational behaviour in the story as it stands? The guest, a passer-by, is suddenly accosted by the king's servants with an invitation to attend a wedding banquet. Why wasn't he wearing a wedding garment? Well, the short answer is we really don't know. But the story makes one thing clear: the guest, and not the king, was in the wrong. We are certain of this because of one key sentence in the gospel, the sentence which gives us the key to the whole riddle. It is a sentence that puts the blame rightly where it belongs: squarely and unmistakably on the shoulders of the guest. And that brief, revealing sentence is: "And the man was silent." He was silent. He didn't have a single word to say in his own defence, as he surely would if he had been unjustly accused. He had nothing to say — no excuse, no explanation, no protest. Perhaps just a shrug of the shoulders, raised eyebrows. But no explanation, no protest. His silence branded him as guilty.[419]

In this allegory the king represents God, and his son is Jesus. The wedding banquet is "the time of divine-human celebration symbolised by the kingdom."[420] The wedding garment is a symbol of repentance and good deeds, "a life in keeping with God's call, a life of justice, of doing God's will."[421] This hapless guest, plucked from the byways to attend the banquet, represents the Gentiles who have been invited to the banquet. But Matthew's gospel makes the point that "the Gentiles are not a new privileged class who can take over from Israel in the history of salvation. For both Jew and Gentile the same truth holds: Belonging to God's people means doing the will of God." This guest has arrived at the banquet "with dirty, rumpled clothing, symbolising a life that has undergone no basic

---

[418] David H. Stern, *Jewish New Testament Commentary*, pp. 64-5.
[419] An insight from William J. Bausch, *Telling Stories, Compelling Stories*, Twenty-Third Publications, Mystic, CT, 1992, p. 53.
[420] Brendan Byrne, *Lifting the Burden*, p. 164.
[421] John P. Meier, *Matthew*, p. 248.

change, a life that has not produced fruits worthy of repentance."[422]

The sting in the tail of the parable can easily make a contemporary congregation feel uncomfortable. It's not politically correct to discriminate against people because they are not dressed correctly. We would prefer to hear "a nice story about God throwing the party open to everyone. We want (as people now fashionably say) to be 'inclusive', to let everyone in. We don't want to know about judgment on the wicked, or about demanding standards of holiness, or about weeping and gnashing of teeth."[423] It's for that reason that I've always felt a little uncomfortable with the words of Deirdre Browne's popular hymn "Come as You Are". True, Jesus did come to call sinners, but he came to call us to repentance. God may invite us to come as we are, but not to stay as we are. The clothes we need for the wedding are love, justice, truth, mercy, compassion and holiness. "If you refuse to put them on, you are saying you don't want to stay at the party. That is the reality. If we don't have the courage to say so, we are deceiving ourselves."[424]

Graham Greene's novel *The Power and the Glory* is the story of a priest who has been condemned to death during the 1930s, an era of religious persecution in Mexico. Paramilitary groups (called the "Red-Shirts") had succeeded in closing all the churches in the state and forced priests to give up the ministry. In this hostile environment where religion has been outlawed, the nameless "whiskey priest" of Greene's novel seeks to minister to the people as best as he can. He is eventually captured and awaits execution. The incredible difficulties that the priest has experienced in this hostile environment have driven him to drink. Greene describes the morning of his execution: "He crouched on the floor with the empty brandy flask in his hand trying to remember an act of contrition. 'O God, I am sorry and beg pardon for all my sins ... crucified ... worthy of thy dreadful punishments.' He was confused, his mind was on other things: it was not the good death for which one always prayed. He caught sight of his own shadow on the cell wall; it had a look of surprise and grotesque unimportance. What a fool he had been to think that he was strong enough to stay when others had fled. What an impossible fellow I am, he thought, and how useless. I have done nothing for anybody. I might just as well have never lived ... Tears poured down his face; he was not at the moment afraid of damnation – even the fear of pain was in the background. He felt only an immense disappointment because he had to go to

---

[422] Donald Senior, *The Gospel of Matthew*, Abingdon Press, Nashville, 1997, p. 155.
[423] Tom Wright, *Matthew for Everyone*, Part 2, p. 82.
[424] Ibid, p. 85.

God empty-handed, with nothing at all. It seemed to him, at that moment, that it would have been quite easy to be a saint. It would have needed only a little self-restraint and a little courage. He felt like someone who had missed happiness by seconds at an appointed place."[425]

Graham Greene's priest, like the wedding guest, must stand silent. They had each accepted an invitation. They had always meant to dress properly for the occasion, but there was never time. It would have been so easy. It was always the very next thing they intended to do.

---

[425] Graham Greene, *The Power and the Glory*, Penguin Books, Reprinted 1967, p. 210.

TWENTY-NINTH SUNDAY IN ORDINARY TIME

(YEAR A)

Give back to Caesar what belongs to Caesar — and to God what belongs to God. (Mt 22:21)

At this stage in Matthew's gospel the opposition to Jesus is heading towards a climax. A seemingly innocuous question about paying taxes to Caesar is the first of four confrontations between Jesus and various power groups in Jerusalem. In Mark's gospel it is set on the Tuesday prior to his arrest and execution.

What is unusual about this scenario is the rather suspect coalition against Jesus between two groups who were normally bitterly opposed to each other, the Herodians and the Pharisees. The Herodians supported the dynasty of Herod Antipas, son of Herod the Great. Herod's tetrarchy consisted of Galilee and Perea, and he held his power by Rome's favour.[426] The Herodians were loyal to Rome because it served their purposes, and such loyalty gained them favour, wealth and relative independence. Herod Antipas had John the Baptist executed and he would have been on the lookout "for other prophets who, like John, might pose a potential danger because of their ability to attract large and enthusiastic crowds."[427] The Pharisees, on the other hand, opposed the Roman occupation and resented having to pay taxes to an occupying power. They argued that the payment of tax to a foreign king was usurping the place of God who alone was king over Israel.

Taxation was a hot issue. The Jewish historian Josephus writes about a Galilean Jew by the name of Judas who rebelled against Roman authority in 6 AD. Quirinius, the Roman governor of Syria had ordered a census of Judea and Samaria in order to establish a basis for taxation. Judas believed that submission to the census was a denial of God's lordship, and so he revolted.[428] The Romans crushed it mercilessly, "leaving crosses around the countryside, with dead and dying revolutionaries on them, as a warning that paying the tax was compulsory, not optional."[429]

---

[426] John P. Meier, *A Marginal Jew, Volume III, Companions and Competitors*, p. 562.
[427] Ibid.
[428] Gareth Lee Cockerill, "Judas. 10", in David Noel Freedman, (Ed), *The Anchor Bible Dictionary, Volume 3*, Doubleday, New York, 1992, pp. 1090-1.
[429] Tom Wright, *Matthew for Everyone*, Part 2, p. 87.

Rome imposed several taxes upon conquered nations, but the tax mentioned here is the poll tax or head tax. This tax had to be paid to Rome, in Roman currency, by men, women and slaves between the ages of twelve or fourteen and sixty-five. It amounted to one denarius, a full day's wage for a labourer.

In this gospel episode we have an attempt at entrapment. In a battle of wits the bait is dangled before Jesus: "Tell us, do we pay tax to Caesar, or not?" If Jesus had rejected the poll tax the Herodians would have immediately alerted the Roman authorities, and Jesus would have been arrested for treason. If he condoned the payment of the poll tax, he would have lost credibility with the population at large, who resented paying taxes to a foreign overlord. Jesus is alert to their ploy and cleverly responds by going on the offensive. Masterfully, he sets a counter trap by asking to see the coin used to pay the tax. They hand him a denarius, a silver coin worth approximately a day's wage. Here they are embarrassingly caught out! And why? In first century Palestine there were two types of coin in circulation. Because the Torah forbade graven images, one type of coin had no human or animal images. This was the only kind of coin that a strict Jew would use. The other type of coin had the emperor's image upon it. In Jesus' day it was that of the emperor Tiberius, together with an inscription that any devout Jew would find blasphemous: *Tiberius Caesar Divi Augusti Filius Augustus Pontifex Maximus* ('Tiberius Caesar, august son of the divine Augustus, high priest')."[430] When those who sought to entrap Jesus produced a coin, which coin was it? Caught out! A denarius with the emperor's image upon it, along with an idolatrous inscription. A flagrant violation of Jewish Law. Their plot to entrap Jesus embarrassingly backfires. His adversaries are exposed as "part of the politics of collaboration."[431] Their hypocrisy is further compounded when we consider where this episode takes place – the Temple courtyard (cf. 21:23). The whole purpose of Temple moneychangers was to make sure that idolatrous images weren't brought into the sacred precinct.

Jesus asks, "Whose head is this? Whose name?" They answer, "Caesar's". He replies, "Give back to Caesar what belongs to Caesar, and to God what belongs to God." This, of course, raises the obvious question about what belongs to Caesar and what belongs to God. For Jesus and many of his Jewish contemporaries the answer is clear-cut: Everything belongs to God. As today's Responsorial Psalm reminds us, "the gods of the heathens (including the pretentious claims of Caesar)

---

[430] Daniel J. Harrington, S.J., *The Gospel of Matthew*, p. 310.
[431] Marcus J. Borg and John Dominic Crossan, *The Last Week*, HarperSan Francisco, 2006, p. 64.

are naught." History is littered with conflicts between church and state, but for Christians the basic principal is crystal clear: if there is a tension between Caesar and God, the demands of God's kingdom must prevail. Allegiance to the kingdom of God takes precedence over allegiance to the kingdom of Caesar.

The German Lutheran pastor Dietrich Bonhoeffer was a leading figure in the church struggle against Nazism following Hitler's rise to power in 1933. The uncompromising message that lay at the heart of his book *The Cost of Discipleship* was that Christians needed to confess Christ concretely. "This meant a categorical rejection of the compromises of the official *Reichskirche*, which had become a 'false church', and following Jesus Christ alone."[432] Bonhoeffer realised that National Socialism "was a brutal attempt to make history without God and to found it on the strength of man alone." In unequivocal terms he denounced a political system "which corrupted and grossly misled a nation and made the 'Fuhrer' an idol and God."[433] American friends got him out of Germany in June 1939, several months before the outbreak of World War II, but he could not stay there. Writing to the American theologian Reinhold Niebuhr, Bonhoeffer explained his decision to return to Germany: "I shall have no right to participate in the reconstruction of Christian life in Germany after the war if I do not share the trials of this time with my people ... Christians in Germany will face the terrible alternative of either willing the defeat of their nation in order that Christian civilisation may survive, or willing the victory of their nation and thereby destroying our civilisation. I know which of these alternatives I must choose; but I cannot make this choice in security."[434] The Gestapo arrested Bonhoeffer on April 5, 1943. He was executed by special order of Himmler at the concentration camp at Flossenburg on April 9, 1945, just a few days before it was liberated by the Allies.

On April 28, 1990, Fr Michael Lapsley received a letter bomb hidden inside the pages of two religious magazines that had been posted from South Africa. In the bomb blast he lost both hands and one eye. His eardrums were shattered, and he suffered serious burns. The bomb had been sent by the De Klerk government, intending to silence Michael's opposition to apartheid. Born in New Zealand, Michael came to Australia to study for the Anglican priesthood with the Society of the Sacred Mission in Adelaide. He arrived in South Africa at the age of 24, shortly after his ordination in 1973. He enrolled at the University of Natal (Durban) and

---

[432] John W. de Gruchy, "Preface", in Dietrich Bonhoeffer, *The Cost of Discipleship*, SCM Press, London, Third Impression, 2004, p. ix.

[433] G. Leibholz, "Memoir", in *Dietrich Bonhoeffer*, p. xv.

[434] Ibid, pp. xvi-xvii.

also served as a chaplain on several campuses. The South African Government exiled him in 1976, and he joined the African National Congress and became one of their chaplains. "No one told me why I was being exiled," Michael said. "But as a university chaplain, and in the wake of the Soweto uprising, when students were being detained and tortured, I was no friend to the apartheid regime. In exile I therefore became a target of the South African government." Michael saw the situation in South Africa as a confrontation between God and Caesar: "I contest the view that Christians can ever, should ever, automatically acquiesce in any tenet the state makes upon us in matters as diverse as requiring permission to enter an African township, to the requirement that you should kill other people at the state's command. Personally, I believe it is often a cop out for a Christian to say that she or he needs to do something because the state commands."[435] Give back to Caesar what belong to Caesar – and to God what belongs to God.

---

[435] Quoted in Michael Worsnip, *Michael Lapsley, Priest and Partisan*, Ocean Press, Melbourne, 1996, p. 43. There are a number of websites on Michael Lapsley and his current work as the Director of the Institute for the Healing of Memories.

THIRTIETH SUNDAY IN ORDINARY TIME

(YEAR A)

Master, which is the greatest commandment of the Law? (Mt 22:36)

The rabbis of Jesus' day were good at quibbling over points of law, and it's a tradition that has endured within Judaism. Consider this case regarding the *yarmulke*, the skullcap worn by Jews during services and by some Jews at all times. A heated debate erupted over whether a religious Jew wearing a toupeé was obliged to wear a *yarmulke*. After a vigorous exchange of views the rabbis arrived at decision: If the toupeé looked like a toupeé, he doesn't have to wear a *yarmulke*.

How many commandments or *mitzvoth* are there? Most Christians would answer "ten" and refer to the Ten Commandments that Moses received on Mt Sinai. But Judaism has trawled thoroughly through the Torah and found not ten but six hundred and thirteen precepts – 365 prohibitions and 268 prescriptions. All *mitzvoth* were to be observed with equal diligence because they had been delivered by God to Moses, but "practical necessity forced distinctions to be made within the 613 commandments between 'light' and 'heavy'."[436] It is against this background that a lawyer (a detail omitted in the *Jerusalem Bible*) asked Jesus for his opinion about which was the greatest commandment in the *Torah*. *Torah* means literally "teaching" or "doctrine", but the Greek text of the New Testament uses the word *nomos*, which means "law." As used in Judaism the word *Torah* has several meanings. It may refer to the Pentateuch, the first five books of the Bible; it may refer to the Tanakh – what Christians call the Old Testament; it may also include the oral *Torah*, which includes the Talmud and other legal materials; and it may include all of that plus religious instruction from the rabbis, including ethical and homiletic materials.[437]

Jesus is asked for his opinion. His response was traditional and orthodox. In one sense he sidestepped the question – refusing to single out any one of the 613 *mitzvoth* as the greatest. Instead, he distilled all of the commandments into

---

[436] John P. Meier, *Matthew*, pp. 256-7.
[437] David H. Stern, *Jewish New Testament Commentary*, p. 25.

a single sentence. He took one verse from the book of Deuteronomy – we are to love God with our whole heart and soul, the commandment that forms part of the *Shema*, the prayer recited by observant Jews several times daily. He joined that to a verse from the book of Leviticus: Love your neighbour as you love yourself (Deut 6:5 and Lev 19:18). Jesus wasn't saying anything new. What he did emphasise, though, was the radical unity of the two commandments: Love of God is impossible without love of neighbour.

The gates of Paradise stood open and a procession of human souls came before the Heavenly Tribunal. First came a rabbi. "I am learned in the Law," he said. "Night and day I studied the Word of God. Surely I deserve a place in Paradise!"

"Wait!" called out the Recording Angel. "First, we must investigate. We must first satisfy ourselves as to the motives behind your study. Did you, for instance, apply yourself to learning for learning's sake? Or was it to gain personal prestige, or honour, standing or monetary reward?"

Next came an ascetic, a saint. "How I fasted in the world I left behind!" he said. "All of the six hundred and thirteen *mitzvoth* did I observe. Several times a day I bathed and studied the mysteries of the *Zohar* without cease. If anyone merits a place in Paradise, surely it is I!"

"Not so fast," cried the Recording Angel. "Of virtue there is plenty, but we are duty-bound to investigate the purity of your intentions."

Then an innkeeper approached. "I simply plied my trade," he said. "I opened my door to the homeless and fed the hungry and gave to the needy, and had little time left for learning, piety and prayer." And the recording Angel stood aside. "Open the Gates of Paradise!" he cried.[438]

Love of God is impossible without love of neighbour, a truth expressed forcefully in the first letter of St John: "Anyone who says 'I love God' and hates his brother or sister, is a liar, since whoever does not love the brother or sister whom they can see cannot love God whom they have not seen" (1Jn 4:20). Ron Fuller had just been installed as an acolyte in an inner city parish. Acolytes were rostered to take Communion to the residents of several nursing homes within the parish, and when Ron's turn came around he set out, feeling honoured and privileged. The Blessed Sacrament was carried in a small vessel called a pyx, which he held in his hand. Ron had just moved from interstate and was still finding his way around the city. He unwisely decided to take a short cut through an alley in order to get to the last nursing home on his list before they began serving lunch to the

---

[438] Serge Liberman, *The Battered and the Redeemed*, Fine-Lit, Balaclava, Vic, 1990, pp. 3-4.

residents. As he walked down the alley he was confronted by some hoodlums who began to threaten him. Ron held the pyx tightly in his hand, but when he was shoved against the wall he lost his balance and the hosts were strewn about the alley. These ruffians ground the hosts into the dirt. Ron was badly beaten, and faced a long recovery in hospital with a broken nose, collarbone, arm, bruised ribs and a lung contusion.

Members of the parish were outraged at this desecration of the Blessed Sacrament, and the story made its way into a local newspaper. The parish priest was pressed for a comment, and he agreed to make the following statement: "The Church is saddened at this senseless act of violence and by the disrespect and desecration of the presence of God in the Blessed Sacrament. However, we are quite sure that God will survive. At the moment, I am more concerned about Mr Fuller. We ask for your prayers that he will recover from his injuries, and from the violence done to the image and likeness of God in him."[439] Catholics have always venerated the Divine Presence in the Blessed Sacrament, but we haven't always been as devout in recognising the Divine Presence in each other. The two cannot be separated.

---

[439] Adapted from *Catholic Lectionary Homilies and Ideas Provided by Fr Jim Mazzone*, http://members.aol.com/homilies/aord30.html. 22/10/99.

THIRTY-FIRST SUNDAY IN ORDINARY TIME

(YEAR A)

The greatest among you must be your servant. (Mt 23:11)

The suicide of a flamboyant Sydney stockbroker featured prominently on page one of the city's two morning newspapers. The obituary published in *The Sydney Morning Herald* described a lavish and narcissistic lifestyle that expressed itself in "Fleets of expensive cars, palatial houses, an enormous gin palace of a boat, art collections lavish enough to turn curators of national museums green with envy." In a society that is "unashamedly materialistic", the obituary noted, we "elevate and honour those with wealth." In certain circles, "almost any sin can be forgiven for those with enough money." This brilliant stockbroker "inflated his persona and fed his ego by perpetuating the myth that he was a superior being, that his destiny was to rise above mere mortals by making far more money than most could dream of." His whole lifestyle screamed: "Look at me."[440] Jesus speaks harshly of the scribes and Pharisees because their religious observance was about drawing attention to themselves, "wearing broader phylacteries and longer tassels" and "wanting to take the place of honour at banquets and the front seats in the synagogues, being greeted obsequiously in the market squares, and having people call them Rabbi." They were pious frauds, hollow and empty people who were desperately dependent on the esteem of others. They lapped up every crumb of privilege and revelled in the limelight. They are "representatives of practical atheism which masquerades as piety."[441]

Jesus' words are as relevant today as they were in the first century. "The charge of pharisaism, that the behaviour of religious people does not always match their principles, is universal; it was noted in the Talmud and in the Dead Sea Scrolls and would resonate through Western history. So there is nothing in these complaints that could not be equally applied to Christian hypocrites, some of whom might have been in Matthew's own community."[442] Religious leaders are called to be

---

[440] Ian Verrender, "Pity the poor man," *The Sydney Morning Herald*, May 3, 2005.
[441] J.C. Fenton, *Saint Matthew*, Penguin Books, Harmondsworth, Reprinted 1968, p. 365.
[442] Howard Clarke, *The Gospel of Matthew and Its Readers*, p. 185.

servants, following the example of Christ who came not to be served but to serve. Jesus' condemnation of the Pharisees in today's gospel, and the condemnation of the priests in the first reading from the prophet Malachi warns religious leaders against becoming ensnared by the trappings of leadership. "We can become satisfied with externals, with buildings completed, lessons taught, or liturgies performed; we can aspire to places of honour and invitations to events where we can associate with important people; we can look for recognition and praise. Even worse than these signs of vanity, we can use our positions of trust to exploit others, whether their resources, their emotions, or their physical persons."[443] Authentic Christian leadership may be likened to the image that St Paul uses in his letter to the Thessalonians, that of a mother feeding and looking after her own children. Paul wishes to hand over not only the Good News but his whole life as well. He slaves day and night so as not to be a burden on anyone.

One of the titles of the Bishop of Rome is "servant of the servants of God." This must never be obscured by grandiloquent titles – Your Holiness, Your Eminence, Your Excellency, Your Grace, My Lord, Monsignor, Father – nor by magnificent vestments or solemn liturgies. Fr Brendan Byrne observes, "scarcely any injunction of the Lord has been so ignored as this ruling out of titles and, by extension, accoutrements of dress and ceremonial." Why, he wonders, has "the Church felt free to ignore literal fulfillment of Christ's clear injunctions in this area, while taking others – for example, the sayings on divorce – with legal rigor. Are fundamental values of the Gospel not as much at stake in the one as in the other?"[444]

Wealthy donors invited the Zen Master Ikkyu to a banquet. The Master arrived at the banquet hall dressed in beggar's robes. His host, not recognising him in this garb, hustled him away: "We cannot have you here at the door step. We are expecting the famous Master Ikkyu any moment." The Master went home and changed into his ceremonial robe of purple brocade, and again presented himself at his host's doorstep. He was received with due respect, and ushered into the banquet room and escorted to the place of honour. He then removed his ceremonial robe and placed it before his host. As Master Ikkyu turned to leave he said to the host, "I came to the banquet hall a short while ago and was sent away with great discourtesy. When I returned dressed in my ceremonial robe you greeted me most obsequiously. And so I conclude that it must be the garment that

---

[443] Dianne Bergant, with Richard Fragomeni, *Preaching the New Lectionary, Year A*, p. 391.
[444] Brendan Byrne, *Lifting the Burden*, p. 172.

you revere, not the person who wears it.[445]

Paul Hofmann, formerly the Rome correspondent for the *New York Times*, has published his reflections on life in the Eternal City in *Rome: The Sweet Tempestuous Life*. He tells of an occasion on which the Knights of Malta held a state dinner at their headquarters, a sixteenth-century palace on the Via Condotti. The guest of honour that evening was to be the Superior General of the Jesuits, Fr Pedro Arrupe. When he arrived, this slightly built ascetic wore a grey civilian suit, an old, ill-fitting jacket, and a white shirt with a badly pressed collar and a dark necktie. "The knights are flabbergasted. What message does the superior general of the powerful society of Jesus mean to convey by showing up without black cassock …? Does Father Aruppe by his modest, not to say threadbare, secular attire intend to hint that he doesn't think much of the knights' aristocratic and archaic pretensions …? The almost ostentatious plainness of the Jesuit chief's appearance when he paid an official visit to the grand master will be endlessly discussed in embassies, curial offices, and convents throughout the city."[446]

---

[445] Adapted from Irmgard Schloegl, *The Wisdom of the Zen Masters*, Sheldon Press, London, 1975, p. 47.
[446] Paul Hofmann, *Rome: The Sweet Tempestuous Life,* Congdon and Lattes, 1982, p. 222, quoted in William J. Bausch, *Storytelling: Imagination and Faith*, Twenty-Third Publications, Mystic CT, Fourth Printing 1986, p. 108.

THIRTY-SECOND SUNDAY IN ORDINARY TIME

(YEAR A)

Stay awake, because you do not know either the day or the hour. (Mt 25:13)

There's a standard format for wedding invitations. They tell us when and where the wedding is to be celebrated, and also the time and location of the reception afterwards. Such invitations are mailed out several weeks beforehand, and guests are requested to reply by a certain date. As far as we know, that wasn't how weddings were arranged in first century Palestine. Wedding invitations in Jesus' day did not state a particular day or time. They simply announced the fact that the wedding was to take place, sometime in the future. In the meantime, parents commenced preparing food, wine, musicians, decorations and fine apparel – in that respect, at least, little has changed over the centuries. When all the preparations were completed, the host dispatched servants to summon the invited guests.

Guests arrived at the house of the bride, revelling in dancing and entertainment. The bridesmaids, ten of them in this story, remained with the bride until the groom arrived. But no one knew for certain exactly when he would arrive. According to an ancient tradition, the groom and his friends had great fun if they caught the bridal party unawares – while they slept, for example.[447]

In the story that Jesus told, the groom arrived at midnight, and the bridal party was aroused at once, "The bridegroom is here! Go out and meet him." Five of the bridesmaids were prepared, and five were caught unawares. When the five foolish bridesmaids finally procured oil for their lamps, it was too late. The door of the wedding hall was closed. And what is the moral of the story? "Stay awake, because you do not know either the day or the hour." What is that saying to us?

Once upon a time, Lucifer, ruler of hell and king of demons, was despondent and dejected. No one, it seemed, was interested in joining him in hell. Demons roamed the earth, but to no avail. Tempting and coaxing mortals with all their

---

[447] *Catholic Lectionary Homilies and Ideas Provided by Fr Jim Mazzone*, http://members.aol.com/homilies/aord32.html, 5/11/99. Cf also, William Barclay, *Gospel of Matthew*, Volume 2, p. 353.

might, they failed to lure a single soul into evil. Lucifer couldn't remember a time when business had been so bad. Tears gushed down his cheeks, before evaporating into steam. Furnace after furnace was extinguished and closed down. Torture chambers stood empty and silent. What to do?

"We need to update," Lucifer thought to himself. "Evil needs a radical makeover, if we are to ensnare denizens of the third millennium." Suddenly, it struck him! "Maybe the internet can help us." Lucifer summoned three of his most mischievous young hackers and commanded them to search the web. "Find me creative and innovative ways to tempt earthlings." And so, the demonic hackers scoured cyberspace, hijacking every available search engine. In no time at all, they gleefully reported to Lucifer. "Your Imperial Wickedness, each of us has discovered a temptation that is guaranteed to repopulate the infernal regions, and hell will be as full as it was in the days of Sodom and Gomorrah."

Lucifer dispatched the first of the three devils to earth and waited impatiently. In due course, he returned and grovelled at Lucifer's cloven hooves, confident that he had done his worst. Together, they ascended the watchtower and focused their binoculars on the gates of hell, awaiting the hoard of evildoers that would soon join them. They waited, and waited, and waited, but only a miserly handful of souls straggled through the gates.

Lucifer exploded. "What a miserable outcome. How did you tempt them? What did you say?" Trembling with fear, he replied, "I told them that God didn't exist, that the universe was the result of random chance, so they could do whatever they like." Lucifer erupted into peals of laughter. "How pathetic! Even Nobel prize winners find such a proposition untenable. Let me tell you what Carl Rubbia said. He is the director of the European Council for Nuclear Research and winner of the 1984 Nobel prize for physics. In a 1992 interview, he said, "... as an observer of nature ... I find the thought that all this is the result of coincidence – or mere statistical diversity – absolutely unacceptable. A higher intelligence exists here – over and above the existence of the universe itself."[448]

The second devil was then dispatched, and again Lucifer waited impatiently. Upon his return, they mounted the watchtower, anticipating a landslide of sinners. But again, nothing much happened. Twenty or 30 people perhaps, but then, not a single soul in sight. "How did you tempt people?" Satan demanded to know. "I told them that 'if it feels good, do it, and hang the consequences. Think first and

---

[448] Quoted in Franz Köing, "The pull of God in a godless age", *The Tablet*, 18 September, 1999, pp. 1248-9.

foremost of your own happiness. Put yourself first. Just do it!'" Again Lucifer laughed. "People have been trying that for thousands of years. It sounds attractive and liberating at first hearing, but they soon recognise that it's little more than a recipe for disaster and disintegration. It's the complete antithesis of authentic love."

Lucifer didn't hold out much hope for the future as he dispatched the third devil. Somewhat despondently he climbed the watchtower stairs. But as he focused his binoculars on the portals of hell, he couldn't believe his eyes. A huge crowd was stampeding through the gates, stretching back as far as the eye could see.

Frothing like a madman, he shouted orders with a frenzied glee, "Ignite all furnaces. Break out the lashes. We're going to have a hell of a time!" Lucifer was ecstatic as he greeted the third devil. "What a brilliant outcome, what a stunning success. What manner of temptation achieved such outstanding results?"

The young devil's face was smeared with smug satisfaction. "Actually, I told them they should love and forgive each other. I told them they should pray and go to Mass more often. I told them to be people of integrity. I told them they should share their good fortune with the poor and needy."

Lucifer was almost overcome with apoplexy. "Whose side are you on?" he spluttered. "Let me finish, Your Imperial Wickedness," said the triumphant demon. I told them they should do all these things, but then I beguiled them with one word. This one word had a hypnotic effect upon them. In no time at all, I had them enthralled; they were under my control, and the results speak for themselves."

"What spell did you cast upon the children of earth? What word? Tell me the word that has saved hell."

"It was so simple, dear Lucifer, and yet so effective," replied hell's saviour. "The word was – 'later'. Love one another, but later. Forgive your enemies, but later. Live the gospel, but later. By all means, get oil for your lamps, but later. Not today, later."

And before you know it, *later* becomes *too late*. No words are so tinged with tears of regret as the sound of the words *too late*. Lucifer and the newly-promoted archdevil chuckled over the success of such a simple mantra. "Later, later," they chanted while stoking the fires of hell.

THIRTY-THIRD SUNDAY IN ORDINARY TIME

(YEAR A)

And he entrusted his property to them. (Mt 25: 14)

In a collection of essays entitled *Dancing at the Edge of the World,* science fiction writer Ursula Le Guin poses a hypothetical question. If the captain of a space ship from a distant galaxy asked the inhabitants of planet earth to spare one human being who would reveal the essence of our human nature, whom should we send? There is room for only one passenger, and on the long return journey home these aliens would seek to learn from this exemplary person the nature of the race. Would we choose a male or a female? A young person at the peek of his or her physical prowess, or an older person steeped in the wisdom of age? A scientist? A poet? A philosopher? Le Guin's choice is interesting. She would choose an elderly woman who "has worked hard at small, unimportant jobs all her life, jobs like cooking, cleaning, bringing up kids, selling little objects of adornment or pleasure to other people. She was a virgin once, a long time ago, and then a sexually potent fertile female, and then went through menopause. She has given birth several times and faced death several times – the same times. She is facing the final birth/death a little more nearly and clearly every day." What does Le Guin find so appealing about this woman (who, incidentally, has a great deal in common with the "perfect wife" in today's first reading) and why should we send her? Quite simply, because only a person who has experienced, accepted, and acted the entire human condition – the essential quality of which is Change – can fairly represent humanity."[449]

Today's parable is about change and the refusal to change. An unscrupulous entrepreneur entrusts varying amounts of money to three of his servants before setting out on a journey. We presume that he's unscrupulous because, in the words of the third servant, he reaps where he hasn't sown, and gathers where he hasn't scattered. Upon his return, the three servants are subjected to an audit. How astutely have they invested his money? The first two servants were truly

---

[449] Ursula K. Le Guin, *Dancing at the Edge of the World*, Grove Press, New York, 1989, pp. 5-6.

industrious, doubling the amount entrusted to them. The third servant played it safe, hiding his money under a mattress. He didn't make a profit, but neither did he risk losing the amount entrusted to him. The third servant is condemned because he played it safe. At the very least, he could have invested his master's capital in a term deposit and gained some interest.

The theme of the parable appears to be straightforward and easy to grasp. The word "talent", as used in this parable, refers to a weight – probably of silver. The value of that weight of silver is somewhere in the vicinity of $12,000 in today's terms.[450] Alternatively, a talent was equivalent to about six thousand denarii, and a denarius was a day's wage. However, the word "talent" is obviously a metaphor for something else, and it's usually interpreted as a symbol for the talents or abilities that each of us has. The parable is therefore saying something to us about being prepared to use our gifts or abilities, however modest they may be. But is that the message of the parable?

Jesus would have startled his audience when he first told this parable, for two reasons. Firstly, many in his audience would have been peasants – poor farmers who were conservative and traditional people. They could not afford to take risks because subsistence level farming in first century Palestine was unforgiving of mistakes and novelty.[451] They would have readily identified with the third servant, who avoided all risk.

Secondly, the Bible forbids usury – charging interest on a loan to fellow Jews. Christians inherited that prohibition, and usury was condemned in England and Germany until the 16th century, and in France until 1789.[452] In refusing to gain interest from investing his master's money, the third servant was faithfully observing the Jewish law. Merchants like the master in this parable were regarded as unsavoury people who amassed a fortune from exploiting others.[453]

So, this parable seems to praise villains and condemn a virtuous servant, according to first century Jewish sensibilities. What, then, is the point of the parable? The focus of the story falls on the third servant, the one who buried his talent. He didn't lose it; in fact, he presented it to the master exactly as he

---

[450] A talent is a weight, usually of silver, equivalent to 34.02 kgms. The price of silver varies daily, but at the time of writing 1 kgm is worth $354 AUD.

[451] Jerome Neyrey, "Reading Matthew: From Womb to Tomb with the Messiah", in Russell H. Hardiman (ed) *At the Heart of the Liturgy*, Twenty-Third Publications, Mystic, CT, 1999, p. 128.

[452] E.A. Livingstone (ed), *The Oxford Dictionary of the Christian Church*, under "usury", p. 1627.

[453] Neyrey, p. 128.

had received it. It was unaltered, unchanged. He had done nothing productive with it.

This parable was originally directed to the Jewish religious authorities. They were like the third servant who had returned his talent unaltered and unchanged. In a similar manner, the Jewish leadership presided over a religious tradition in which change and development were anathema. The tradition had succumbed to paralysis; there was an in-built resistance to change.

Change involves risk and uncertainty, and it is understandable why many of us are extremely resistant to change — in all areas of life. I was amused to read a letter to the editor of the London *Times*, dated May 8, 1903. The letter was written by a Lieutenant-General Dunham Massy, Colonel of the 5th Royal Irish Lancers. He is lamenting the demise of the lance as a weapon of war:

Sir,

I am glad to see that Sir D. Drury-Lowe and Sir Henry Wilkinson, who have both served in and commanded lancer regiments, and have seen the lance used in war, have written strongly in favour of its retention. I also have served for over 21 years in a lancer regiment, and held command of it for more than a third of that period, and have commanded a brigade on active service composed exclusively of British and Indian lancers. I desire to add my testimony in favour of that 'queen of weapons.' Both in moral and physical effect, the lance is incomparably superior to the sword in all situations, except the close melee. It is difficult to understand why it is proposed to abolish the lance for all except ceremonial purposes."[454]

An amusing reflection on the innate human resistance to change, and how ironic that in just over forty years after Lt General Dunham's letter decrying the abolition of the lance in warfare, the first atomic bomb was dropped on the Japanese city of Hiroshima, flattening an area of 10 square kilometres and killing or injuring almost 130,000 people.

To be open to change is to be truly human. As Fr Edmund Campion points out, "much of what we consider to be immutable, even divinely ordained, is in reality only a matter of the imagination. If we cannot imagine them to be different, they will never be ordered differently." Consider the example of the Papal States. "Once upon a time, the Pope was a great Prince. His principality stretched across the middle of Italy, reaching deep into the north and south. His armies kept other princes at bay; his civil service, carabinieri, and prisons kept the populace in its

---

[454] Kenneth Gregory (ed) *The First Cuckoo: A selection of the most witty amusing and memorable letters to The Times since 1900*, Unwin Paperbacks, London, 1978, pp. 47-48.

place. It has been like that for centuries and people assumed it would stay like that forever. They could not imagine the papacy without the papal states. Then, less than 150 years ago, there were no papal states; they were done away with. Now, we find it hard to imagine our pope with armies and prisons and the other structures of a civil state. Preserving the status quo is a matter of the imagination, not of doctrine or theological rhetoric."[455]

The one factor that counted against the Pharisees was their refusal to change. They were so self-confident, so self-assured in their religious outlook that they failed to hear the invitation that God extended to them in the person, in the words, in the ministry of Jesus. A cynic once observed that the only person who looks forward to a change is a baby with a wet nappy. It was Cardinal Newman who said, "In a higher world it is otherwise, but here below to live is to change and to be perfect is to have changed often."[456]

---

[455] Edmund Campion, "Clerical Celibacy", in *The Sydney Papers*, Vol. 15 No. 2, Autumn 2003, pp. 19-20.
[456] Ibid, p. 20

CHRIST THE KING

(YEAR A)

In so far as you did this to one of the least of these brothers of mine, you did it to me. (Mt 25: 40)

Today's feast of Christ the King is a comparatively recent addition to the Church's liturgical calendar. Pope Pius XI established the feast in 1925 during a time of political upheaval in Europe. Mussolini's fascists had just seized power in Italy, the Bolsheviks under Lenin had taken control in Russia, and the Nazi party led by Adolf Hitler was growing at an alarming rate in Germany.

These empires have crumbled. Hitler and Mussolini met ignominious deaths, the Soviet Union is no more, and the city named after Lenin has reverted to its former name, St Petersburg. One is reminded of Percy Bysshe Shelley's poem *Ozymandias*. Ozymandias is the Greek name of the Egyptian monarch Ramses II who lived in the thirteenth century BC, and he apparently erected a huge statue of himself. According to Shelley's poem, the following words were inscribed on the pedestal of the statue:

My name is Ozymandias, king of kings:
Look on my works, ye Mighty, and despair!

The irony of these words becomes obvious from the following lines of the poem:

Nothing beside remains. Round the decay
Of that colossal wreck, boundless and bare
The lone and level sands stretch far away.

* * *

On today's feast of Our Lord Jesus Christ, Universal King, we are presented with the image of the Shepherd-King, and the gospel likens the day of judgment to a shepherd separating sheep from goats.

One of the most confronting experiences of my life was visiting Calcutta. Although I had been forewarned, nothing really prepared me for the all-pervasive poverty that makes such a massive assault upon the sensitivities of the average

Westerner. People sleeping on footpaths; whole families living in huts made of cardboard cartons. The pollution and dirt, the squalor, the oppressive smells, the constant noise, and no escape from the crowds. And the persistent appeals for a handout: *baksheesh, baksheesh!* At first I felt guilty — in the face of abject poverty I felt guilty that I even had the price of an air ticket to fly me away from this incredible squalor. Then there were feelings of total helplessness – a kind of paralysis. Even if I gave away all that I had, it wouldn't make the slightest difference — except, perhaps, to myself.

It was on September 10, 1946 that Mother Theresa experienced what she has described as a "call within a call". Teaching in a school for middle and upper class Indian girls, she could not remain unmoved by the massive poverty beyond the school gates. And so, over fifty years ago, she founded the order of nuns we know today as the Missionaries of Charity. They are committed to serving the poorest of the poor.

One might imagine that the most basic need of the poorest of the poor in Calcutta is for food and drink, clothing and shelter. But Mother Theresa found that there was an even more basic need. In her own words: "The biggest disease in the world today is not leprosy or tuberculosis, but the feeling of being unwanted and uncared for. The greatest evil in the world is lack of love, the terrible indifference towards one's neighbour. What the poor need even more than food, clothes, and shelter, is to be wanted."

And so, when the King comes in judgment, he might well say to those on his left hand: Depart from me for I was hungry, not for food, but for a smile. And all I got from you was sour, disapproving looks. I was hungry for a word of encouragement and appreciation, but all you did was point out my mistakes. I was thirsty, not for a drink, but for a word of recognition. But all you did was belittle me. I was a stranger, a refugee fleeing from tyranny, seeking compassion. But you held me in detention, behind wire fences for years on end. I became a non-person. I was naked, not because I lacked clothing, but because I lacked self-esteem, and you tore me to shreds to bolster your own fragile ego. I was in prison, not one made of iron bars, but a prison of loneliness, and you shunned me. I was homeless, not for want of a house made of bricks and mortar, but for the want of tenderness and affection, for care and love, for acceptance, and you closed the door.

When one is confronted by the Calcuttas of this world there is a temptation to conclude that nothing can be done. Nothing that I could do would make a scrap of difference. But an Albanian nun teaching in India in the 1950s did make a difference. Her order now has over 3,000 nuns and brothers working among the poor in over seventy countries, and over three million volunteers assist them.

The Spanish mystic St John of the Cross once wrote that "In the evening of life we shall be examined on love." Those turned away by the King in Jesus' graphic account of the judgment had all failed to love. In the words of the Russian writer, Dostoyevsky, "Hell is the suffering of one who can no longer love."

If you're a fan of the Peanut's cartoon strip you'll be aware of the ongoing saga of Lucy's unrequited love for Schroeder, the young musician. As Schroeder plays his piano Lucy poses a question, "Do you know what love is?" Schroeder offers a perfect dictionary answer: "Love (luv) n. to be fond of; a strong affection for or attachment or devotion to a person or persons." And then continues playing without batting an eyelid. Somewhat crestfallen, Lucy replies, "On paper he's great."[457] It's not only Schroeder who looks good on paper; it's a temptation that all of us face. Our faith must be more than mere words, although that's a lesson that Charlie Brown and Linus are yet to learn. It's snowing, and Snoopy is shivering. "Snoopy looks kind of cold, doesn't he? asks Charlie." "I'll bet he does," replies Linus. "Maybe we'd better go over and comfort him." And so they do. "Be of good cheer, Snoopy," says Linus, and Charlie adds: "Yes, be of good cheer." And together they walk off, leaving a puzzled Snoopy still shivering in the snow.[458]

The world's media gave saturation coverage to the events of September 11, 2001, when terrorists crashed two airliners into the Twin Towers of the Trade Centre in New York, and a third airliner into the Pentagon, killing three thousand people. What we didn't hear about was that on the very same day, September 11, 2001, about 27,000 children died from avoidable causes, and that has been happening every day since then.[459] How many millions of dollars have been spent combatting the "war on terror" since then? If only a fraction of that amount were to have been dedicated to combatting infant mortality! Like Linus and Charlie, we can express our concern, and then walk off. Like Schroeder, we can look good on paper!

On a cold, wintry day a man noticed a small girl standing on a street corner.

---

[457] Charles M. Schulz, *The Complete Peanuts, 1969 to 1970*, Fantagraphics Books, Seattle, WA, 2008, p. 133.
[458] Charles, M. Schulz, *The Complete Peanuts, 1955 to 1956*, Fantagraphics Books, Seattle, WA, 2004, p. 151.
[459] Matthew Hall, "The controversy king's new cause", *The Sun-Herald*, November 23, 2008.

She was shivering with the cold, and starving for want of a decent meal. The man got angry and said to God: 'Why do you allow this to happen? Why don't you do something about it?" And God replied: "I have already done something about it. I made you."

Ultimately it is not a question of doing great things, but rather of doing little things with great love. Nor in most cases is it even a question of giving things. It is rather a question of giving of ourselves — of our time, our energy, and our love. The Christian writer, C.S. Lewis, once wrote: "When we get to heaven, there will be three surprises: First, we will be surprised by the people that we find there, many of whom we surely had not expected to see. The second surprise is that we will be surprised by the people who are absent – the ones we did expect to see but who are not there. The third surprise, of course, will be that we're there."

Why surprise, though? Another great Christian writer, Frederick Buechner, offers an answer: "Many an atheist is a believer without knowing it. Just as many a believer is an atheist without knowing it. You can sincerely believe there is no God and live as though there is one. You can sincerely believe there is a God and live as though there is not." At the great judgment, when the sheep are separated from the goats, labels such as believer or atheist will count for nothing. In the evening of life we shall be examined on love.

BIBLIOGRAPHY

Horst Balz and Gerhard Schneider, *Exegetical Dictionary of the New Testament, Volume 2*, William B. Eerdmans Publishing Company, Grand Rapids, MI, 1981

William Barclay, *Gospel of Matthew*, Volume 1, The Saint Andrew Press, Edinburg, 1956

William Barclay, *The Plain Man Looks at the Lord's Prayer*, Fontana Books, London, 1964

William Barclay, *New Testament Words*, SCM Press, London, 1964

William Barclay, *Gospel of Matthew*, Volume 2, The Saint Andrew Press, Edinburgh, Seventh Impression, 1969

William Barclay, *And Jesus Said*, The Saint Andrew Press, Edinburgh, Republished 1970

William J. Bausch, *Storytelling: Imagination and Faith*, Twenty-Third publications, Mystic, CT, 1984

William J. Bausch, *Telling Stories, Compelling Stories*, Twenty-Third Publications, Mystic, CT, 1992

William J. Bausch, *A World of Stories*, Twenty-third Publications, Mystic, CT, 1998

William J. Bausch, *The Word In and Out of Season*, Twenty-Third Publications, Mystic CT, 2000

William Bausch, *Once Upon a Gospel*, Twenty-Third Publications, Mystic, CT, 2008

Dianne Bergant, with Richard Fragomeni, *Preaching the New Lectionary, Year A*, The Liturgical Press, Collegeville, MN, 2001

Dietrich Bonhoeffer, *The Cost of Discipleship*, SCM Press, London, Third Impression, 2004

Marcus J. Borg, *The Heart of Christianity*, HarperSan Francisco, 2003

Raymond E. Brown, *The Gospel According to John*, I-XII, Doubleday & Company, New York, 1966

Raymond E. Brown, *The Gospel According to John XIII-XXI*, Doubleday & Company, New York, 1970

Raymond E. Brown, *The Virginal conception & Bodily Resurrection of Jesus*, Paulist Press, New York, 1973

Raymond E. Brown, *The Birth of the Messiah*, Doubleday, New York, 1979

Raymond E. Brown, *The Critical Meaning of the Bible*, Paulist Press, New York, 1981

Raymond E. Brown, *Responses to 101 Questions on the Bible*, Paulist Press, New York, 1990

Raymond E. Brown, *The Death of the Messiah*, Volumes 1 & 2 Doubleday, New York, 1993

Raymond Brown and John Meier, *Antioch and Rome*, Paulist Press, New York, 1983

Brendan Byrne, *Romans*, The Liturgical Press, Collegeville, MN, 1996

Brendan Byrne, *Lifting the Burden*, St Paul's Publications, Strathfield, NSW, 2004

Joseph Campbell, *The Hero With a Thousand Faces,* Fontana Press, London, 1993

Edmund Campion, *Rockchoppers*, Penguin Books, Ringwood, Vic, 1982

Edmund Campion, *Australian Catholics*, Penguin Books, Ringwood, Vic, 1988

Howard Clarke, *The Gospel of Matthew and Its Readers*, Indiana University Press, Bloomington, IN, 2003

W.D. Davies and D.C. Allison, *Matthew 1-7*, T & T Clark International, London, Reprinted 2006

W.D. Davies and D.C. Allison, *Matthew 8-18*, T & T Clark International, London, Reprinted 2006

W.D. Davies and D.C. Allison, *Matthew 19-28*, T & T Clark International, London, Reprinted 2006

Christina Feldman and Jack Kornfield (Eds), *Stories of the Spirit, Stories of the Heart*, HarperCollins, New York, 1991

J.C. Fenton, *Saint Matthew*, Penguin Books, Harmondsworth, 1963

Joseph A. Fitzmyer, *Romans*, The Anchor Bible: Doubleday, New York, 1993

Viktor E. Frankl, *Man's Search for Meaning*, Hodder and Stoughton, London, 1964

Daniel J. Harrington, *The Gospel of Matthew*, The Liturgical Press, Collegeville, MN, 1991

Wilfrid J. Harrington, *Revelation*, The Liturgical Press, Collegeville, MN, 1993

Alan Jones, *Soul Making*, HarperSan Francisco, 1989

Alan Jones, *Passion for Pilgrimage*, Morehouse Publishing, Harrisburg, PA, 1999

Alan Jones, *Living the Truth*, Cowley Publications, Cambridge, MA, 2000

Craig S. Keener, *The Gospel of Matthew*, William B. Eerdmans Publishing Company, Grand Rapids, Michigan, 2009

Jack Kornfield, *After the Ecstasy, the Laundry*, Bantam Books, New York, 2000

Mark Link, *Illustrated Sunday Homilies, Year A, Series II*, Tabor Publishing, Allen, TX, 1990

Mark Link, *Vision 2000*, Tabor Publishing, Allen, TX, 1992

E.A. Livingstone (Ed), *The Oxford Dictionary of the Christian Church*, Oxford University Press, Third edition 1997

John P. Meier, *Matthew*, Liturgical Press, Collegeville, MN, 1980

John P. Meier, *A Marginal Jew, Volume 2: Mentor, Message, and Miracles*, Doubleday, New York, 1994

John P. Meier, *A Marginal Jew, Volume 3: Companions and Competitors*, Doubleday, New York, 2001

Francis J. Moloney, *This is the Gospel of the Lord*, Year A, St Paul Publications, Homebush, NSW, 1992

Francis J. Moloney, *This is the Gospel of the Lord: Year B*, St Paul Publications, Homebush, NSW, 1993

M. Scott Peck, *Further Along the Road Less Travelled*, Simon & Schuster, New York, 1993

Ronald Rolheiser, *Seeking Spirituality*, Hodder & Stoughton, London, 1998

Donald Senior, *The Gospel of Matthew*, Abingdon Press, Nashville, 1997

John Shea, *Stories of Faith*, The Thomas More Press, Chicago, IL, 1980

Geza Vermes, *The Passion*, Penguin Books, London, 2005

Rick Warren, *The Purpose Driven Life*, Zondervan, Grand Rapids, MI, 2002

Tom Wright, *Matthew for Everyone*, Part 1, SPCK, London, 2002

Tom Wright, *Matthew for Everyone*, Part 2, SPCK, London, 2002

Tom Wright, *John for Everyone, Part 1*, SPCK, London, 2002

Tom Wright, *John for Everyone, Part 2*, SPCK, London, 2002

Philip Yancey, *What's so Amazing About Grace?* Zondervan, Grand Rapids, MI, 1997

Philip Yancey, *Soul Survivor*, Hodder & Stoughton, London, 2001

Steve Zeitlin, *Because God Loves Stories*, Simon & Schuster, New York, 1997

www.ingramcontent.com/pod-product-compliance
Lightning Source LLC
Chambersburg PA
CBHW050900160426
43194CB00011B/2236